Serge A. Theriault

MSGR. DOMINIQUE M. VARLET

ORIGINATOR OF THE OLD CATHOLIC EPISCOPAL SUCCESSION

1678 - 1742

His Life and Work

To the glory of God, in memory of the Rev. Jean Venne (1940-2008), priest of the Christian Catholic Church in the Canadian Capital Area (Ottawa-Gatineau).

Dedicated to my wife Diane, our daughter Melanie, our two sons John and Justin, and our granddaughter Veronica.

Apocryphile press
BERKELEY, CA

Apocryphile Press
1700 Shattuck Ave #81
Berkeley, CA 94709
www.apocryphile.org

© 2008 by Serge A. Theriault

ISBN: 978-1-933993-96-6

No parts of this book may be reproduced in any form without the express written permission of the author.

Copies of this book are available from www.amazon.com
or by writing:

The Christian Catholic Church in the Capital Area
Saint Bernard and Saint Gregory
30 Briermoor Crescent
Ottawa (ON), Canada K1T 3G7

TABLE OF CONTENTS

Foreword	5
INTRODUCTION	7
Notes	13

I
BIOGRAPHICAL SKETCH — 17

The Years of Preparation — 23

- Childhood and Adolescence — 24
- Saint Magloire Seminary and École de Sorbonne — 32
- Parish Ministry — 39
- Missionary in New France — 45

The Resistance — 57

- Towards a National Dutch Church — 61
- Religious Life at Rijnwijk and Schonauwen — 63
- Unity Talks with the Russian Orthodox Church — 67
- Indochina Mission Project — 69

The Last Years — 71

Notes — 77

II
DEVOTION AND REFORM — 101

- The Relations of New France — 107
- From the Church of Quebec to the Reform of Utrecht — 113
- The Pursuit of the Lordship of Christ: the Reform Program — 127
- The Consolidation of the Doctrine — 143
- The Interpretation of Scripture — 165
- To Sum Up — 185

Notes — 191

III
BISHOP VARLET AND OLD CATHOLICISM   209

- The Gallicano-Jansenist Alternative: Its Organization into an Independent Church   213
- The Instrumentality of the Apostolic Succession   219
- The Instrumentality of a Body of Doctrine   229

Notes   255

CONCLUSION   271

Notes   278

APPENDIXES:

- The 5 Propositions condemned by the Bull Cum Occasione   281
- The 101 Propositions condemned by the Bull Unigenitus   283
- Letters Patent Issued by Bishop St. Vallier   293
- The Holy Trinity in Bishop Varlet's Theology   295
- Bishop Varlet's Plan of a Method to Study Theology   307
- The Declaration of Utrecht   311
- Old Catholic Episcopal Succession, 1739-1910   315

Notes   317

Chronology   323

Index   331

Bibliography   397

Abbreviations and Illustrations   411

This book makes available in English the results of our research for the doctorate in theology at the University of Berne (Switzerland), for the *Series Dominique Marie Varlet* at the Bibliothèque et Archives Nationales du Québec, for a university course called *Productions québécoises des origines*, for articles published in the Revue d'histoire de l'Amérique française, the International Kirchliche Zeitschrift and elsewhere, and for the book Dominique-Marie Varlet, Lettres du Canada et de la Louisiane published by Quebec University Press. Contributions that have all been made in the French language.

It may interest the scholars and theologians, as well as individuals, groups and churches who claim Bishop Varlet for the apostolic lineage of their ministry.

May all find here a useful presentation of the life and work of this great churchman who is at the origin of the Old Catholic Church.

INTRODUCTION

Bishop Dominique M. Varlet has entered history for having transmitted the Apostolic Succession to the Dutch opponents to the papal bull *Unigenitus*,[1] consuming the rupture of the Chapter of Utrecht with the See of Rome and facilitating the formation of the Old Catholic Church.[2]

We have on him two sets of testimonies: (1) those of his opponents, who present him as a naive and reckless adventurer, who threw off the mask in Europe, after having masquaraded a few years in the Church of Quebec as a pious and devoted missionary; (2) those of his friends and supporters who see in him a providential figure, led by God to preserve from error a small group of Catholics, gathered around the Appellant[3] clergy of Utrecht. The first interpretation, widely disseminated by Ultramontane[4] historiographers, makes him a fatal character after his excommunication by Pope Benedict XIII in 1725.

There is no doubt that Bishop Varlet was at the same time the providential man of Old Catholicism and the troublemaker of Roman Catholicism because, by helping the dissenting Chapter of Utrecht to become a parallel church, he directly challenged the ecclesiastical system that he ironically called "papal court". Also, it is futile to try to defend the legitimacy of either interpretation. We must study the man and his work apart from the partisanship that has characterized so far the various interpretations of his life. It is the goal that this book wants to pursue.

Organization of the Book

To achieve the objective, we organized our book in three parts. The first part is a biographical sketch. We will place Varlet in his family context; characterize the formative years that led to his priestly ordination and will follow his ecclesiastical career since entering the Société des Missions Étrangères and his missionary activity in New France, to his episcopal consecration, his suspension, his excommunication and his involvement with the Oud-Bisschoppelijke Clerezij[5] (O.B.C.) of Holland.

In the second part we will describe the change sought by the reformer, from what he saw as an egocentric and domineering church to a church called to be servant of the kingdom of God and sacrament of salvation. This, taking into account his millenariarist convictions, the relationship between his activities and his writings, and the change he recommended in matters of doctrine, ecclesiology, morals and ministry.

In the third part we will demonstrate how instrumental to the formation of the Old Catholic Church was the episcopal succession that he transmitted to the O.B.C. We will also analyze the rapport between the doctrine behind the alternative Church he helped to put in place in the Netherlands and the present day Old Catholics.

Acknowledgements

This book would not have been possible without the collaboration of the following persons, to whom we express our deepest gratitude:

- Dr. Peter Amiet, our Th.D. Supervisor, the late Dr. Herwig Aldenhoven, former Dean of the Christian Catholic Faculty of the

University of Berne, Switzerland, and the late Dr. Kurt Stalder, Emeritus Professor, who have shared their knowledge of Old Catholicism and gave us useful advices for the conduct of our research.

- The late Right Reverend Leon Gauthier, former Bishop of the Christian Catholic Church of Switzerland, and former Secretary of the Old Catholic Bishops Conference of the Union of Utrecht, who facilitated in every way possible our studies in Berne.

- The late Dr. Denise Bindschedler-Robert, former Judge at the European Court of Human Rights and member of the Société des Amis de Port-Royal, who put at our disposal her rich collection of Jansenist books, allowing us to access a wealth of information that would have been difficult to obtain otherwise.

Our gratitude goes equally to the following organizations and persons:

- The Museum Catharijneconvent, Utrecht, and Mr. Kees van Schooten, Bibliotheek en Documentatie, for permission to reproduce the pictures of Msgr. Varlet and of the Old Catholic Archbishops of Utrecht that appear in this book.

- The authorities of the Royal Archives (Rijksaarchief) of Utrecht, who generously placed at our disposal the Port Royal Collection that contains the manuscript works of Bishop Varlet.

- The late Dr. Max Krämer, former officer of the Swiss Church Synod, and late Liliane, his wife, who shared with us historical publications related to Old Catholic Congresses, including the report on the one held in Vienna in 1909 that contains the picture of English bishop Arnold H. Mathew which appears in this book.

- Mr. Daniel Abel, photographer, for permission to reproduce the picture of the old Seminary of Quebec.

Finally, we do not forget the assistance received from the Dean of Research, the librarians and the secretaries of the Department of Human Sciences of the University of Quebec at Gatineau at the origin of our research project (1980-1985).

May all find here the expression of our deep appreciation.

Notes

---

[1] *Unigenitus* (named for its Latin opening words *Unigenitus Dei Filius*, or "Only-begotten Son of God"), is an apostolic constitution promulgated by Pope Clement XI in 1713, which opened the final phase of the Jansenit controversy in France. *Unigenitus* condemned 101 propositions of Pasquier Quesnel's *Réflexions morales sur le NouveauTestament* as suspected of heresies, especially those contained in the book *Augustinus* by Cornelis Jansen (1585-1638). The propositions can be found in Appendix 2. http://en.wikipedia.org/wiki/The_Bull_Unigenitus.

[2] The Old Catholic Church in this book means *a federation of several independent national Churches united in the Union of Utrecht on the basis of the faith of the undivided Church of the first ten centuries. They are Catholic in faith, order and worship but reject the Papal claims of infallibility and supremacy. Since the Bonn Agreement of 1931, they have been in full communion with the Churches of the Anglican Communion. They have participated in the World Council of Churches since its beginning and are in formal dialogue with both the Orthodox Churches and the Roman Catholic Church. Among them the Archbishop of Utrecht holds a primacy of honour not dissimilar to that accorded in the Anglican Communion to the Archbishop of Canterbury.* http://www.willibrord.org/who_en.html

We are aware that since the defence of our thesis, the Union of Utrecht has undergone major changes and that since the Polish National Catholic Church (P.N.C.C.) ceased to be a member in 2003, it has been "exclusively a European body." Laurence J. Orzell, *Disunion of Utrecht....*, Touchstone, The Fellowship of St. James, Chicago, 2004.

There are other Old Catholic groups in North America, some with real churches and membership. Unlike the P.N.C.C., they have never been affiliated or recognized by the Union of Utrecht. The Old Roman Catholic Church, founded in England by Bishop Arnold H. Mathew and no longer part of the Union of Utrecht, has a good presence in the United States.

Terminology. The term "Old Catholic" is often used by groups ranging from 'Continuing" or "Traditionalist" to "New Age". The Bishops of many of these groups trace lines of Apostolic Succession to Bishop Varlet and the Old Catholic Church. They are regarded as Episcopi Vagantes (Wandering Bishops) by the churches of the Utrecht Union.
http://en.allexperts.com/e/o/ol/old_catholic_church.htm

[3] *Appelant* is the name given to those of Jansenist and Gallican sentiments who rejected the condemnation by Unigenitus (1703) of Pasquier Quesnel's book. In 1717 four bishops appealed against the Bull to the next General Council. They were soon joined by other bishops, the Sorbonne, and some clergy. In 1718 pope Clement XI formally condemned and excommunicated them. Oxford Concise Dictionary of the Christian Church, Oxford University Press, 2006, p. 34.

[4] From Latin *ultra* and *mons*, beyond the mountain, the Alps (from France), *Ultramontanism* places strong emphasis on the prerogatives and powers of the Pope. In particular, it asserts the superiority of Papal authority over the authority of local or national hierarchies.

[5] The Dutch church was recognized by the state under the name "Kerk Genootchap der Oud-Bisshoppelijke Clerejiz" in 1912.

Bishop Varlet's Coat of Arms

As prescribed by canon law to the new bishops, Msgr. Varlet took a coat of arms. He used the oval shield that his father had registered in the Armorial Général de France: *d'azur au rocher d'or posé sur une onde d'argent et au chef d'or chargé d'un rameau d'olivier et d'une palme de sinople posés en sautoir* (in azure, a gold rock laid on a wave of silver and above, a gold chief charged with an olive branch and a green palm branch laid crosswise and bound with gules). The shield, topped with a miter and a crosier, is stamped with a prelatice hat with 10 tassels on each side, which is nowadays that of archbishops.

I
BIOGRAPHICAL SKETCH

Dominique Marie Varlet was born in Paris on March 15, 1678. The Church of France was grappling with the Jansenist controversy. The authorities were shaken by the supporters of the new doctrine and opinion movements appeared, favoring the emergence of militant spiritual centers such as the Abbey of Port Royal, that rallied important personalities such as Jean Duvergier de Hauranne, Abbot of Saint-Cyran, Antoine Arnauld and Blaise Pascal. We must also mention the founding of the Prêtres du Calvaire (Priests of Calvary) on Mont-Valérien near Paris, by Hubert Charpentier, a disciple of Saint-Cyran. These different environments, under the impetus of the book <u>Augustinus</u> (1640) by Cornelis Jansen,[1] taught a purity of faith and morals which, because of all sorts of intrigues, seemed possible only by distancing oneself from the official church.

Jansen (Jansenius) *Augustinus* *Saint-Cyran*

Alongside the efforts of these reform movements, the Church of France in the wake of Charles Borromeo, Archbishop of Milan, experienced a renewed enthusiasm in the service of God called for by the Council of Trent (1545-1563).[2] So, reducing everything to the

Jansenist controversy would distort the perspective. The French religious world was complex. Many Christian communities had a real fervor. The problem was not due to a lack of faith but rather to aging institutions.

The Jansenists preached a greater rigor of life[3] based on the Bible and the Church Fathers. The more they led their contemporaries to reflect on the meaning of their Christian life, the more they provoked confrontation of ideas. This gave rise to a literature of controversy in the 17th and 18th centuries. The dispute got polarized around the book *Réflexions morales sur le Nouveau-Testament* (1671) published by Oratorian[4] priest Pasquier Quesnel. It was in line with the Gallican theses of Edmond Richer.[5] From that moment, the French Catholicism would be divided into Ultramontane and Jansenist factions. Unable to restore order in his church, King Louis XIV made an appeal to Pope Clement XI who in 1713, issued the Bull *Unigenitus* condemning Father Quesnel's book.

Pasquier Quesnel

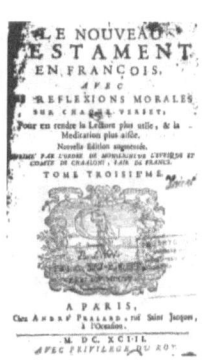

Réflexions morales

A group of bishops opposed the bull, invoking the secular freedoms of the Church of France (Gallican Articles[6]) and the sacred rights of its episcopate. They were followed in their protest by many theologians and pastors who saw in the condemnation an abuse of authority and a disregard for the jurisdiction of the pastors, and (new phenomenon at the time) for the right of the faithful to confirm doctrinal decisions. In the midst of this ideological germinal appeared the figure of Dominique M. Varlet. He was to become one of the most illustrious representatives of the resistance to the Bull Unigenitus and of the *Appeal to the General Council*. He was to prepare himself for that during some forty years.

1
THE YEARS OF PREPARATION

We know the life of Bishop Varlet after 1719 because it pervades the history of the conflict of the Chapter of Utrecht with Rome. It is reported by the historians of Old Catholicism and fragments of it are found in the works on Jansenism in the 18th century. We also have a good idea of his missionary activity in New France from 1713 to 1718. But we lack information about his youth, his years as a seminarian and the period when he did parish ministry before becoming a missionary. It is important to know the phase between 1678 and 1713 to understand the meaning of his action in favor of the O.B.C. of Holland. This is the goal we will persue in the following pages.

Two books give us much of our data. The first, written by Emile Jacques, is entitled *Les années d'exil d'Antoine Arnauld* (1976). It covers the years 1679 to 1694, a period that corresponds to the childhood and the adolescence of Varlet, in the context of the first Jansenism (controversy on grace). The second book, by Edmond Préclin, is called *Les Jansénistes au 18e siècle et la Constitution civile du clergé* (1929). It is a comprehensive study covering the development and spread of the Gallican doctrine of Edmond Richer. Adopted by the second Jansenists, who wanted to win the support of priests and laity in their struggle with the pope and the bishops, this doctrine gives the framework and tools of the resistance to the Bull *Unigenitus*. This is the context into which Varlet has evolved from childhood until his departure for New France.

Childhood and Adolescence

Dominique was the son of Achille Varlet and Marie Vallée, two actors of the Troupe de Molière[7] who lived on Nevers Street, near the Pont Neuf in Paris. They were married on November 25, 1673, ten years after Marie had joined the Troupe and met Achille who was playing along-side his brother Charles, the famous La Grange.[8] The daughter of a cloth merchant in Normandy, Marie was playing *Amalasonte*[9] in Rouen when she was discovered by Pierre Corneille[10] in the sixties.

Charles Varlet dit La Grange

We know little about the youth of Madame Varlet, except that she attended drama school and belonged to the middle class. On the other hand, we have a comprehensive documentation on the Varlet family.[11] Achille was the son of Hector Varlet, who was steward of Marshal Schomberg,[12] a lieutenant general for the King in the government of Languedoc. Qualified as a noble man in the parish register of St. Germain l'Auxerrois in Paris, when he married Marie Lagrange on May 9, 1634, he had the titles of Squire and Captain of the Castle of Nanteuil at the baptism of his children Charles and Marie-Justine on February 12, 1642.[13] The term squire in the Ancien Régime,[14] designated a person who belonged to nobility.[15] There is no doubt that Hector Varlet had ties to the ruling class.

At the baptism of Achille, it is Msgr. Achille de Harlay, Counselor of the King and Bishop of Saint-Malo, and the widow of the Marquis de Maignelay, Claude-Marguerite de Gondi, who were godparents. Also, in the parish register of St. Nicolas-des-Champs in Paris, Marshal Schomberg and his wife Marie Helluin are indicated as godparents at the baptism of Charles and Marie-Justine. However, the Varlet sons did not maintain the social position of their father. This is confirmed in official documents such as the marriage certificate of Charles, Sieur de La Grange, and Marie Ragueneau in 1672. He is identified as *bourgeois de Paris*.[16] Their two daughters also had for godparents two bourgeois de Paris, Molière and Armande Béjart.[17]

Marshal Schomberg

It is obvious that in the seventies, the Varlet family no more had the aristocratic connections it had before. This is perhaps ascribable to the fact that Achille and Charles chose to be actors. This trade was badly seen by the Church and the discredit of the actors was so great in the public that it became impossible for a noble to play theatre.

But although they did not have the privileges of the nobility, the Varlet brothers lived on a grand scale. Charles inhabited, on rue Royale, a house rented from the Marquis de Bellefond.[18] Achille, in 1679, had in addition to his residence on Nevers street, a country house he had bought from Armande Béjart, Molière's widow.[19] It was located in

Rueil, a suburb west of Paris, on the high road leading to the *Mont-Valérien* that would become, in 1696, a major reference point in the direction Dominique would give his life.

The family often went to Rueil. They could even stay for weeks when the Comedy had no performance. During the long stays, relatives and friends came to visit and the conversation would focus on the topics of the hour: the affair of the régale[20] and its politico-religious implications, the exile of Antoine Arnauld and the persecution of the Jansenists, the revocation of the Edict of Nantes and the exodus of the Protestants, the rise of Cartesianism[21]...

Most often, the visitors belonged to the milieu of theatre and most of them evolved in the entourage of Molière. But this did not prevent them from alluding to Jean Racine.[22] Though still young, his tragedies had taken precedence over those of Pierre Corneille. He captured the audience and critics were full of praise for him. The dramatist who had been in bad terms with the religious of Port-Royal, who had raised him in their school,[23] had just reconciliated with them and

The Mont-Valérien lies to the West of Paris, on the other side of the Bois de Boulogne. In 1633, a graduate of the Sorbonne, Hubert Charpentier, obtained from the king the permission to plant on the top of the mountain three crosses representing Mount Calvary, to erect a church dedicated to the Holy Cross, and to build a house for the priests in charge of the site.[24]

The Calvary at Mont Valérien

there was a great to-do about it.[25] At his marriage with Catherine de Romanet in 1677, it is Father Pasquier Quesnel who officiated.[26]

All this might have been puzzling for the followers of Molière, whose principles were more aligned with the Epicurean ideal of philosopher Pierre Gassendi[27] than with the rigorism of the Port-royalists.[28] It is likely that the name of Jean Racine was evoked in the conversations at Rueil. The residence of the Varlets was at a short distance from the Jansenist shrine of the Mont-Valérien and certain of the priests might have been frequent visitors of the Varlets.[29]

The Jansenist party, motivated by the desire to provide a strong spiritual background to the man who was to become the Originator of the Old Catholic Episcopate, gave a version for the less moving of that period of his life. His father *touched by God*, supposedly built a small house on Mont-Valérien and ended his days there, seclused with his family, in prayer and penance.[30]

But let's set the facts straight. Achille Varlet was 37 years old when he purchased the house in Rueil. He still played theatre and was probably more attracted to the luxuriant receptions organized by his brother Charles than to the austere disciples of Hubert Charpentier. Besides, if he came to be touched by grace as mentioned in the Nouvelles Ecclésiastiques,[31] this did not happen before he attained the age of retirement, which was around 1700.

It is doubtful that the father had that sort of spiritual influence on his son. Achille Varlet was not a man to get involved with the Jansenists. He could, as other free thinkers of his time, have taken an interest in their movement because it favoured individual rights and personel thought.[32]

His mother is more likely to have played a key role. It is more her who frequented the Mont-Valérien. And this, not for ideological reasons, but in response to an inner desire to ensure her salvation. In the correspondance that Dominique had with her she appears as a deeply religious woman, vertuous[33] and manifestly pious.[34] But although she attended church at Mont-Valérien when the family was in Rueil, it is in all probabilities at Saint-André-des-Arts, the church of the artists and actors, of which she knew the clergy,[35] that she was involved during the childhood of Dominique. It skirted famous Jansenists, such as the notary Philippe Galois, in front of whom *Antoine Arnauld* deposited, in 1661, his protest against the attitude adopted towards him by the Faculty of Theology of Paris.[36] They transported there, in 1710, the

Antonius Arnaldus
Doctor in fide et veritate
(6-II-1612 — 8-VIII-1694)

remains of Jansenist historian Sébastien LeNain de Tillemont that were at Port Royal Abbey.

Dominique was attached to that parish.[37] It is possible that he received there the rudiments of the catechism; that he served Mass and that it is through his contact with the clergy in charge that was awaken his priestly vocation. Perhaps it is there that he was confirmed and attended his sister's marriage with the attorney Antoine Olivier. In any case, it is certain that the funeral of his father took place there on August 26, 1709[38] and that he administered in that church the sacrament of confirmation on March 17, 1719.[39]

The biographers have not made any link between Saint-André-des-Arts and the pastoral vocation of Dominique, preferring to focus on his relationships with the Priests of Calvary. It is true that his affection for the work of the Holy Cross of Mont-Valérien became so strong that he solicited from the Priests an aggregation that was granted on October 6, 1699.[40] But should we see there an exceptional event? Isn' it not rather the result of a gradual spiritual evolution already begun in childhood?

To sum up, Dominique was raised in a time when Western thought and sensitivity "were taking a tragic turn".[41] He grew up with a father who had a mind rather independent (possibly interested in Jansenism because it challenged absolutist authoritarianism) and a devout mother who, in her quest for salvation, exposed him early to the influence of the Jansenists, transmitting him a taste of God's things that was never to cease.

The child was not different from other kids when he was in primary school. However, he should have kept in his heart what he saw and heard with a precocious intensity, until came the time when the meaning of all this was going to be revealed. It is in the period from 1691 to 1697, when he was doing his humanities, that the revelation began. In 1688, there was an event in Paris which was not without causing a stir in intellectual circles. This is the famous meeting of the Académie Française, when Charles Perrault read in front of Nicolas Boileau[42] his poem *Le Siècle de Louis le Grand*. This poem, which took a stand for contemporary writers, revived the Quarrel of the Ancients and the Moderns. Boileau, a supporter of the Ancients, was quick to give the reply. His response, directed against Perreault,[43] was inserted in a new edition of his works which appeared in 1694. Varlet could not ignore this publication that was mentioned in class. It was known that Boileau had the support of Arnauld and a common sympathy for Port Royal had brought them together.[44] This could have encouraged Dominique to read Boileau and other works presenting the opposite view such as Digression des Anciens et des Modernes by Fontenelle.[45]

It is not impossible that his passion for reading began at that time, as well as his interest for the Ancients. The love of books, was one of his worldly passions, the only likely, and also, perhaps, the object of his spending. When he died in Holland, his library, made with care and equipped with an engraved ex-libris, was the best part of his estate. Jacob van Bosveld took stock of the library and published in 1743, the list of the books it contained, under the title Bibliotheca

Varletiana (Kribb & Weyde). In a section called *Polygraph, Poetae and Orators*, there are 103 books listed, of which only 4 are from contemporary authors: La Bruyère's *Caractères*, La Fontaine's *Fables*, Boileau's *Works* and Voltaire's *Henriade*. His favor went to: Xenophon, Hesiod, Pindar, Sophocles, Euripid, Aristophanes, Homer, Virgil, Terence, Horace, Ovid, Esope, Lucretia, Aristotle, Cicero, Pliny. This shows his predilection for the ancient authors. We know that he was interested in the quarrel between the ancients and the moderns because he had read the *Histoire de la querelle des Anciens et des Modernes* (no. 496 of the list).

When he studied philosophy, his teachers certainly mentioned René Descartes, whose doctrine (cartesianism) disturbed the Church, and Nicolas Malebranche, who inspired Oratorian priest Michel Le Vessor to develop the course of positive theology that he was giving at Saint-Magloire. Arnauld, admirer of Descartes, criticized the philosophy of Malebranche,[46] and in his frequent interaction with the Priests of Calvary, Dominique surely has addressed these questions.[47] His rapports with the Mont-Valérien intensified especially in 1696-1697, which corresponds to the period when he studied philosophy.

If we believe the proverb *tell me who you frequent and I will tell you who you are*, there is no doubt that Varlet belonged to the Jansenist party when he entered the diocesan seminary of Saint Magloire in the fall of 1898. To suggest, as did Auguste Gosselin[48] and others before him, that until 1719, that is to say until his episcopal ordination, he had concealed his Jansenist tendencies and was not known as such in his circles, is the highest fantasy.[49]

Saint Magloire Seminary and the École de Sorbonne

Dominique was twenty when he began, at the École de Sorbonne, [50] his theological studies as a student of Saint Magloire seminary. Aware of his positions and rich of what he had learned from the Priests of Calvary and those of Saint-André, he entered seminary with a relative confidence. He knew he was to find teachers and classmates[51] with whom to share his religious convictions while having no illusions about the difficulties he was to face.

It was not easy to be a Jansenist in France in the early 18th century. The heyday of the movement had passed.[52] There were sympathizers and militants in the dioceses, rectories, religious communities and schools of theology,[53] and it was still possible to frequent spiritual centers such as the Mont-Valérien. However, their influence was becoming more discreet. Leaders like Arnauld and Quesnel had taken the road to exile to avoid persecution. Cases of intimidation, arrest and even imprisonment were numerous.[54] Religious communities were being dissolved and Port Royal was not safe[55] since the death of the Duchesse de Longueville, protector of the nuns.

Nuns being forcibly removed from the Abbey of Port-Royal in 1709.

With the *affair of the régale*, who opposed him to the pope, about the administration of the bishoprics of Alet and Pamiers, prompting the adoption, in 1682, of the Gallican Articles,[56] Louis XIV was fighting the Jansenists he held responsible for the failure of his negotiations with Rome.[57] He had as an ally Bishop François de Harlay, the Archbishop of Paris, who put as much zeal to persecute the followers of Cornelis Jansen as he did with those of John Calvin after the revocation of the Edict of Nantes (1685).[58] So, it is not at Saint-Magloire in the nineties, that one could expect to receive teaching on grace and predestination according to the treaty Augustinus. Bishop de Harlay had seen that the faculty of his seminary be purged of all its suspicious elements. The balance that the seminary had maintained in the past between Jansenist and Anti-jansenist trends had been broken since 1678. Father Abel-Louis de Sainte-Marthe, the superior, had been defeated at a meeting held in the Oratoire de France, and at the request of the archishop, he was relegated to Saint-Paul-aux-Bois in the forest of Saint-Gobain near Loan, in 1682.[59] Two years later, on December 25, the Oratorians were forced to sign a formulary affirming their compliance with the resolutions of the Assembly of 1678. It was forbidden to teach the doctrines condemned by the Church or suspected of the sentiments of Jansen and Baius[60] for theology, and of Descartes for philosophy. Father Quesnel, who was then at Saint-Magloire, did not want to sign without explanation and had to flee to Brussels on February 23, 1685.[61]

Although Saint Magloire was recognized as a center for the dissemination of Jansenist ideas in Paris,[62] it is not there that

Dominique developed his Augustinian[63] convictions. In the years he was there (1698-1706) the dominant ideas were those of Richerist Gallicanism, [64] and he certainly spent more time studying the positions of Quesnel, Duguet, Juénin and Habert, transferring to the clergy and the faithful the authority previously vested in a council of bishops, than the theses of Arnauld and the Port-royalists. At the time he received the doctor's cap in 1706,[65] he had endorsed the teaching of Father Quesnel. In his <u>Première Apologie</u> published in 1724 to justify his conduct in the consecration of Archbishop Steenoven, he wrote that the right to elect the bishop belongs to the cathedral chapter which represents the clergy and the people.[66] If he joined the movement of the Appelants, it is because Rome had used the pretext of the Bull *Unigenitus* to suspend him from the episcopate. But his argumentation is more Gallican than Jansenist, invoking the superiority of the council over that of the pope[67] and the discipline formulated in the ancient church canons. And when he discussed the doctrine of the bull, he used arguments that were more pastoral than theological as shown in this passage: *Such a strange censure could only diminish the faith of the Christians of the Levant,[68] loosen the knots that tie them more closely to Jesus Christ and disarm them in the midst of temptations. Because in the violent temptation where they are of losing faith, the bull is only fit to make several of them fall into apostasy, by fomenting the hope of making their salvation outside the Church.*[69]

He did not study the authors of the first Jansenism thoroughly in the seminary. This is what suggests the *Varlet Collection* kept at the Royal Archives (Rijksaachief) in Utrecht. In his papers are the notes, summaries and reviews of the books he had to read, after his excommunication (1725), to acquire the arguments used in his later works, such as the <u>Lettre aux missionaries du Tonkin</u> (1734), which incorporates the controversy initiated by the first Jansenists. He took his inspiration from Arnauld and followed his approach: presentation of the Augustinian conception of grace, rejection of the moral theology of Jesuit[70] priest Luis de Molina,[71] criticism of the biblical exegesis of the Protestants and of their theology of the sacraments, particularly of the Holy Eucharist. [72]

There is a marked contrast between the apologies and his later works. He seemed more comfortable when he wrote Gallican minded texts than when he worked at refuting the Bull *Unigenitus* on substantive issues. The first writings are clear and limpid, the others laborious and weighed. Clearly, having associated his destiny to that of the Dutch dissenters after 1725, he had to master a church culture of which he had acquired only the rudiments around 1700. This "ecclesiastical culture" consisted mainly of the First Jansenist ideology because of the influence of Arnauld and other Port-royalists who had found refuge in Holland, including Pontchâteau and Nicole. Quesnel also had influence, but his richerism was affirmed only after the arrival of the Benedictine Thierry de Viaixnes after 1722. He played the key role in the affair of the election and the consecration of Archbishop Steenoven.[73]

The energetic and stirring monk made sure that two of Richer's works get printed: <u>Demonstratio Libelli</u> and <u>Libellus de Ecclesia</u>. De Viaixnes became secretary of Bishop Varlet after his establishment in Amsterdam (1722). It is he who urged the prelate to proceed with the consecration and who planned the ceremony in all details.[74]

The Jansenism of Bishop Varlet was spiritual and pastoral,[75] in line with the Case of conscience,[76] not with the theories of the Port-royalists. Besides, how could it be otherwise? The masters of the first Jansenism had left France and enjoying the protection of Bishop J.B. van Neercassel, were gaining a following in Holland.[77] It is there in the early 18th century, that was the best expertise on the questions of grace and predestination. The tolerant attitude of the Dutch Government doubled with the resistance of the clergy of Utrecht[78] had contributed to the immigration of many French dissidents. Some were based in Amsterdam, but the largest concentration was in Utrecht and the surrounding areas. Neercassel, an Oratorian, had studied and taught in Paris around 1645. This made him familiar with the French theological circles in the days when Cornelis Jansen had better press.

J.B. van Neercassel

The Treaty of Nijmegen, on August 10, 1678,[79] encouraged the dissemination of Jansenist ideas after the resumption of the relations between the Oratories of Malines and Paris. Several Belgian and Dutch students were sent to do their theology at Saint-Magloire. Among them were Peter Codde, the successor of van Neercassel (removed from office by Rome),[80] and Cornelis Steenoven and Cornelis Barchman Wuytiers, the two Archbishops of Utrecht Varlet would consecrate in 1724 and 1725. Soon was to appear the conflict of trends mentioned earlier, that led to the defeat of Father de Sainte-

Marthe and the Formulary of 1684. However, despite the ban on teaching the "sentiments of Jansenius", the conflict was not to stop. It would resurface in 1717 in the Appeal to a general council of the Bull *Unigenitus* by Bishops Soanen, Colbert, De la Broue and De Langle.[81]

We felt it necessary to present the ideological context in which Varlet has evolved during his years in the seminary. This was desirable because in most cases, the analysts have inserted him in the milieu of Saint-Magloire without the necessary nuances. For a seminarian in the jurisdiction of the Archbishop of Paris, it was natural to go there because it was the diocesan seminary. However he did not go there as someone who opts for a party. Surely he was a Jansenist, but of a spiritual sort, that was no stranger to the ideal proposed by Pierre de Berulle, the founder of the Oratoire de France.

It is not easy to separate what was Berullian from what was Jansenist.[82] There were similarities between the two. An example is their shared view on the sacrament of penance. The Oratorians were as rigorous as the Jansenists regarding priestly absolution of penitents.[83] They shared the view that one cannot be validly absolved unless one has the love of God (contrition) as a motive for one's repentance, and that fear of punishment (attrition) is not a sufficient motive.

This question was one of the warhorses of the Counter-reformation, a revival which began with the Council of Trent. It included focusing on a personal relationship with God in Christ. Archbishop Charles Borromeo of Milan made contrition a requirement in his <u>Instructions to</u>

Confessors (1657). Bishop van Neercassel, suspected of being Jansenist,[84] wrote Amor Poenitens (1683) for his clergy who, seduced by attritionnism, sulked the Instructions of Archbishop Borromeo.

The sacrament of penance was important for Bishop Varlet. In the following explanation, we can see that he made in application the Berullian lessons learnt at Saint-Magloire: *We could expose the Catholic religion to the reproaches and insults of the schismatics if they heard that fear without the love of God has so much virtue that with its help, the heart is freed from sin without having to be led by the love of justice, and that we are not guilty before God, though we refrain from evil only by fear of punishment.*[85]

This is not the only similitude between him and the Oratory. There was at the heart of the Oratorian spirituality a christocentricity recommended by Bérulle, that profoundly nourished Varlet. Indeed, when he challenges the validity of imposing the Bull Unigenitus in his apology, or comments on the Acts of the Apostles, or another book of the New Testament such as the Epistle to the Romans, there is always, at the center of his discourse, the same christological articulation. "*My title are the words: habebis thesaurum in coelo. Can you offer me something better? But to enjoy my title, I must satisfy the prescribed condition: veni, sequere me.*" [86] This trait which is dominant in his writings, is as Berullian as Jansenist.

We have now assembled enough data to be able to draw the major traits Varlet had when he became priest. He was, we will remember, particularly concerned with his salvation. Awakened early in childhood, under the influence of a devout mother, his quest was to find at Mont-Valérien, the anchor for his passionate and generous soul. Having become a candidate for Holy Orders, he entered seminary and took courses at the École de Sorbonne, more specifically at the Collège de Navarre.[87]

For eight years, his generosity was sollicited at two complementary levels: that of a rigorous exploration of the revealed truth (bible exegesis and patristics[88]) and ecclesiology (conciliarism, richerism and canon law[89]) with the doctors of the Faculté de Paris. He internalized Christ the Savior with what it entailed for the service of the Church, inspired by Jansenist and Oratorian spirituality. This is what, in our view, would determine his attitude and actions in the Netherlands.

Parish Ministry

It is failing to leave France and go to work as a missionary abroad that brougth Father Varlet to the parish ministry after his priestly ordination in 1706. It seems that this dream "haunted him for some time and it is reasonable to think that he received the call to be missionary in his early years in the seminary.[90] We have mentioned the Berullian christocentrism and the urgent calls to serve the Church, and we showed how Jansenism had been an anchor point for his adolescent enthusiasm. Two factors must be added to that. The first is the interest shown in the Collège de Navarre, in the early 18th century, for the fabulous discoveries supposedly made in Louisiana and the Illinois country, by the men of the expedition of Cavallier de la Salle.[91] The second is the dispute over the Chinese Rites, which opposed the Jesuits to the Priests of the Missions Étrangères.[92] Msgr. Artus of Lionne, Bishop of Rosalie (whom the Jesuits had done much publicity by attacking him when he returned from China in 1702) went to meet Navarre College students in 1706 to talk about the distant missions and to give them his views on the Chinese Rites. We know that this contact Varlet had with the Bishop of Rosalie in 1706 contributed to his determination to devote himself to abandoned works.[93] However, he would not reach the goal before 1712. Is it because of his mother? It is possible. Madame Varlet, once a widow, went to live with him. Jean-Achille and Anne-Marie, both married and absorbed by their responsibilities, had left to Dominique to care for her.[94] Moreover, the affection that he had for her would have rendered difficult to consider a possible separation.

From 1706 to 1708, he was assistant priest in several Parisian parishes.[95] He was busy on Sunday but had free time during the week. So, he took advantage of the situation to renew contact with former colleagues. One of them was Jacques Jubé (1674-1745), with whom he had, in 1699, taken the course of Hebrew, Arabic and Syriac taught at the Collège Royal by Brother Fétix de la Croix.[96]

Jubé had six years of experience as parish priest and this gave him credit in the eyes of the newly ordained Varlet, whose goal was to be a good curé in default of being a missionary. He had just left Vaugrigneuse, where he had been curé since his ordination (1700),[97] to start a new parish at Asnières, two miles from Paris. This offered him the opportunity to implement the liturgy he had been working on at Vaugrigneuse.

Inspired by Father Quesnel, that liturgy[98] had for objective to provide the faithful with the knowledge they needed in the truths of religion to exercise their power of authority (that was restricted to a council of bishops in old traditional Gallicanism). Father Quesnel saw the faithful exercize that authority in three circumstances: to excommunicate bad Christians, the elect pastors and to confirm doctrinal definitions.[99] There was in this position a laicist (synodal) bias similar to the one foreseen in 1700 by the Assembly of the clergy of France when it labeled as "reckless and outrageous Presbyterian audacy" the proposals contained in the request presented to their bishop, on May 15 of that year, by the members of the Cathedral Chapter of Chartres.[100] Edmond Préclin believes that Richerist ideas taught at the time by Calvinist Pastor David Blondel were not foreign to this request. The first two propositions, inspired by Chapter 20 of the Acts of the Apostles (St. Paul's speech to the elders of Ephesus) denied, as did Edmond Richer, that there is a difference between the bishops and the priests: *It is only because of a use, which was generalized into a rule, that we distinguish the priests from the bishop, establishing one over the others, with the name of Bishop.*[101]

We get an idea of Jubé's objectives by examining the accusations made against the Cérémonial d'Asnières: (1) priestly prerogatives extended to the faithful; (2) the priest at the altar acting as delegate of the parish community; (3) believers made real priests.[102] Nicolas Petitpied, who made several visits to Asnières, denied that there were Protestant elements in the liturgical reform of his future refuge companion.[103] But when we examine closely the Cérémonial, it is difficult not to see Reformed connotations.

The liturgy was celebrated in a "temple" (term preferable to that of church), where paintings depicting the lives of saints were replaced by gravures representing scenes from the Bible. The eucharistic table, imitating the form of a tomb, was covered with a linen only during the celebration of the Mass. Finally, no cross nor candles were seen on the altar during the actualization of the Sacrifice. As for the structure of the liturgy, it included the following changes: (1) the celebrant was going to his seat after having said the Confiteor and stayed there throughout the first part of the Mass (until the offertory); (2) the laity gave the reply to the celebrant, answering "amen" to the prayers of the sacrifice, including the Secret;[104] (3) after the Gospel, the celebrant read only the little prone of the ritual, leaving the long instruction (homily) to the deacon; (4) there was no singing during the anaphora.[105]

Inside view of the parish church of Asnières, built in 1704, that reflects Father Jubé's liturgical reform

We know from the content of his library, what type of reference material Varlet might have used during his working sessions on liturgy with Jubé. Were found, beside the 1664 edition of the Roman Pontifical and that of 1685 of the Liturgie Gallicane by Marbillon: the De Antiquis Ecclesiae Ritibus by Edmond Martene (1700), the Discipline des Églises Réformées de France and the Book of Common Prayer of the Church of England. [106] Jubé's intention to "restore the ancient discipline of primitive Christianity" was coupled with an interest in the Reformation.[107] He was representative of a tendency that was current in France and the United Provinces. The spokesmen were: Guy Drappier (Du Government en commun par les évêques et les curés, 1707) and Vivien de la Borde (Le Témoignage de la vérité, 1714). The latter, who became Superior of Saint Magloire in 1708, is said to have gone so far in the direction of Calvinism (Non-Sacerdotalism) that he won the praise of Pastor Jacques Basnage. In his book L'Unité, la visibilité, l'autorité de l'Église... published in 1715, he spoke of the work of De la Borde as being "tout protestant."[108]

Varlet and Jubé did not go as far, in their reform, as to recognize the multitude of the Christians as superior to the Ecumenical Council.[109] But did they dissociate themselves from extreme positions, like that of Aegidius de Witte of Malines (Belgium), who merged the episcopate and the priesthood? This is not clear.[110] In any case, they advocated the election of the pastors by the people.[111]

In 1708, Msgr. de Noailles, the Archbishop of Paris, entrusted to Father Varlet the Parish of Conflans, a north-western suburb of Paris,

15 miles from the center. Wanting to evangelize his flock the way Jubé did, he tried to establish in his parish the *Cérémonial* d'Asnières.[112] But the Parish of Conflans was close to a Benedictine monastery[113] and he was soon opposed by the monks, who tried to stop him.

Msgr. de Noailles   *Conflans and its parish church*

"Frustrated by the behavior of the Benedictines, perhaps also by the indifference of his parishioners,[114] he taught the time had come to realize his dream of going overseas to dedicate himself to the abandoned works.[115] In 1711, he went to see the directors of the Séminaire des Missions Étrangères (S.M.É.); offered his services and requested to be admitted to their congregation. He was appointed as successor of Father Marc Bergier, missionary to the Tamaroa indians at Cahokia (near St. Louis East, Illinois) as well as Vicar General of the Bishop of Quebec for the Mississippi Valley and Superior of the priests of the S.M.É. in that region. The mission had been without a pastor since the passing of Father Bergier on November 9, 1707.[116]

Because of certain technicalities, he could not depart before the fall of 1712 and continued his parish ministry. Finally, he took leave of his mother in December and went to Port-Louis,[117] in southern Brittany, the place of his boarding. He left on February 7 but because of bad weather, he had to call at La Rochelle two days later, leaving from there on March 8. He had to call again after two days, this time at Brest, also because of bad weather. Finally, he left for good on March 28, arriving in New France on June 6, after a stop at Cap-Haïtien, then called Cap-Français (April 30-May 3) and another one at Havana (May 12-13).[118]

Missionary in New France

Contrary to what some historians[119] have said, he did not land in Quebec City but at Mobile, Alabama, then called Fort Louis de la Louisiane.[120] From there, he was supposed to go directly to the Mission of the Holy Family in Cahokia, to minister to the Tamaroas.[121] But he was prevented from leaving because of a bloody flux (dysentery) that almost killed him[122] and forced him to stay at Mobile longer than expected. It is only on April 7, 1715 that he would leave for Cahokia, taking advantage of an expedition organized by the Governor of Louisiana, La Mothe Cadillac,[123] to search for silver mines[124] in Upper Louisiana via the Mississippi.

Varlet's letters give us interesting information on that portion of the Diocese of Quebec located in Lower Louisiana. We learn that the area was not as they believed in France, the promised land expected from the trade concession granted to the financier Antoine Crozat in

1712.[125] To his brother who wanted to join him to make money, Varlet wrote: there is nothing to gain here, except for those seeking souls to convert, and a lot of zeal is needed, even more than in any other place of the world. *The only affair that is important is the salvation of souls.*[126]

New France at its apogee

He was preoccupied with the evangelization of the Native people. But since his arrival in Louisiana, he had seen only the Amerindian who was assisting the missionaries and who brought them the (wild) animals they needed for their meals. His colleagues and himself were all occupied with the French who were living in Mobile and in a settlement ten miles away from the fort.[127] His name appears in the *Register of the Parish of Notre Dame de la Mobile, his signature being* as Vicar General.[128]

Exact replica of the old French fort at Mobile

Although he had been there since June 1713, it was not until November that he went outside the fort to go celebrate Mass in a small village of Christian Indians.[129] It is only in January 1714 that he ventured to make God known to other Native people of the area.[130] He returned one month later with a good idea of what awaited him at Cahokia, among the Illinois, a confederacy of Algonquian tribes.[131] He knew it was not a context to make progress quickly. *We have to learn languages of which there are no rules, no books, no teachers,* and it is *a great job to expose the Holy Mysteries in languages so numerous and so different from each other.*[132]

Among the Tamaroas at Cahokia

The first communication we have from Varlet after his departure for the Illinois country dates from November 2, 1716. It is a letter to his brother, written from Cahokia, saying that he had left the vicinity of the sea (Mobile) to come revive one of the old missions of the Seminary of Quebec.[133] An allusion to the Governor of Louisiana "who went up from the sea to the Illinois country along with him"[134] confirms that he left for the Mission of the Holy Family in April 1715.[135]

Log Church of the Holy Family at Cahokia, rebuilt in 1759

The ministry to the Tamaroas includes two phases: one that took place in Cahokia; the other in Quebec city for "the interest of the missions."[136] These years are critical in the life of Varlet. Not only did he realize his dearest wish, which was to work with the abandoned souls,[137] but also he acted as vicar general of the vast Diocese of Quebec, which included "the full extent of the lands discovered by the French and which had been taken possession of on behalf of the King."[138] It is understandable that he used that experience in his apology to justify himself against his critics after the events of Holland.[139]

Arrived at Cahokia, he worked with zeal,[140] even to the point of spending winter with the Tamaroas at their hunting territory.[141] It is surprising how easily the docteur de Sorbonne has adapted to these Natives that Jesuit priest Gabriel Marest presented as "cowards, traitors, fickle, treacherous, brutal, without honor and without any recognition."[142]

Varlet is rather stingy with details about his dealings with the Natives. The only time he did was in a letter written from Mobile. He said they were "fairly mild and quite manageable."[143] If he came to have such troubles that he had to go to Quebec in the spring of 1717, it was not because of the Indians but because the Jesuits were fighting over a territory they considered reserved for them[144] and because he did not suffice to the task due to the growing needs of the mission.

The Tamaroa conflict dated from 1698, when Bishop St. Vallier had taken from the Jesuits the Mission at Cahokia (granted to them in 1690) and entrusted it to the Priests of the S.M.É.[145] The Jesuits refused to leave the village and maintained a rival ministry. "Two chapels were ringing their bells, calling the Indians for the morning and evening services at the same time".[146] Father Marc Bergier found the situation unedifying upon his arrival in 1700 because the village was divided into two clans. The Bishop of Quebec went to Paris to take part in a commission ordered by the King to settle the dispute and a decision favorable to the S.M.É was made on June 7, 1701. However, the problems continued. Father Bergier claimed that his powers of vicar general extended to all the French in the country of the Illinois, even to the parishes of the Jesuits.[147] When he died in 1707, this second dispute had not been resolved. As the mission has remained without a priest until 1715, one can imagine in what state of ambiguity Varlet found things when he arrived there. It is not surprising that he went to obtain from Bishop St. Vallier, a confirmation of the letters patent issued in 1698, in favour of the S.M.É.

One Year in Quebec City

After a journey of 6 months of which he made a detailed description (found on the following page), Varlet arrived in Quebec for a stay of nearly 13 months. His first goal was to settle the dispute on the Tamaroa Mission with the bishop and the directors of the seminary.[148] Two weeks after his arrival, St. Vallier acquiesced to his request and confirmed by new letters patent, the privileges obtained by the Seminary of Quebec for missionary work among the Tamaroas.[149] He could therefore address the problem of the shortage of missionaries and to that end he occupied the long winter months of 1718. Housed in the seminary which he hoped not to leave too often because of the cold "extremely harsh in this country",[150] he strove to transmit to the clergy his zeal for the salvation of souls and the evangelization of the Amerindians. The best testimony to this effect comes from what Pierre Hurtubise calls the "relations inédites de l'Illinois".[151]

Old Seminary of Quebec

Journey to Quebec

I left my mission on March 24. The spring drought had lowered the level of the Illinois River, which made things difficult. It took almost 25 days to do 30 leagues. Finally, the Lord has sent a big storm which came just in time. It facilitated the portage to the height of land and, at the end of May, we embarked on the lake (Michigan). The newly-made peace with the Fox has facilited our trip because we did not fear the wars of years past. It took a month to do 130 leagues to get to Michilimakinak. We were not well equipped to navigate the lakes because we had wooden boats that do not support the bad weather as well as bark canoes.

On June 20, we went to Michilimakikak where I was welcomed by the commander and the Jesuits. I stayed with these fathers. It took us 8 days to prepare to continue our journey. We had to pay our people, to buy a canoe because the wooden boat could not go further, even though it was still in a good condition. We gave it to the Jesuits in appreciation for their kindness and we bought a bark canoe, which costed me 50 crowns. We still had to stock up on food. All this done, we left on June 28. We wanted to take the shortest route, but there are many rapids that make it dangerous. So, we took the longest route but the safest and easiest: the route of the (Great) Lakes. The first is Lake Huron, where we did 100 leagues before entering the Detroit River which is 20 leagues long. It is the discharge of the lakes where is the Fort Detroit. We arrived there on July 19. I stayed with the chaplain of the fort, a Franciscan priest. After having made provisions, we resumed our journey.

We entered another lake (Lake Erie) on which we did about 100 leagues. We were often stopped by bad weather... Finally, on August 10, we arrived at very famous falls (Niagara Falls), almost as tall as the towers of Notre Dame. All the water of the lakes flows there. This is what forms the St. Lawrence River. We did the portage which is 2 ½ leagues, and on August 17, we embarked on another lake (Lake Ontario) where we did about 80 leagues. After ten days, we left the lake and entered the St. Lawrence River where, after 40 leagues and having passed (the) rapids (of Lachine), we arrived on September 2 in Montreal, the first city of Canada. I stayed 5 days in the seminary of that city, which is led by the Priests of St. Sulpice, and after 60 leagues, we arrived on September 11 in Quebec City, at our seminary.

Varlet to his mother, from Quebec City, October 6, 1717

The *relations of Illinois* are letters sent to Varlet by Jean-Paul Mercier and René Thaumur de la Source, two missionaries that he had recruited at the Seminary of Quebec. Their letters "reveal the spiritual ascendancy Varlet had on those with whom he came in contact."[152] One recalls having told him that *he was his father and would be forever.*"[153] The other is *pleased that through him the Lord makes Varlet continue exercizing his a zeal: Your Grace has, by my hand, baptized in this mission last year, 17 children and an adult... You are doing, through me and my dear colleague Mercier, every day, the catechism, and we hope it will bear more fruits in the future.*[154]

Other letters between Varlet and the Bishop,[155] the Vicar General[156] and other clergymen[157] of the Diocese of Quebec reveal around what turned their conversations during the years he spent in the capital of New France. There was a firm opposition to the Jesuits. This emerges from the letters of Charles Glandelet[158] and Thomas Thiboult, [159] the superiors of the seminary. Each time they refer to the mission of the Illinois, they mention the conflict with the Jesuits and this is typical of the mentality of the diocesan clergy at that time.

Under Bishop St. Vallier, the Church of Quebec had characteristics different from those it had under his predecessor, Francois de Laval, formed by the Jesuits at the College of Laflèche. Jean-Baptiste Chevrière de la Croix de St. Vallier, a graduate of the Faculty of Paris, was formed according to the Augustinian principles. He had been strongly influenced by the Bishop of Grenoble, Étienne Le Camus, who opposed the Bull Unigenitus and appealed to a General Council of the Church.[160] We also know that St. Vallier had been in contact with the

Bishop of Alet, Nicolas Pavillon (1597-1677), whose name is associated with the first Jansenism. Moreover, the ritual of Quebec was based on that of Alet, wich contained propositions condemned by the Church.[161]

Bishop St. Vallier

St. Vallier, a former chaplain of the King, attached a great importance to the Gallican Articles and the liberties of the Church of France. He reportedly opposed the institution of vicars apostolic in New France because they were more devoted to the papacy than to the king.[162] The second bishop of Quebec was a Regalist Gallican. In his diocese, it is the King who made the appointments; controled the religious orders, paid the priests and assured the temporal administration of the Church.

St. Vallier had the reputation for being friendly with Jansenists. Quebec was, next to Utrecht, a place of refuge for partisans of the new doctrine. Father André de Merlac came and was appointed canon; Varlet became vicar general and Georges F. Poulet, a Benedictine monk, settled later in the diocese because he did not have to endorse the Bull Unigenitus. François-Xavier Garneau said that Varlet left after him proselytes of Jansenism in the Church of Quebec. "Father de Villermola of the Seminary of Montreal, Father Thiboult, curé of Quebec, and Father Glandelet, dean of the cathedral chapter, began to think as the author of the Lettres Provinciales".[163] Pierre Hurtubise wrote: *it would be surprising if the future bishop of Babylon did not have the opportunity, in thirteen months of contact with religious houses of the capital, to transmit to them a little of that spirit which would make him known to all Europe.* [164]

2
THE RESISTANCE

In the fall of 1718, Varlet was recalled to Paris by his superiors, who had recommended him to the pope for the position of coadjutor of the bishop of Babylon (Baghdad, Iraq), Msgr. Pidou de St. Olon.[165] "He was consecrated on Quinquagesima Sunday 1719 (February 19), wrote Cardinal de Noailles, in the chapel of our Séminaire des Missions Etrangères. The consecrator was the Bishop of Condom (Gers), Jacques Goyon de Matignon, assisted by the Coadjutor Bishop of Quebec, Louis François Duplessis de Mornay, and the Bishop of Clermont, Jean-Baptiste Massillon."[166]

Duplessis de Mornay, Coadjutor Bishop of Quebec

Eventually St. Vallier would distance from Varlet even if the latter stayed attached to the Church of New France.[167] *The Bishop of Quebec did not approve the 4 bishops who did not accept the condemnation of Jansenius, and the 19 prelates who took their side. What weight,* he said, *may have in the Church such a small number of bishops, while others have taken an opposite view? He claimed strongly from Cardinal Le Camus*, wrote Dom Georges-François Poulet (Récit simple de ce qu'un religieux bénédictin a souffert au Canada au sujet de la bulle

Unigenitus).[168] Poulet was ordered to leave Canada on March 14, 1718 and he left on October 2,[169] possibly on the Mutine together with Varlet. The assumption is made by Pierre Hurtubise and Auguste Gosselin.[170] Anyway, Rome reproached Varlet his relations with the Benedictine monk.[171]

After his consecration, en route for his diocese of Babylon, Varlet stopped at Amsterdam, and he was asked to confirm 604 persons[172] who had not received the sacrament because of the vacancy of the see of Utrecht, due to the conflict with Rome.[173] He wrote in his Première Apologie that he was not aware of these troubles.[174] It is as if he wanted to transpose in Holland the model of church functioning he had experienced in the Church of New France.[175] However, there was no question of liberties of Gallican type in that church, which was administered on behalf of Rome by the Internuncio of Brussels.[176] The fact that he did confirmations without the permission of the Internuncio would never be forgiven.

When he arrived in Persia, a Jesuit gave him a letter from the Bishop of Isfahan (Iran) telling him he had been suspended by Rome of the exercise of the episcopate.[177] Unable to occupy his see, he returned to the Netherlands in the spring of 1721 and lived in Amsterdam, with Arnould de Brigode Dubois, a French librarian, established on the Keysersgracht. There he recovered from the negative experience in had in Persia and he took steps to have the suspense canceled. He liaised with Cardinal de Noailles and the directors of the S.M.É. of Paris and they promised to make every effort to have him reconciled with

Rome. Father François de Montigny, who had recommended him for the bishopric of Babylon,[178] represented him to the Propaganda, but a condition was imposed: he had to return to France so that he be not accused of associating himself with the refractory clergy of Holland. He met the condition and spent part of the year 1722 with Msgr. Charles de Caylus, Bishop of Auxerre.[179] Jean-Pierre Gibert, one of the best French canonists of the time was consulted. He believed that the suspense was invalid and suggested to ignore it. This opinion was shared by many theologians of Paris and Louvain. Canonist Bernard van Espen of Louvain went as far as saying that in all antiquity, no bishop was so badly treated.[180] Varlet composed a memorandum to the attention of the Propaganda. He added the report of Gibert and the summer was spent in negotiations. In August, he said to De Montigny he would never accept the Bull Unigenitus; that he would not apologize for having done confirmations in Amsterdam and that he would not abandon his rights to the see of Babylon.[181] In the circumstances, said De Montigny, your situation is hopeless. Varlet returned to Amsterdam at the beginning of 1723.

Caylus, Bishop of Auxerre

Immediately after moving to Holland, he resumed by letters the negotiations with the Propaganda and Pope Innocent XIII but there was no response. He decided to follow the example of several French bishops and of the Chapter of Utrecht, and on February 15, 1723, he appealed to a general council against the suspense received in Persia and the Bull Unigenitus which was the pretext of it.

Meanwhile, the Cathedral Chapter had resolved to elect an archbishop and put an end to the vacancy of the see of Utrecht. The see had been vacant since May 7, 1702 when Archbishop Peter Codde was deposed by Rome. A letter had been sent to the pope on June 11, 1721 but it remained unanswered. It was followed on September 30 of that year, by a <u>Mémoire sur l'Église et le clergé d'Utrecht</u> demonstrating the necessity of a bishop.[182] As there was no answer there either, they appealed to the canonist Bernard van Espen and to two other doctors of Louvain. The result of the consultation, published under the title <u>Dissertatio de misero statu ecclesiae ultrajectinae</u>,[183] included the following: (1) it is necessary to have a bishop in a national church, (2) the canons of the chapter have the right to elect a bishop, (3) if Rome refuses to issue the bulls, the chapter may nevertheless proceed with the election and the consecration, (4) the nearest bishops have the duty, in such a situation, to provide assistance for the consecration.[184]

Once this consultation was approved by 19 doctors of the Sorbonne and several other from Reims, the Chapter decided to consult with government officials to have their view regarding the consecration of an archbishop of Utrecht. The results were favorable and a Protestant lawyer named Slicher expressed the opinion that it could be avantageous to the state that the Catholics be under the jurisdiction of a national bishop.[185]

Towards a National Dutch Church

Knowing that there was nothing to hope from Rome, the Chapter met at The Hague on April 27, 1723 and proceeded with the election of an archbishop. The majority of the votes went to Canon Cornelis Steenoven, the vicar general of Utrecht.[186] A series of letters were sent to the pope. The day of the election, the Chapter asked him to be excused from the canonical rule requiring three consecrating bishops. Then the archbishop elect sent him his profession of faith. The Chapter renewed its request of April 27 on August 4 and on December 29, but it remained unanswered. On March 9, 1724, a circular letter was sent to all Catholic bishops, exposing the sufferings of the Church of Utrecht. Meanwhile, the death of Innocent XIII had left the See of Rome vacant. The cardinals assembled in conclave, sent a letter on April 8, in which they made severe reproaches to the Chapter of Utrecht. It was followed by a circular letter from the Internuncio of Brussels to all the Catholics of Holland. He explained that in the eyes of Rome, the pretensions of the supposed canons of Utrecht were inadmissible, the chapter having been abolished by the pope in 1702.[187] As for the need of a bishop, it was a chimera: the majority of the Catholics acknowledged Jan van Bijlevelt (appointed on October 2, 1717) as provicar apostolic. The refractory parishes had to do the same and stop their unjustified disobedience.[188] The Chapter responded with a letter sent to all Catholic chapter deans begging them to stand with the canons of Utrecht against the invasion of their common rights. They also wrote to the new pope, Benedict XIII, as well as to the prelates of neighboring countries. Dom Thierry de

Viaixnes, the secretary of Bishop Varlet,[189] took it upon himself to get the sentiments of the French bishops. In a letter to the Chapter on September 10, 1724, he wrote that the bishops of Montpellier, Senez and Auxerre were in favor of the consecration as well as those of Bayeux, Pamiers, Macon, Rhodes, Angouleme , Metz and Troyes.[190]

Having unsuccessfully sought the assistance of the neighboring bishops, the canons on October 13, 1724, addressed a letter to Bishop Varlet asking him to consecrate their Archbishop Elect Steenoven. The latter proceeded with the consecration in the oratory of Brigode Dubois in Amsterdam, where Father Quesnel had taken refuge and celebrated his religious services. He was assisted by Johannes van Erkel, dean of the chapter, and Willem van Dalenoort, one of the canons.[191]

When the new archbishop wrote to the pope to inform him of his consecration, the latter replied, on February 22, 1725, by the brief *Qua Sollicitudine* which pronounced his excommunication and that of Bishop Varlet and of all those involved in the election and the consecration. The Church of Utrecht, from that moment, would have to begin the career of an Independent Church. She would eventually be recognized by the state and granted a budget of some 12.000 florins.[192]

Msgr. Steenoven

Archbishop Steenoven died on April 3, 1725, only six months after his consecration. It is his successor, Cornelis Barchman Wuytiers[193] (whose episcopate was predicted by Father Quesnel)[194] who would consolidate the positions of the Kerk der O.B.C. Bishop Varlet consecrated him on September 30, 1725, in the same manner as his predecessor. Three events particularly distinguished his episcopate: (1) the establishment of religious houses for refugees from France and Luxembourg, (2) unity talks with the Russian Orthodox Church and (3) a project of a mission in Indochina.

Msgr. Barchman Wuytiers

As these events are likely to inform us about the type of relationship that Bishop Varlet had with the Church of Utrecht, we will discuss them briefly.

Religious Life at Rijnwijk and Schonauwen

The accession of Barchman Wuytiers to the Metropolitan See of Utrecht brought more more than 100 letters of praise and communion signed by some 2,000 clergy of France and the Austrian Netherlands (actual Belgium).[195] These signatures were those of bishops who had welcomed Archbishop Steenoven and it is reported that about thirty others in France, had said verbally they were sympathetic.[196] This is because the cause of Utrecht had become that of all the Appellants. The new archbishop was known in Jansenist circles outside the

Netherlands since he had studied at Huissen, at Louvain and at the Seminary of Saint Magloire in Paris. In addition, he had been ordained a priest by the Appelant Bishop of Senez, Jean Soanen.[197]

Very soon after he had become the leader of the Kerk der O.B.C., thirty-one French Carthusians and forteen Cistercians from the Abbey of Orval in Luxembourg, persecuted for their refusal to accept the Bull Unigenitus, came to place themselves under his protection. He wrote constitutions for them in collaboration with Bishop Varlet and established them in two houses which have become famous in the history of the Church of Utrecht: Schonauwen and Rijnwijk. Bishop Varlet who acted as Episcopal Visitor in conjunction with the Archbishop,[198] lived in both houses, spending the summers at Schonauwen and the winters at Rijnwijk.

House at Rijnwijk

The importance of these houses, particularly that of Rijnwijk is highlighted in the *Inventaire* of the Port Royal Archives by Bruggeman and van de Ven, which devotes to them a large section (nos. 1826 to 4175) titled *French and Belgian Refugees*.[199] Moreover, in the preface of the book, van de Ven shows the role played by the house at Rijnwijk in the conservation of the papers listed in the Inventaire.[200] These papers give us a good idea of the activities that took place there.

We learn that shortly after the establishment of the monks of Orval in 1726, French clergymen came as refugees there and that they soon founded a school of theology which was in operation until they moved to Utrecht in 1772: St. Mary's Cloister on the Mariaplaats.[201] To answer the needs of their theology students, they developed a vast library that received, between 1730 and 1740, the papers related to the Abbey of Port Royal and its circle[202] which form the core of the Inventaire by Bruggeman and van de Ven.

Schonauwen and Rijnwijk are two small villages located a few miles from the city of Utrecht. Although quite distant from each other, the two houses appear to have been under the same administration.

House at Schonauwen

The *Inventaire* indicates that L. Paris Vaquier de Villiers was administrator of Rijnwijk and Schonauwen.[203] This, although each community had its own superior. For example, one of Brigode Dubois' lodgers, Benoît Honasse, was Prior of the Carthusians at Schonauwen after 1712. This may explain why Bishop Varlet, his companion of refuge, moved there with his secretary De Viaixnes and that Jacques Jubé, former pastor of Asnieres, joined them in 1730.

Each house had its special vocation. At Rhijnwijk, they did theological training, at Schonauwen, agriculture.[204] Bishop Varlet, because of his training and interests, felt closer to the house at Rijnwijk. The *Plan d'une méthode pour étudier la théologie et l'histoire de l'Église* that was found in his papers, along with his *Annotations sur divers sujets d'ordre historique, théologique et moral*,[205] indicate that he gave courses.[206] He was in the public eye and Barchman Wuytiers, who lived there, must have told him he had something in mind for him. On June 16, 1727, he invited him to participate, as a suffragan,[207] in a meeting of the Metropolitan Chapter, called to elect a bishop for the diocese of Haarlem.[208] It is not excluded that the archbishop wanted him to occupy that see. In a memorandum sent to the chapter, he told the canons that he would himself appoint a bishop if they could not elect one within three months.[209] We know that ultimately, the choice fell on Theodore Donker who was never consecrated because of *various writings of his own on the subject of usury (that) raised a storm which threatened the welfare if not the existence of the National Church.*[210]

Unity Talks with the Russian Orthodox Church

Among the aspects that marked the episcopate of Barchman Wuytiers, we must speak of his role in unity talks with the Russian Orthodox Church. They began in 1717, during a visit of Emperor Peter II to the Faculty of Theology of Paris. A group of doctors, deploring the division that separated the Eastern Christians from those of the West, proposed to prepare a memorandum to the bishops of the Russian Church. This occurred one year before similar talks started with Archbishop William Wake of Canterbury.[211] Events precipitated when Princess Irina Petrovna Dolgoruki,[212] who lived in Holland, made profession of Catholic faith in front of Archbishop Barchman Wuytiers on June 11, 1717 and asked that a priest be sent to minister to her family in Russia.[213] The archbishop asked Father Jacques Jubé to assume the charge. After a visit to Paris, where he obtained the agreement of the doctors of Sorbonne and of Cardinal de Noailles, he went to Moscow and remained there until the death of the Emperor in 1730. The accession of the Empress Anna to the throne of Russia put an end to the project. Having conceived a mortal hatred for the Dolgoruki family, she did everything in her power to compromise their interests. Jubé returned to Holland where he joined his friend Varlet in Schonauwen.

We do not know exactly what was the participation of the Bishop of Babylon in the project. His correspondence is silent on the matter and says nothing on the theological implications of such an undertaking. What is certain is that as a suffragan and adviser of the archbishop, his cooperation was sought.

We can get an idea of these ecumenical exchanges from the findings made by Edmond Préclin in his study on richerism.[214] Hence, it is possible to speculate on the involvement that Bishop Varlet had. The objective of these exchanges, in the wake of the Appeal, was to "bring the Bull Unigenitus to nothing".[215] This, by holding a general council in which would participate the Church of Rome, that of Russia and soon that of England, regenerated under the presbytero-episcopal influence of the Church of Utrecht.[216] Even if it may have seemed utopian, this ideal made some people dream as evidenced by an anonymous manuscript preserved in the Library of Nantes. The author, full of respect for Msgr. Barchman Wuytiers, gives him the surprising title "Our Holy Father the Pope Patriarch of Utrecht".[217] Such a craze for the archbishop is indicative of what he represented for these Appellants that Voltaire considered more dangerous than the Presbyterians of England.[218] *They have a populist conduct*, said Bishop Lafiteau of Sisteron, *and they want to overthrow at the same time the ecclesiastical and the monarchical orders*.[219]

We do not address the political dimension of the Utrecht church reform.[220] Our interest is for aspects of the work of Bishop Varlet that illustrate the support that he gave to Archbishop Barchman Wuytiers. It is in the <u>Annotations sur divers sujets</u> ... that we find the most relevant information. We have identified two. The first, in line with the ecumenical efforts, is the necessity to build the communion of the Church on the unity of the faith.[221] A unity that only the See of Utrecht could guarantee, Rome having lost, by its greed, her function of guardian of the deposit.[222] The second is the need to end the schisms caused by sin[223] because it is a scandal that put the believers at risk of losing their faith.[224] This explains why pastoral assistance was provided to the Dolgoruki family in Moscow. Bishop Varlet also shared the sollicitude of Msgr. Barchman Wuytiers for the Christians of India who were opposing the Bull Unigenitus. All these pastoral situations made the strings of his heart vibrate.[225]

Indochina Mission Project

During the two years he exercised jurisdiction in Russia, while negotiations were underway with the Russian Orthodox Church, Msgr. Barchman Wuytiers, possibly at the instigation of Msgr. Varlet who had long corresponded with missionaries in these regions,[226] had his attention put on another project of interest: that of organizing a mission for the Christians of India who opposed the Bull Unigenitus, with a view that the islands of Malabar be evangelized from there. Bishop Varlet had an interest for the Eastern Christians. This dated back to his early university years. He studied Oriental languages and his library contained books on the history and civilization of these people.[227] He worked hard on the project using for this purpose the relations he still had in Paris. A French Oratorian, Father Gaspard Terrasson, had even been designated as superior.[228] Unfortunately, while they were preparing to send the first missionaries, the Bishop of Rosalie, who was Vicar Apostolic of Siam, desisted from the enterprise. He did not want to antagonize Rome for the uncertain benefits this mission could bring.[229] As the cooperation of the Vicar Apostolic was needed for the project, they did not go ahead with it.

3
THE LAST YEARS

The failure of the mission project in Indochina was not the last disappointment of Bishop Varlet. On May 13, 1733, Msgr. Barchman Wuytiers died at Rijnwijk, carrying in his grave the noble ideals which had almost made the French refugees forget that they were in exile. The Bishop of Babylon was 55 years old when took place the funeral of the man who liked him enough to consider having him as successor. The rumor was that he would succeed him, but it did not happen. On July 27, 1733, the chapter unanimously elected Theodore van der

Archbishop van der Croon

Croon[230] as Archbishop of Utrecht. As with previous archbishops, an election notice was sent to Rome with a request for permission to proceed with the consecration with a single consecrating bishop. Having received no response after one year, Archbishop-elect van der Croon sent another letter to the pope and he invited the bishops of neighboring countries to attend the ceremony.

Despite attempts by the Portuguese and French Ambassadors to dissuade him,[231] Bishop Varlet proceeded with the consecration on

October 28, 1734.[232] Rome responded with a brief of excommunication, which was followed by the traditional appeal to a general council by the archbishop and the chapter.

Van der Croon, who did not have the stature of his predecessor, has employed the five years of his episcopate to defend himself against the Cardinals, who accused him of being a false bishop. Restrained by the moderate Gallican party which did not want to offend Rome, he reduced the Church of Utrecht to a local reality at the mercy of the Dutch merchants, favorable to usury.[233] It was a dark period for Bishop Varlet. But instead of becoming bitter, he engaged in intense reflections on the importance of being configured to Christ and he wrote his most profound texts on the spiritual role of the bishop. He sees him as one who assumes in an exemplary fashion, the lordship of Jesus in his diocesan church. In his view, the direction taken by the chapter was running counter to this vision.[234]

Disappointed by his co-religionists, he turned to the French convulsionists,[235] then under intense persecutions. He saw them as blessed by God in that miracles were operated through the intercession of deacon Francois de Pâris who sided with the Jansenists in their opposition to the Bull Unigenitus.

François de Pâris

He died on May 1, 1727 in the midst of the debate over the Bull, and was buried in the parish cemetery of Saint-Medard in Paris. Soon worshippers began to gather at his tomb and reported miraculous healings and events. They also began to go into strange convulsions, and empassioned followers filled the streets writhing as though in a trance.

Usually held in suspicion by most of the Jansenists, those last hour Appelants had few supporters. The fact that Bishop Varlet got interested in their fate and defended them from the Bible, made him an expert who was consulted on the question of miracles.

When Archbishop van der Croon died in 1739 (June 9), he refused to consecrate a successor.[236] Along with Jacques Jubé, he retired to Zwolle, in a secret location in order not to be solicited. Finally, he accepted to lay his hands on Peter Meindaerts, a canon of stature who strengthened his position by consecrating bishops for the former dioceses of Haarlem and Deventer.[237] It was a providential decision because it is through the bishops of these dioceses that the episcopal succession would be maintained in the Dutch church and transmitted outside the Netherlands, starting with German Old Catholics.[238] It is

Archbishop Meindaerts

also Archbishop Meindaerts who convened the first synod in 1763, inviting the Dutch Old Catholics to define their faith.

Msgr. Meindaerts was the last archbishop of Utrecht to be consecrated by Bishop Varlet. When he conducted the ceremony on October 18, 1739, he was 61 years. His health, which already worried Archbishop Barchman Wuytiers in 1727, continued to decline. He lived three more years at Rijnwijk and died there from a stroke. Jaque Lohof, burial crier of the city of Utrecht, prepared the following burial certificate:

I hereby certify that on the 14th month of May 1742 has died at Rijnwijk Msgr. Dominique Marie Varlet, Bishop of Babylon, and that his body was buried by me in the church of St. Mary in Utrecht on the 18th of the said month of May 1742.
"We did a solemn funeral, wrote the superior, Vaquier de Villiers.[239] His body was carried by 16 clergymen, most of whom were French priests or religious. There was a large crowd and nearly 100 people in black robes and cloaks. The body was placed in the vault

Burial place of Bishop Varlet in Utrecht

near the coffin of the Princess of Auvergne... [240] The Archbishop (Meindaerts) officiated pontifically."

Already in 1724, when he published his Première Apologie, Bishop Varlet was in full possession of his means. His character and his thoughts were fixed. It is this spiritual master that we will discover in the second part, detailing his efforts to make the Church more conformed with the mission dictated to her by the Holy Scripture and the Tradition.

Notes

[1] Cornelis Jansen, known by his Latinized name Jansenius, was Bishop of Ypres in Belgium. He became the father of the theological movement known as Jansenism, which is characterized by moral rigor and derived its position on grace from Saint Augustine. See note 63 on Augustinism. Other characteristics include the idea of the sinfulness of humanity and predestination (God determined the fate of the universe throughout all of time and space). Although they were condemned by the pope, the Jansenists continued to have a following among those who tended to reject papal authority. The archdiocese of Utrecht, Holland, was influenced by the Jansenists and it separated from the Roman Catholic Church in the 18th century, leading to the development of the Old Catholic Church.

[2] The spread of Protestantism and the need for moral and administrative reforms had let to widespread demands for a council. Summoned by Pope Paul III, the Council of Trent embodied the ideas of the Counter-reformation and established a base for the renewal of discipline and spiritual life in the Roman Catholic Church. Oxford Concise Dictionary..., 2006, p. 597. The counter-reformation included the foundation of seminaries for the proper training of priests and new spiritual movements focusing on the devotional life and a personal relationship with Christ, including the Spanish mystics and the French school of spirituality.

[3] The main feature of Jansenism was the concept of a Christianity deeply demanding, lived without compromises or concessions. Louis Cognet, Le Jansénisme, Presses Universitaires de France (P.U.F.), Paris, 1961, p. 124.

[4] The Oratorians are a congregation of priests and lay-brothers founded by St. Philip Neri (1515-1595) in Rome. Pierre de Bérulle (1575-1629) in 1611 founded the French branch of the Congregation of the Oratory destined to propagate educational institutions. It did not submit to the formulary condemning Jansenism until 1749.

[5] Gallicanism (originating among the French clergy) favored the restriction of papal control and the achievement by each nation of individual administrative autonomy of the church. It is in opposition to Ultramontanism. Edmond Richer (1559-1631) is the author of De ecclesiastica et politica potestate (1611), a short but influential brochure which summarizes his positive Gallicanism. It also expresses his 'democratic' view of authority in the Church as something that is shared by all the members. This 'richérisme' strongly influenced 18th-c. Jansenism.
http://www.answers.com/topic/edmond-richer

[6] Under the name Gallican Articles, four claims were made by an Assembly of the French clergy in 1682. They denied that the Pope had dominion over things temporal and affirmed that kings are not subject to the Church in civil matters. They reaffirmed the authority of a General Council over the Pope;

	insisted that the ancient liberties of the French Church were inviolable; and asserted that the judgement of the Pope was not irreformable. http://www.encyclopedia.com/doc/1O95-GallicanArticlestheFour.html
7	Jean-Baptiste Poquelin, known by his stage name Molière (1622-1673), became an actor in 1643. He cofounded a troupe (Illustre Théâtre) that was established in a permanent theatre in Paris under the patronage of Louis XIV (1659). He then won acclaim in the court and among bourgeois audiences. His major plays include *The School for Wives*, *Tartuffe*, *The Misanthrope*, *The Miser*, *The Bourgeois Gentleman*, and *The Imaginary Invalid*. http://www.answers.com/topic/moliere
8	La Grange, Charles Varlet, sieur de (1639-1692). Male lead in Molière's company from 1659, and administrator of the company after Molière's death. He kept a detailed register of productions, takings, etc., which is an essential source of information for the history of the theatre. http://www.answers.com/topic/charles-varlet-la-grange
9	Tragedy by Philippe Quinault (1635-1688) written in 1658.
10	Pierre Corneille (1606-1684) wrote his first comedy, *Mélite*, before he was 20; other comedies followed. He responded to the call for a new approach to classical tragedy by writing *Le Cid* (1637), an instant success that established him as the creator of French classical tragedy. http://www.answers.com/topic/pierre-corneille
11	Madeleine Jurgens & Elizabeth Maxfield-Miller, <u>Cent ans de recherches sur Molière, sur sa famille et sur les comédiens de sa troupe</u>, Paris, Imprimerie Nationale, 1963.
12	Friedrich Hermann, duc de Schomberg (Schönberg), 1616-1690, was a marshal of France. Descended from an old family of the Palatinate, he was the son of Hans Meinard von Schönberg and Anne, daughter of Edward Sutton, 5th Baron Dudley. He began his military career under Frederick Henry, Prince of Orange, and entered into the service of France in 1635. http://en.wikipedia.org/wiki/Frederick_Schomberg,_1st_Duke_of_Schomberg
13	Auguste Jal, <u>Dictionnaire critique de biographie et d'histoire</u>, Paris, Calman-Lévy, 1887, p. 105.
14	During the time of the *Ancien Régime* (Old Regime), French society was broken down into three orders or classes. The most important class of the three consisted of the rebellious Nobility of the Second Order which contained about 400,000 individuals who held all the public offices in the kingdom. The First Order consisted of the Clergy, or the Church. The Third Order consisted of citizens who weren't classified as either Clergy or Nobility (the Peasants, the Middle Class, and the Urban Workers).
15	D. Cogné, *Les armoiries de Dominique-Marie Varlet (1678-1742)*, <u>L'Héraldique au Canada</u>, Vol. XVI, No. 2, June 1982, p. 9-11.

[16] The bourgeoisie (adjective: bourgeois) is a social class of people, characterized by their ownership of capital. They are a part of the merchant class, and derived social and economic power from employment, education, and wealth, as distinguished from social classes whose power came from being born into an aristocratic family of titled land owners. *Bourgeois* and *bourgeoisie* originate from the French word *bourg*, (cf. German *Burg*) meaning city-dweller. http://en.wikipedia.org/wiki/Bourgeoisie

[17] D. Cogné, op. cit., p. 10.

[18] Bernardin Gigault, marquis de Bellefond (1630-1694), maréchal de France.

[19] Pierre Hurtubise, *Dominique-Marie Varlet, missionnaire en Nouvelle-France (1713-1718)*, Bulletin de la Société canadienne d'histoire de l'Église catholique, Vol. 35, p. 21.

[20] The *régale* was the royal right to the revenues and the administration of vacant sees. Initially, it existed only in a part of France but Louis XIV in 1673 wanted to extend it to all provinces of the kingdom. He met the opposition of two bishops: Nicolas Pavillon of Alet and François de Caulet of Pamiers. Émile Jacques, op. cit., p. 17, note 34.

[21] Cartesianism is the doctrine of René Descartes (1596-1650) that viewed the mind as being wholly separate from the corporeal body. Sensation and the perception of reality were thought to be, potentially, lies, with the only truth to be had in the existence of a metaphysical mind. Such a mind can perhaps interact with a physical body, but it does not exist in the body, nor even in the same physical plane as the body. In France, it was very popular, and gained influence among Jansenists such as Antoine Arnauld, though it became opposed by Roman Catholic authorities.
http://en.wikipedia.org/wiki/Cartesianism

[22] Jean Racine (1639-1699) was a dramatist, one of the "Big Three" of 17th century France (along with Molière and Corneille). He was primarily a tragedian, though he did write one comedy. Experimenting with poetry yielded high praise from France's greatest literary critic, Nicolas Boileau with whom he would later become great friend, and Boileau would often claim that he was behind the budding poet's work.
http://en.wikipedia.org/wiki/Jean_Racine

[23] He received his education at the *Petites écoles de Port-Royal*, an institution which would greatly influence other contemporary figures including Blaise Pascal. Racine's interactions with the Jansenists in his years at this academy would have great influence over him for the rest of his life. At Port-Royal, he excelled in his studies of the Classics and the themes of Greek and Roman mythology would play large roles in his future works.

[24] A.M. Lefebvre, Calendrier historique et chronologique de l'Église de Paris, 1747, p. 391-396.

[25] C.A. de Sainte-Beuve, Port-Royal, Bibliothèque de la Pleiade, Paris, tome III, p. 575-76.

[26] Émile Jacques, op. cit., p. 689.

[27] Pierre Gassendi (1592-1655) wrote numerous philosophical works, finding a way between scepticism and dogmatism. His best known intellectual project attempted to reconcile Epicurean atomism with Christianity. He was one of the most illustrious libertine of the 17th century.
http://en.wikipedia.org/wiki/Pierre_Gassendi

[28] The Port-royalists were dwellers in the Cistercian Abbey of Port Royal des Champs, near Paris, when it was the home of the Jansenists in the 17th century, among them being Arnauld, Pascal, and other famous scholars.
http://www.thefreedictionary.com/Port-royalist

[29] B.A. van Kleef, *Dominicus Maria Varlet*, Internationale Kirchliche Zeitschrift (I.K.Z.), Berne, 1963, Hefte 2-4, p. 7.

[30] Mentionned in the Nouvelles Ecclésiastiques, Paris, July 8, 1742.

[31] Idem.

[32] Accoring to Louis Cognet (op. cit., p. 124-25) Jansenism helped prepare the way for modern consciousness by the intense desire it had for human rights and especially personal thinking in front of absolutist authority. After 1675 the Jansenists got closer to the Second Order of society, whose dignity had been offended in the requirement to sign the Formulary of Alexander VII and the continual progress of episcopal authority which weakened the jurisdiction of parish priests. E. Preclin (op. cit., p. 21). On October 16, 1656, in the Bull Ad Sacram, Pope Alexander VII condemnent as heretical five propositions supposedly found in the book Augustinus by Cornelis Jansen. The Jesuits who then enjoyed predominant political and theological power, persuaded the Pope to force all Jansenists to sign a formulary leading them to admit the papal bull and to confess to their faults. The Assembly of the French Clergy hereafter decided to impose on all priests the signature of an anti-Jansenist formulary, in which each one accepted the papal condemnation.

[33] *Nothing encourages me more to undertake the holy work into which God wants to use me than the example of your virtue and of your submission to his will*. D.M. Varlet to his mother, December 18, 1712, in S.A. Thériault, Lettres de Dominique-Marie Varlet se rapportant aux missions du Séminaire de Québec et de l'Orient, au mouvement de l'Appel au Concile général de la bulle Unigenitus et au clergé vieil-épiscopal d'Utrecht, 1713-1739, Université du Québec en Outaouais, 1982, in Bibliothèque et Archives du Québec (BAnQ.), Centre de l'Outaouais, Collection Réforme catholique (C.R.C.), Document No. P103, S2, D3/5, p. 11, 19, 22. Also in Basil Guy, Domestic

[34] Correspondance of Dominique M. Varlet, Bishop of Babylone, E.J. Brill Editor, Leyden, The Netherlands, 1986, p. 43.

Basil Guy, op.cit., p. 43, 48, 51, 53. Also in our edition of Bishop Varlet's Lettres du Canada et de la Louisiane, Presses de l'Université du Québec (P.U.Q.), 1986, p. 48.

[35] D.M. Varlet to his mother, January 25 1713 in Lettres... se rapportant aux missions du Séminaire de Québec..., BAnQ, 1982, p. 19 & 23.

[36] E. Jacques, op. cit., p. 239.

[37] Lettres... se rapportant aux missions du Séminaire de Québec..., op. cit., p. 19 & 23.

[38] D. Cogné, op. cit., p. 11.

[39] Maximin Deloche, *Un missionnaire français en Amérique au 18e siècle: contribution à l'histoire de l'établissement des Français en Louisiane*, Bulletin de la section géographique du Comité des travaux historiques de l'Instruction publique et des beaux-arts, Paris, 1930, Vol. 45, p. 58.

[40] This is recorded in the Registre des délibérations de Messieurs les Prêtres du Calvaire du Mont-Valérien (1664-1744), Archives Nationales de France, Paris, LL1591, p. 38-39. Also mentioned in the book by E. Préclin and E. Jarry, Les Lettres doctrinales aux 17e et 18e siècles, Paris, Bloud & Gay, 1955, Tome 1, p. 220-233.

[41] Ernest Lavisse, Histoire de France, 1926, Tome VII, p. 88.

[42] Nicolas Boileau-Despréaux (1636-1711) was brought up to the law, but devoted to letters, associating himself with Jean de la Fontaine, Jean Racine, and Molière. He is the author of *L'Art poétique* in which he attacked and employed his wit against what he perceived to be the bad taste of his time. He did much to reform the prevailing form of French poetry, as Blaise Pascal did to reform the prose. http://en.wikipedia.org/wiki/Nicolas_Boileau-Despreaux

[43] Charles Perrault (1628-1703) laid the foundations for a new literary genre, the fairy tale. His best tales include *Little Red Riding Hood, Sleeping Beauty, Puss in Boot, Cinderella...* A major participant in the Quarrel of the Ancients and the Moderns, he attempted to prove the superiority of the literature of his century. http://en.wikipedia.org/wiki/Charles_Perrault

[44] E. Jacques, op. cit., p. 692

[45] Bernard le Bovier de Fontenelle (1657-1757) was received into the Académie Française in spite of the efforts of the partisans of the Ancients in this quarrel, especially of Racine and Boileau.

46   About Malebranche's Traité de la nature et de la grâce, he wrote: *Regarding metaphysics which has always been his forte, he was strangely misguided.* E. Jacques, op. cit., p. 259-260.

47   We know by the content of his library that these questions did not let Bishop Varlet indifferent. In the section called *Philosophi et Mathematici*, there was one book by Malebranche (Recherche de la vérité) versus 7 related to Descartes (Doc. No. 171-174, 176, 198-199).

48   Auguste Gosselin, L'Église du Canada depuis Mgr de Laval jusqu'à la Conquête, Laflamme & Proulx, Quebec, Tome I, pages 331-335.

49   P. Hurtubise, op. cit., p. 25.

50   We use the terms *École de Sorbonne* to designate the Faculty of Theology because in the 17th century it held its meetings in this college. But the doctors who represented its doctrine belonged to various colleges, including that of Navarre. (Aimé-Goerges Martimort, Le Gallicanisme, P.U.F., Paris, 1973, p. 77). Varlet prepared the license (L.Th.) and the doctorate (D.Th.) at the Collège de Navarre, but he took courses in other colleges. For example, around 1699, he studied Hebrew, Arabic and Syriac with Brother Fétis de la Croix at the Collège Royal. E. Préclin (op. cit., p. 181) found the information in a letter of Jacques Jubé to his brother dated January 26, 1726 (Troyes, Dossier Jubé, Folio 13).

51   The professors to whom he has been exposed include: Louis Ellies Dupin (1694-1704), Jacques Vincent Asfeld (who was doing figurative exegesis), Noël Alexandre, Nicolas Petitpied (Holy Scripture), and C. Vitasse (he had in his possession two treaties written by him: De Deo and De Trinitate). Studied at Saint-Magloire, besides Jacques Jubé and a friend of the family, J.B. Paulin d'Aguesseau: Cornelis Barchman Wuytiers (the future Archbishop of Utrecht), Boulenois (the future author of the Mémoire pour l'Église et le clergé d'Utrecht and theologian of the bishop of Senez) and Jean Soanen (the future Appelant Bishop of Senez). B.A. van Kleef, op. cit., p. 8.

52   The rumor was that they would push Port-Royal to its limits. It was the story of the time and the conversation of those who, for or against, took part in this affair. P. Guilbert, Mémoires historiques et chronologiques sur l'Abbaye de Port-Royal-des-Champs, Utrecht, 1755-1756, p. 107-109.

53   Among them: Jean Le Noir, theologian of the Diocese of Séez, the Sisters of the Visitation of Angers, the Oratoire of Paris, the University of Louvain, the archbishop of Malines, the Diocese of Ghent, the Diocese of Sens, the Abbey of Hautefontaine and that of Orval in Luxemburg. E. Jacques, op. cit., p. 13, 15, 49, 50, 54, 96, 105.

54   Jean Le Noir of the Diocese of Séez was imprisoned in the Bastille in 1671; Mathieu Feydeau, theologian of the Bishop of Beauvais, exiled to Bourges in

[55] 1677. De Sainte-Marthe of the Seminary of Saint-Magloire was defeated in 1678. On May 17, 1679, Arnauld and the other Solitaires of Port-Royal were ordered to leave. E. Jacques, op. cit., p. 14, 16, 21, 36.

[55] E. Jacques, op. cit., p. 16.

[56] The bishops Pavillon and De Caulet brought to Rome their opposition to extending the right of régale, provoking a conflict that lasted until 1693. A.G. Martimort, op. cit., p. 84. On May 19, 1682 were published the *Quatre Articles Gallicans* that a royal edict made official on March 22. The crisis peaked on September 27, 1688 with the appeal of the King to a future general council. A.G. Martimort, op. cit., p. 101. But the King was to lay arms the following year before the new pope, Innocent XIII, sounding the death knell of the Royal Gallicanism. The *Quatre Articles* remained and they continued to be taught in schools of theology. In that context where developed the ecclesiological theories on which relied the Jansenists of the 18th century in their struggle against the royal, pontifical and episcopal authorities. In this developement inspired by Richerist principles, the book of Father Quesnel (Réflexions morales...) had the same importance as the book by C. Jansen on the doctrine of grace (Augustinus).

[57] E. Jacques, op. cit., p. 16.

[58] Idem, p. 10.

[59] Idem, p. 52, 68, 345.

[60] Michel de Bay (1513-1589), known by his Latin name Baïus, was a Belgian theologian (Louvain), whose work powerfully influenced Cornelis Jansen. http://www.britannica.com/EBchecked/topic/49375/Michael-Baius

[61] E. Jacques, op. cit.

[62] A. Degert, Histoire des séminaires français jusqu'à la Révolution, t. II, Paris, 1912, note 38.

[63] Augustinism designates Saint Augustine's explanation reconciling the theories of the fall, grace, and free will in the solution of the problem of freedom and grace, i.e., of the part taken by God and man in salvation.

[64] Already in 1678, Father Jacques Joseph Duguet, professor at Saint-Magloire, taught that the clergy and the people once had the right to sit in councils (E. Préclin, op. cit., p. 24). Around 1695 the ideas of Edmond Richer were prevalent in France, due first and foremost to the various editions of the Réflexions morales (A. Gazier, Histoire générale du mouvement janséniste, Paris, 1922, Tome 1, p. 234-35), and then to the manuals of theology by Louis Habert and Gaspard Juénin for the use of seminaries (E. Preclin, p. 27). A summary of the theology of Habert is found in the Compendium

Theologicae Dogmatae et Moralis Parisiis, 1736, p. 547, 661, 685). As for the ideas of Juénin, they are presented in his Institutiones Theologicae ad usum seminariorum published in 1694. According to Preclin (p. 27), the Institutiones of Juénin were taught in Paris and Varlet was surely exposed to those ideas at Saint Magloire.

65   His Th.D. dissertation was titled *Claude Caille: Quaestio theologica: quis solus habet immortalitatem (1 Tim. 6:16)*. His defence was on July 8, 1706.

66   *Seconde Plainte et Appel de Mgr l'Évêque de Babylone à l'Église catholique*, in Première Apologie, Amsterdam, 1724, p. 99.

67   The Council of Constance (1414-1418) gave the sanction of its high authority to this Gallican principle. In its fourth and fifth sessions it declared that the council represented the Church and that every person, no matter of what dignity, even the pope, was bound to obey it in what concerned the extirpation of the schism and the reform of the Church; that even the pope, if he resisted obstinately, might be constrained by process of law to obey it in the above-mentioned points.

68   Levant are the countries bordering the Mediterranean from the east, which are Turkey, Syria, Lebanon, Israel, Palestine, and Egypt.

69   Première Apologie, op. cit., p. 16.

70   The label *Jesuit* is applied to the Society of Jesus, a Roman Catholic order founded by St. Ignatius of Loyola in the 16th century as part of the wider Catholic Counter-reformation.

71   Molina was professor of theology at Evora in Portugal, when he published Liberi Arbitrii cum gratia donis, divina praescientia, praedestinatione et reprobatione (1595), a book in which the Jansenists saw the heresy of Pelagius (354-430) condemned by Saint Augustine. The doctrine put forward by Pelagius (called pelagianism) denies original sin and affirms the ability of humans to be righteous.

72   This Varlet Collection is numbered 3626 to 3803 in the Inventaire des pièces d'archives françaises se rapportant à l'Abbaye de Port-Royal-des-Champs et son cercle et à la résistance contre la bulle Unigenitus by J. Bruggeman & A.J. van de Ven (Martinus Nijhoff, The Hague, 1972). The Inventaire is abbreviated A.P.R. (Archives of Port Royal) for future reference. Varlet said he had established in the dissertation for his L.Th. principles that were so orthodox and moderate on grace that not only the Thomists, but also the most stubborn Molinists of the faculty did compliment him. D.M. Varlet, Lettre à Brisacier, June 14, 1719, A.P.R., No. 3643. Thomism is the doctrine which aims at harmonizing grace and free will on principles derived from St. Thomas Aquinas (1225-1274). The Thomist attempt to explain the attitude of the will towards grace, beginning with the idea of efficacious grace. It contains the

idea that by it and with it the free will does precisely that which grace desires should be done. Molinism is a system developed by Jesuit priest Luis de Molina (1535-1600), which purposes to reconcile grace and free will. Molinism tries to clear up the mysterious relation between grace and free will. It emphasizes the unrestrained freedom of the will, without detracting from the efficacy, priority, and dignity of grace.

[73] E. Preclin, op. cit., 201.

[74] Letter of Dom de Viaixnes to the Abbé de Vlierbeek, November 11, 1724 in A.P.R., No 1610.

[75] By Spiritual Jansenism we mean that of devout circles, more concerned with practical spiritual problems than with theological speculation. Louis Cognet sums up the view when he recalls the advice given by St. Francis de Sales: it is better to focus on making good use of grace than to talk about it (op. cit., P. 18). Madame Varlet was probably part of one of these groups of devotees. This is suggested by a demand made to her by Dominique in a letter written from New France on November 23, 1713: *please ask the good souls that you know to pray earnestly to God that He send laborers into this great harvest.* As for Pastoral Jansenism, it follows from the first. B.A. van Kleef pointed it out in his article about Bishop Varlet (op. cit., p. 10): *Healing what was sick and seeking what was lost were for him the highest task of a Christian. This is why he considered the parables of the Good Samaritan and the Prodigal Son as the center of the gospel.* He wrote in his Première Apologie (p. 24) to justify having administered the sacrament of confirmation in Holland: *We have looked upon the poor flock scattered and languishing, as having no pastor, and instead of being carried away by the outrageous example of the Priest and the Levite, we were imbued with the sentiments of mercy of the charitable Samaritan, and fearing God more than earthly powers, we confirmed those who had a pressing need of it.* The books he has left in Cahokia (Illinois) are concerned mostly with the pastoral ministry. Among them are: the first seven volumes of the Morale de Grenoble, the 9th volume of Essais de morale, the Tradition of the Church on repentance and the Pastorale de Saint-Grégoire. Archives of the Seminary of Quebec, Missions, No. 105b. More information on Bishop Varlet's pastoral theology can be found in our article published in I.K.Z., July-September 1985, p. 180-188.

[76] The "cas de conscience" is as follows: is it possible to absolve a penitent who, on the fact of Jansenius said he could not go further than the respectful silence? This problem was submitted to the doctors of the Sorbonne by a parish priest in Clermont-en-Auvergne, Abbé Fehel. One of the doctors, Nicolas Petitpied, wrote an affirmative answer that was signed by forty of his colleagues. Denounced on February 12, 1703, this position was formally condemned by Pope Clement XI in the *Bull Vineam Domini Sabaoth* on July 16, 1705.

[77] E. Jacques, op. cit.

78   The subject of that resistance is developed in: Gabriel du Pac de Bellegarde, <u>Histoire abrégée de l'Église métropolitaine d'Utrecht</u> (1765), C.B. Moss, op. cit., p. 90-123, J.M. Neale, <u>A History of the So-Called Jansenist Church of Utrecht</u>, Apocryphile Press, Berkeley, 2005, and E. Préclin, op. cit., 197-207. This can be supplemented by the two following articles that present a Roman Catholic perspective: E. Allmang, *L'Église janséniste d'Utrecht* in <u>Annuaire Pontifical catholique</u>, 1912, p. 438-456, and J. Carreyre, *Église d'Utrecht* in <u>Dictionnaire de théologie catholique</u>, columns 2390-2446. Here follows a summary of the facts. In 1702, the Apostolic Vicar of Utrecht was suspended by Rome because of Jansenism, and replaced by Theodore van Cock. The Chapter refused to acknowledge him because he had been appointed directly by the Vatican, as if The Netherlands were a mission country. Rome answered that this was indeed the case. The Canons replied that at the time of Vicars Apostolic Rovenius and Neercassel there was a Cathedral Chapter in Utrecht; that it had always existed and that Rovenius had even erected it canonically in a Vicariate (J. Visser, <u>Rovenius und seine Werke</u>, van Gorcum, Assen, 1966). Moreover, Neercassel and his successor, Peter Codde, had been elected by the members of that Chapter. The Church of Holland was not a mission. If Codde and his predecessor have not taken the title of Archbishop of Utrecht, it was to avoid the ill will of the States General. But they were indeed, in fact, archbishops of Utrecht. According to the laws of the Church, they said, the canons are entitled to elect their bishop and the Pope, who is not above the law, cannot take away that right. Hence the election of Cornelis Steenoven on April 27, 1723 and his consecration by Bishop Varlet on October 15 1724. If there has been schism, they said, it was caused by Rome, which violates the laws of the Church. Bishop Varlet used the same arguments in his <u>Deuxième Apologie</u>, Chapters I-XXVIII.

79   E. Jacques, op. cit., p. 49.

80   Compromised with Father Quesnel, whom he had taken as an adviser, he was suspended from the exercise of the episcopate in 1702. The see remained vacant until 1724. E. Jacques, op. cit., p. 390-392.

81   E. Jacques, op. cit., p. 719.

82   Idem, p. 66-67; B.A. van Kleef, op. cit., p. 8. The term "Berullian" comes from Pierre de Bérulle who in 1626 founded, after that of France, the Oratory of Louvain at the request of Msgr. Jansen, Bishop of Ypres. E. Jacques, op. cit., p. 66-67.

83   L. Cognet, op. cit., p. 43-44; B.A. van Kleef, op. cit., p. 8. Also Guy Plante, <u>Le Rigorisme au 17e siècle, Mgr de Saint-Vallier et le sacrement de pénitence (1685-1727)</u>, J. Duculot Ed., Gembloux, 1970.

84   E. Jacques, op. cit., p. 94.

85   D.M. Varlet, <u>Première Apologie</u>, p. 17. The same argument is found in his *Lettre aux missionnaires du Tonquin* (<u>Lettres de D.M. Varlet</u>..., op. cit., p. 128 ff) and in his *Annotations sur divers sujets d'ordre historique, théologique*

[85] *et moral* (edited under the title <u>Recueil Alphabétique des annotations de D.M. Varlet sur divers sujets</u>..., Vol. I, Université du Québec en Outaouais, 1982, p. 3 (absolution) and p. 162 (contrition). Document kept at BAnQ: C.R.C. No. P103, S2, D5/5.

[86] *Lettre à un correspondant parisien*, 13 March 1723, in <u>Lettres de D.M. Varlet se rapportant...</u>, p. 59. More on Bishop Varlet's christology and its rapport to ecclesiology in Part II. Also in on our article *L'articulation christologique comme forme de la thématique ecclésiologique dans trois textes de Dominique-Marie Varlet aux origines du vieux-catholicisme*, I.K.Z. 1990, Vol. 80, No. 389, p. 40-58.

[87] The College of Navarre was one of the colleges of the historic University of Paris. It was founded by Queen Joan I of Navarre in 1304. The regulations allowed the theological students a fire, daily, from November to March after dinner and supper for one half-hour. On the festival days, the theologians were expected to deliver a collation to their fellow-students. The students wore a special dress and the tonsure and ate in common.
http://en.wikipedia.org/wiki/College_de_Navarre

[88] The Gallican doctrines affirmed by the Assembly of the Clergy of 1682 were taught in the schools of theology (Martimort, op. cit., p. 102). These doctrines assume that the authority of the Church is subordinate to the Holy Scripture and the Tradition (perpetual, universal and unanimous). This is a rampart against the ambitious undertakings of the Court of Rome (Mignot, op. cit., p. 10).

[89] The traditional interpretation of the Scriptures, which is the rampart against the abuses of papal authority, is guaranteed by the common maxims and the old usages. (Mignot, op. cit., p. 4). They are contained in the Code of the Universal Church (p. 5). These canons are the only basis of the Gallican liberties (p. 8). They are the fruit of the conciliar experience representing the whole Church militant. Its power comes directly from Jesus Christ and everyone, of whatever state or dignity, even the pope, is required to obey it (p. 106). This is why in the University of Paris, we hold the authority of the council over that of the pope and are censored as heretics those who hold the contrary (p. 107).

[90] P. Hurtubise, op. cit., p. 26.

[91] Loc. cit.

[92] Idem. The Chinese Rites controversy was a dispute within the Catholic Church from the 1630s to the early 18th century about whether Chinese folk religion rites and offerings to the emperor constituted idolatry. Pope Clement XI decided in favor of the Dominicans (who argued that Chinese folk religion and offerings to the emperor were incompatible with Catholicism), which reduced Catholic missionary activity in China.
http://en.wikipedia.org/wiki/Chinese_Rites_controversy

93	*I admit that the abandoned works attract me very much. To them I am dedicated and they are the sole reason that brought me to America. They are the reason why I have accepted to revive the Mission of the Tamaroas: nobody wanted or could do it. I will always remember that 18 years ago, the late Bishop of Rosalie, urging us to dedicate ourselves to foreign missions, did not talk of China nor of Tonkin, or Siam, but only of the abandoned works.* Lettre au doyen Vivant in Paris on August 25, 1725, A.P.R. No. 3749.
94	This is what suggests the letters of the Attorney of the Séminaire des Missions Étrangères of Paris, H.J. Tremblay (A.P.R., No. 3742). When she died in 1720, Madame Varlet bequeathed most of her material possessions, including he house on Nevers Sreet, to Dominique.
95	B.A. van Kleef, op. cit., p. 9.
96	E. Préclin, op. cit., p. 181.
97	Loc. cit.
98	Jacques Jubé, also called Jubé de la Cour, lived in exile duiring the second half of his existence, mainly in the Netherlands where he published most of his works. Jubé had befriended at Saint Magloire his classmate Cornelis Barchman Wuytiers, who became Archbishop of Utrecht. http://en.wikipedia.org/wiki/Jacques_Jube
99	E. Préclin, op. cit., p. 26.
100	<u>Minutes of the Assembly of the Clergy of August 7,1700</u>, Paris, 1703, p. 465.
101	Condamnation par NN.SS. de l'Assemblée du clergé des propositions de la Requête signifiée, au nom du Chapitre de Chartres, à Mgr l'Évêque de Chartres le 15 mai 1700, p. 2.
102	The essential document of the <u>Cérémonial d'Asnières</u> was lost. The sources used are at the Records Office in London (Edgmont, Mss 67). The accusations that we present were collected by E. Préclin (op. cit., p. 183) from the following documents: J. de la Beaune (<u>Réflexions sur la nouvelle liturgie d'Asnières</u>), P. Colonia (<u>Bibliothèque Janséniste</u>, Vol. II, p. 139-140), <u>Collections Languet</u>, Vol. III, doc. 49, Bibliothèque Municipale de Sens. Favorable comments were made by Nicolas Petitpied based on the observations on the <u>Cérémonial</u> by Grancolas (Bibliothèque Nationale de France, Paris, doc. 24,877) and in his *Lettre à l'abbé Vaissière* dated November 17, 1740.
103	In 1724, suspected of smuggling in bundles of Jansenist writings, Jubé took refuge in Holland, near the Archbishop of Utrecht, "whose chapel he accommodated to the taste of Asnières" (Préclin, op. cit., p . 185). In the fall of 1728 he was joined by Nicolas Petitpied who had escaped from the Bastille (Préclin, op. cit., p. 115).

104   The Secret (Latin: Secreta, oratio secreta) is a prayer said in a low voice. In the Roman Rite the *secreta* is said by the celebrant at the end of the Offertory in the Mass. It is the original and for a long time was the only offertory prayer. It is said in a low voice merely because it was said at the same time the choir sang the Offertory, and it has inherited the special name of Secret as being the only prayer said in that way at the beginning. http://en.wikipedia.org/wiki/Secret_(liturgy)

105   E. Préclin, op. cit., p. 183.

106   Bibliotheca Varletiana, op. cit., p. 22 & 43.

107   E. Préclin, op. cit., p. 181-182. It is difficult for him not to see a Protestant inspiration in Jubé's liturgy (p. 233).

108   Basnage, Jacques, L'Unité, la visibilité, l'autorité de l'Église..., 1715, p. 33 & 46.

109   The Protestants recognize, in their synods, the assistance of the Holy Spirit, and they want that we abide by them as if they were infallible (Recueil Alphabétique de D.M. Varlet sur divers sujets..., Vol. I, p. 141). For other points of disagreement between Bishop Varlet and the Protestants, see the same Recueil: pages 28 (invocation of angels and saints), 30 (the Pope as Antichrist), 31 (meaning of the Seven Beasts in the Book of Revelation), 50-51, 76-78, 82-89 (bible interpretation), 54-55 (the authority of the Church), 80-84 (the real presence in the Eucharist), 89, 199 (justification and works), 91 (baptism of children), 92 (original sin), 114, 153 (the sacrament of confirmation), 115 (morality), 116 (the canon of scripture), 118-119 (observance of Lent), 120-121 (doctrinal content of the catechism), 122-125 (clergy celibacy), 128 (liturgical signs), 128 (certainty of salvation), 135-136 (the possibility of God's commandments), 183-188 (the use of the Church Fathers in religion) and 208 (clergy discipline).

110   For Bishop Varlet, "believers are priests as members of the High Priest Jesus Christ (Recueil Alphabétique..., p. 35) and he does not seem to see a difference of nature between the priesthood and the episcopate . "It is probable that this was the practice of the Apostles to confer the episcopate to those they were ordaining priests (Recueil..., p. 222). Maybe he shared the position of Edmond Richer to the effect that the episcopate is an extension of the priestly ministry which is granted by the Synod of the Church. In his Commentaire sur le Concile de Ries (held in 439) he presents the ordination as "the election and everything that attaches a bishop to a see and gives him jurisdiction" (Recueil..., p. 139). But he agreed with the Council of Trent that it is necessary to proceed with the episcopal consecration "no later than six months", otherwise the bishop "is deprived of his church" (Recueil..., p. 222).

111   E. Préclin, op. cit., p. 33.

112   P. Hurtubise, op. cit., p. 26.

113	The Priory of Notre Dame attached to the Abbey of Bec Hellouin (Eure).
114	B.A. van Kleef, op. cit., p. 9.
115	P. Hurtubise, op. cit., p. 26.
116	Marc Bergier was born in 1667 at Tain (Dauphiné), France (today Tain-l'Hermitage, Department of Drôme). He arrived in Quebec in 1698. On 30 July 1699 he was received as a member of the Séminaire des Missions Étrangères of Quebec, and the next day he was appointed Vicar General of Bishop Saint-Vallier for the Mississippi region. On 7 Feb. 1700, after a six-month trip, he arrived among the Tamaroas with the young priest, Michel de Saint-Cosme, who helped him until 1703. The Vicar General was to succeed the founder of the Sainte-Famille mission, Jean-François de Saint-Cosme (1667–1706), his companion's older brother. Bergier applied himself to his ministry with fervour and great rigour. He was an ascetic whose austerity caused fears for his health. These fears were justified since he died 9 Nov. 1707 with his stomach full of abscesses resulting from an epidemic during which he had lavished his attentions without stint upon his Indian prishioners. They mourned him and bestowed upon him their highest praise, saying that he was truly a man. Dictionary of Canadian Biography Online, Volume II (1701-1740). http://www.biographi.ca/
117	It was the port of call of the first *Compagnie des Indes*. The directors and captains of the *Compagnie* kept their residences in Port-Louis. In 1690, Port-Louis became the capital city of a department of the Royal Navy.
118	Details provided by Varlet in a letter to his brother Jean-Achille written on January 5, 1714 from Mobile (Alabama), in Lettres du Canada et de la Louisiane, P.U.Q., op. cit., p. 38-40.
119	F.X. Garneau (Histoire du Canada, Felix Alcan, Paris, 1913, Tome 1, p. 235) makes him arrive in Canada, as well as Anselme Rhéaume (Mgr D.M. Varlet, Bulletin de recherches historiques, III, Québec, 1897, p. 18), M. Tremblay (Mémoire, Archives of the Seminary of Quebec) and Auguste Gosselin (op. cit., p. 33).
120	The colony had a population of 400 persons.
121	The Tamaroas were one of the tribes of the Illinois Confederacy of the Algonquian linguistic family. The name is said to be from the Illinois term *tamarowa*, "cut tail," having reference to a totemic animal, perhaps the bear or the wildcat.
122	To his mother from Mobile, July 13, 1713, in Lettres du Canada et de la Louisiane, P.U.Q., op. cit., p. 41.
123	Antoine Laumet de La Mothe, sieur de Cadillac (1658-1730) was an explorer in New France. Rising from a modest beginning in Acadia in 1683, he achieved

various positions of political importance in the colony. He was the commander of Fort de Buade, modern day St. Ignace, Michigan, in 1694. In 1701, he founded Fort Pontchartrain du Détroit, the beginnings of modern Detroit, which he commanded until 1710. Between 1710 and 1716 he was the governor of Louisiana.

[124] Bénard de la Harpe, Journal historique de l'établissement des Français en Louisiane, Nouvelle-Orléans, 1834, p. 116.

[125] *Édit du Roi portant l'établissement de la Louisiane par le Sieur Crozat, du 14 septembre 1712*, in Édits, ordonnances royaux, déclarations du Conseil d'état du Roi concernant le Canada, Tome I, Quebec, p. 327-331.

[126] To his brother Jean-Achille from Mobile on January 5, 1714, in Lettres du Canada et de la Louisiane, op. cit., p. 37.

[127] Idem.

[128] John G. Shea, The Catholic Church in Colonial Days, 1521-1763, J.G. Shea Ed., New York, 1886, p. 556.

[129] To his mother from Mobile on November 23, 1713 in Lettres du Canada et de la Louisiane, p. 43.

[130] To his mother from Mobile on April 7, 1714, in Lettres…, BAnQ., p. 48.

[131] The confederation included the Kaskaskia, Peoria, Michigamea, Moingwena and Tamaroa. http://www.rootsweb.ancestry.com/~itquapaw/illinois/illinois.html#tamaroa

[132] To his brother from Mobile on January 5, 1714 in Lettres du Canada et de la Louisiane, p. 43.

[133] To his brother from Cahokia on November 2, 1716 in Lettres du Canada et de la Louisiane, p. 44.

[134] Loc. cit.

[135] The Journal historique of Benard de la Harpe (p. 116) tells us that in effect La Mothe Cadillac went to the Illinois country early in the year 1715 in order to verify the existence of silver mines allegedly found in that region by Canadians.

[136] To his mother from Quebec City on October 6, 1717, op. cit., p. 46.

[137] The theme of the abandoned souls appears several times in the work of Varlet. He said that it is his concern for the abandoned souls that brought him to New France and led him to take a stand for the Church of Utrecht. See his letter of 1725 to a missionary (Nouvelles Ecclésiastiques, Paris, July 8, 1742), the preface of the Première Apologie and the Deuxième Apologie, p. 42.

[138] Archives des colonies, B, Vol. II, Mémoires sur les missions du Canada, May 19, 1865, p. 283, Library & Archives Canada (L.A.C.).

[139] *Our vocation to the episcopate after several years as vicar general of a large diocese is a proof of the integrity of our doctrine*, Plainte à l'Église catholique in <u>Première Apologie</u>, p. 2.

[140] J.B.A. Ferland, <u>Cours d'histoire du Canada</u>, Tome II, Hardy ed., 1882, p. 407.

[141] Letter to his mother, from Cahokia, November 3, 1716, <u>Lettres du Canada et de la Louisiane</u>, P.U.Q., p. 45.

[142] Letter of Father Gabriel Marest dated November 9, 1712, in <u>Lettres édifiantes et curieuses</u>, Paris, 1781, IV, p. 320 ff.

[143] To his brother, from Mobile on January 5, 1714, op. cit., p. 42.

[144] Pierre Hurtubise, op. cit., p. 30.

[145] Bishop St. Vallier, *Confirmation de privileges en faveur du Séminaire de Québec*, October 6, 1717. Text in Appendix 3.

[146] Letters of Father Marc Bergier published by Gilbert Garraghan, S.J. in the <u>Illinois Catholic Review</u>, October 1928.

[147] F. Emile Audet, <u>Les Premiers établissements français du pays des Illinois</u>, F. Solat ed., Paris, 1938, p. 41.

[148] To his mother, from Quebec City, October 16, 1717, in <u>Lettres</u>..., P.U.Q., p. 48-49.

[149] Text of the Letters Patent in Appendice 3.

[150] To his mother, from Quebec City, October 16, 1717, op. cit.

[151] Pierre Hurtubise, *Relations inédites des missions de l'Illinois, 1720-1724*, in <u>Église et Théologie</u>, 8, 1977.

[152] P. Hurtubise, op. cit., p. 271.

[153] Letter of Jean-Paul Mercier from Cahokia, September 10, 1722 in <u>Lettres</u>..., P.U.Q., p. 74-79.

[154] Letter of René Thaumur de la Source from Cahokia, September 22, 1720, op. cit., p. 81-82.

[155] Bishop St. Vallier wrote to him on July 20, 1719, op. cit., p. 60.

[156] Joseph Ceré de la Colombière wrote November 8, 1719, op. cit., p. 63-64.

[157] Thomas Thiboult, curé of the Cathedral of Quebec, wrote on October 21, 1722 & October 13, 1723, Charles Glandelet, dean of the Chapter and lord of the Seminary of Quebec, on September 27, 1719, October 12, 1720, 6 & 21 October 1722, September 16, 1723 and October 17, 1724.

[158] Charles Glandelet, letter of October 6, 1722, op. cit., p. 67.

[159] Thomas Thiboult, letters of October 21, 1722 and October 13, 1723, op. cit., p. 70-73. Father Thiboult succeeded Father Glandelet as superior of the seminary in 1723.

[160] Guy Plante (op. cit., p. 31, note 9) and Alfred Rambaud (*La Croix...de St-Vallier, J.B.*, Dictionary of Canadian Biography, Tome II) mention the influence of Msgr. Le Camus on Bishop St. Vallier, as well as Sister Helena O'Reilly (Mgr de St-Vallier et l'hôpital general de Québec, 1882, p. 23) and Louis Bertrand (Correspondance de Louis Tronson, III, Paris, 1904, p. 222-223). The name of Bishop Le Camus appears in the Inventaire of Bruggeman & van de Ven: A.P.R. No. 286, 420, 863, 918, 922, 938, 1067, 1126, 1217, 2595, 3220, 4271, 6132, 6133, 6672, 6912 & 6969. Among his correspondents were: Antoine Arnauld (No. 286), Pasquier Quesnel (No. 1067), Nicolas Pavillon (No. 4271) and Jean Soanen, bishop of Senez (No. 6672 & 6912).

[161] This ritual that the opinion attributed to Antoine Arnauld and Martin de Barcos, contained "doctrines and propositions, false, strange, dangerous and wrong in practice, contrary to the established custom of the Church", Brief *Credita Nobis* dated April 9, 1668.

[162] Henri Têtu (Les Évêques de Québec, Granger ed., Montreal, p. 133-34) mentions the opposition of Bishop St. Vallier to the erection of vicars apostolic in New France to give preference to the bishops. The reason is that "the bishops serve the interests of the king better than the vicars apostolic, who seem more attached to those of Rome". These words, taken from a *mémoire* that St. Vallier presented to the King in 1714 when Louis Duplessis de Mornay was nominated co-adjutor bishop of Quebec, reflect the tendency of the French bishops "to please the king first and then the pope."

[163] F.X. Garneau, op. cit., p. 235.

[164] P. Hurtubise, Dominique-Marie Varlet..., op. cit., p. 691-693.

[165] Varlet was appointed bishop of Ascalon and coadjutor to the bishop of Babylon by Pope Clement XI on September 17, 1718. He became titular bishop of Babylon on November 20 of that year, the death of Bishop Pidou de Saint-Olon having left the see vacant.

166 Certificate of consecration in A.P.R. No. 3626. B.A. van Kleef, op. cit., p. 19.

167 This is what he confided in a letter to his sister Anne-Marie on December 31, 1733 in Lettres du Canada et de la Louisiane, P.U.Q., p. 33.

168 Quoted by Guy Plante, op. cit., p. 153.

169 L.A.C., Archives des colonies: C11A, No.106, 269 and C11A.

170 Pierre Hurtubise, D.M. Varlet, op. cit., p. 32, note 50. Auguste Gosselin, op. cit., p. 330.

171 Fourth letter to his agent in Rome, in Lettres, BAnQ, p. 48.

172 Having taken refuge in Holland upon his arrival in Europe, Dom Poulet might have informed the canons of the Chapter of Utrecht of the forthcoming passage of a bishop sympathetic to their cause. Ref: Correspondence of Bishop Varlet with Dom Thierry de Viaixnes, A.P.R. No. 3903.

173 The alleged powers of the Chapter of Utrecht are inadmissible in the Court of Rome. Letter of Father François de Montigny to Bishop Varlet, dated April 12, 1721, A.P.R. No. 3709.

174 Letter to the Sacred Congregation "de Propaganda Fide", in Première Apologie, p. 39.

175 The role of Gallicanism in French Canada is shown in the following articles: Joseph Cossette, *Jean Talon, champion au Canada du gallicanisme royal*, Revue d'histoire de l'Amérique française (RHAF) *IX,3, 1957, p. 327-352)*, Lionel Groulx, *Le gallicanisme au Canada sous Louis XIV*, RHAF 1,1, June 1947, p. 54-90, and Jean-Guy Lavallée, *L'Église dans l'État au Canada sous Mgr de Saint-Vallier*, 1685-1727, Revue de la Société canadienne d'histoire de l'Église catholique, 39, 1972, p. 29-40.

176 While the chapters of Utrecht and Haarlem claimed to exercise jurisdiction sede vacante, Rome kept its own jurisdiction delegated, in the absence of vicar apostolic, to the nuncio of Cologne or to the internuncio of Brussels. At the time Bishop Varlet made the confirmations in Amsterdam (1719), it is the internuncio of Brussels who was in charge of the affairs of Holland.

177 *Nos F. Barnabas Dei et Apostolicae Sedis gratiae Episcopus Aspahanensis. Universis et singulis has nostras litteras inspecturis notum facimus, quatenus decimâ quinta Decembris anno ut infra, ad nos pervenerunt Epistolae S. Congregationis de Propaganda Fide, in quibus de mandato summi Pontificis dato sub die septima Maii currentis anni, non non S. Congregationis nobis committur suspendere omni exercitio Ordinis et Juridictionis Illustrissimum D.*

Dominicum Mariam Varlet Episcopum Electum et consecratum et destinatum pro Episcopatu Babilonensi, in Première Apologie, p. XX. Details on the Babylonian (Persian) phase are provided in his Journal du voyage vers Babylone (P.R.A. No. 3753) and in his letters to his agent in Rome, to Innocent XIII and to Benedict XIII (Lettres de D.M. Varlet, BanQ, p. 31, 36, 39, 53, 68, 74). He left Amstserdam at the end of May 1719 and arrived in Persia in late October of that year, after a short stay in St. Petersburg (with Jesuits) and in Astraquan (with Capuchins). His destination was Hamadan, his see city, but he never reached it. He spent six months in Shamakè in Iran, waiting for the permission to cross the Iraqi border. He befriended a Jesuit priest (Father Bash?) and celebrated with him the Holy Mysteries in his church. It was there that Father Bachoud, S.J. came to present him, on March 15, 1720, on behalf of F. Barnabas, Bishop of Isfahan, the suspension decreed by the Propaganda Fide on May 7, 1719. As the matter had been disclosed in Iran and that Capuchin priests had already seized his house and his church in Hamadan, he decided to stay in Schamakè and await there the clarifications of the Propaganda.

[178] Archives of the Congregation « de Propaganda Fide », Rome, vol. 615 (1718). Copy at Library & Archives of Canada, Ottawa, microfilm MG17-A25.

[179] Leader of the Appellants' party, Bishop Caylus gave wages to the second order; convened his cooperators in synod and with the Richerists, tried to make the Gallican Church a clerical democracy. E. Preclin, op.cit., p. 142-143. He may have influenced Bishop Varlet in the direction of Presbytero-episcopal Gallicanism.

[180] Claude B. Moss, The Old Catholic Movement. Its Origins and History, Apocryphile Press, Berkeley, 2005, p. 122.

[181] J.M. Neale, op. cit., p. 246. C.B. Moss, op. cit.

[182] Préclin (op. cit., p. 201) is of the opinion that Bishop Varlet and Dom Thierry de Viaixnes have put the case on.

[183] B.A. van Kleef, op. cit., p. 50.

[184] Bernard van Espen, Oeuvres, Tome V, p. 396-415.

[185] J.M. Neale, op. cit., p. 250.

[186] Cornelis Steenoven (1662-1725) studied at Louvain and at Rome. He exercized his ministry in Amsterdam and in Amersfoort, where he became parish priest in 1693. He delivered the funeral oration of Father Quesnel in December 1719.

[187] Émile Préclin, op. cit., p. 198.

[188] The majority of the 300,000 Dutch Catholics submitted to papal orders and agreed to the abolition of elections, but the minority, inspired by parish priests Dalenoort and Steenoven, disobeyed the orders of the pope. The Chapter of Utrecht refused to disband; retained the allegiance of 300 parishes and entrusted its government to elected vicars general. Émile Préclin, op. cit., p. 198.

[189] A.P.R. Numbers 3747, 3794 & 3923.

[190] J.M. Neale, op. cit., p. 255.

[191] B.A. van Kleef, op. cit., p. 52. J.Y.H.A. Jacobs, Joan Christian van Erkel, 1654-1734, Academic Publishers Associate (APA), Amsterdam, 1981.

[192] E. Allmang, op. cit., p. 444.

[193] Cornelis Barchman Wuytiers (1693-1733) studied theology at Saint Magloire, on the recommendation of Father Quesnel and was ordained priest on April 8, 1719 by the bishop of Senez, Msgr. Jean Soanen. He studied law at Louvain, graduating in 1725 with a degree in *utroque jure*. He succeeded Msgr. Steenoven as Archbishop of Utrecht. P.J. Maan, C.J. Barchman Wuytiers Erzbischof von Utrecht, van Gorcum & Co., Uitgevers Assen, 1949.

[194] C.B. Moss, op. cit., p. 125.

[195] J.M. Neale, op. cit., p. 129.

[196] A gentleman by the name Dilhe is said to have presented a list of these bishops to Msgr. Barchman Wuytiers in October 1725. J. Neale, op. cit.

[197] He was convicted based on his pastoral letter of August 28, 1726, which is a real vindication of Father Quesnel. Archbishop Pierre-Paul Guérin de Tencin, his Metropolitan, presided the council of the ecclesiastical province of Embrun, held from 16 August to 28 September 1727. Bishop Soanen was suspended by the council from all episcopal functions, reduced to a layman and exiled to the Abbey of Chaise-Dieu in the Haute-Loire department in south-central France. He died there of old age in 1740. E. Preclin, op. cit., p. 119.

[198] A.J. van de Ven, *La communauté cistercienne de la Maison de Rijnwijk près d'Utrecht*, I.K.Z. (Berne), April-June 1949, p. 131. René Tavenaux (Le Jansénisme en Lorraine, 1640-1789, Paris, 1960, p. 540) said that Bishop Varlet was already considered in 1719 as the head of the refugee community in Amsterdam and that he watched with a jealous care to any alteration of principles. He wrote: *Father Quesnel resented the meddling control of the Bishop of Babylon, and he wanted to free himself from this tutelage*. This statement is surprising. Bishop Varlet spent only a month in Amsterdam in 1719 and he lodged with Jacob Krys, not with Brigode Dubois (with whom Father Quesnel was lodging).

[199] Inventaire by Bruggeman & van de Ven, p. 71-170.

[200] Idem, p. VI.

[201] Loc. cit.

[202] Loc. cit.

[203] Idem, p. 159.

[204] This is reflected in the tax receipts for the maintenance of windmills and polders at Schonauwen mentioned in the Inventaire by Bruggeman & Van de Ven, p. 72 (A.P.R. No. 1837).

[205] Inventaire, p. 155 (A.P.R. No. 3768). The Plan d'une méthode... is reproduced in Appendix 5, p. 295.

[206] A.P.R. 368, 3798 & 3799. It may also be teaching responsibilities that led to his collections on the Epistle to the Romans, Isaiah, Justin, Tertullian and St. Augustine (No. 3768), his annotations and extracts on the affairs of the Church (No. 3796) and his annotations on Holy Scripture (No. 3800).

[207] B.A. van Kleef, p. cit., p. 83.

[208] J.M. Neale, op. cit., p. 272.

[209] C.B. Moss, op. cit., p. 130.

[210] J.M. Neale, op. cit., p. 273. Usury is an older term for the idea of earning interest on money, and is prohibited or at least limited in the Bible. *Thou shalt not lend upon usury to thy brother* (Deut 23:19). *Thou oughtest therefore to have put my money to the exchanges, and then at my coming I should have received mine own with usury.* (Matt 25:27). The successor of Barchman Wuytiers, van der Croon (and later Meindaerts), who belonged to the Dutch party, approved the loan with interest and stood out from the French influence (Préclin, op. cit., 207) represented by Poncet (J.B. Désessart), Nicolas Le Gros and Varlet, Bishop of Babylon (idem, p. 205). The former were more Presbyterians and more favorable to the laity, the latter, Richerists moderates opposed the calvinist laicism present in the Gallican parochism of the Renversement des libertés gallicanes (by Le Gros). Préclin, op. cit., p. 207. René Taveneaux (Jansénisme et prêt à intérêt, J. Vrin, Paris, 1977, p. 59-71 & 139-162) confirms this distinction. More on Gallican parochism and the influence of Father Quesnel, in J. Tans' article *Kerkpolitiek tussen gallicanism en Verlichting*, Kracht in Zwakeid van een kleine Wereldkerk, Oud-katholiek Seminarie, Amersfoort, 1982, p. 9-19.

[211] At the beginning of the 18th century, at the Seminary of Paris, there were unity talks with the the Anglicans. A Swiss Calvinist pastor, the Rev. Jean Aymon, left a letter written from The Hague on August 23, 1712, in which he mentioned the propensity of some French clergymen for a reconciliation with the Church of England and their interest in the English reformation (La France protestante I, J. Cherbuliez ed, 1859, p. 202). Even the superiors were involved in the discussions which had been undertaken by two doctors of the University of Paris, Louis Ellies Dupin and Pierre de Girardin, with Archbishop William Wake of Canterbury. Jacques Gres-Gayer, Paris-Cantorbéry (1717-1720). Dossier d'un premier oecuménisme, Beauchesne, 1989.

[212] Wife of Prince Vasily Vladimirovich Dolgoruki (1670-1746), a Russian diplomat and statesman who acquired political power for himself and his family during the reign of Tsar Peter II (1727–1730). He served as Russia's ambassador to France (1721–1722).

[213] Paul Pierling (La Sorbonne et la Russie, 1717-1747, Paris, Leroux, 1882) addressed the issue as well as E. Preclin, op. cit., p. 59, J.M. Neale, op. cit., p. 270, and P.J. Mann, op. cit., p. 73-74.

[214] Le Jansénisme et la constitution civile du clergé, op. cit., p. 431 ff.

[215] Idem, p. 437.

[216] Préclin wrote (op. cit., p. 234) that it is his synodalist convictions that brought Bishop Varlet to establish a parallel hierarchy in Holland. This view was shared by the chargé d'affaire Chambéry. *I know, he wrote, that this bishop of Babylon and Dom Thierry de Viaixnes were in Utrecht, Rotterdam, The Hague and Haarlem. They have assembled the pastors and the Jansenist priests, and encouraged them to do an episcopal election. They are currently in Amsterdam, where they try to enlist the support of the judiciary. A part of them is favorable and they hope soon to elect a bishop with the approval of the government.* State Archives, Holland, Correspondance politique, Tome 350, Folio 55.

[217] Constitution de Notre Saint Père le Pape Patriarche d'Utrecht, 1730, Bibliothèque de Nantes (France), Manuscript No. 2113, Folio B.

[218] François Marie (Arouet dit) Voltaire, Correspondance, Tome 42, 1838, p. 557. Cited by Préclin, op. cit., p. 439.

[219] Pierre-François Lafiteau, Entretiens d'Anselme et d'Isidore sur les affaires du temps, 1756, p. 119.

[220] This aspect is developed by Préclin in Le Jansénisme et la constitution civile du clergé, op. cit., p. 438 and following: *Les idées politiques des jansénistes*.

221 When he disputes the notion of authority among the Protestants (In the Catholic Church, we do not have to give our assent to the truths without indubitable evidence, Recueil alphabétique..., p. 55) and in his critique of the Catechism of England (which rails without proving or refuting by the Scripture, p. 112; an Anabaptist and a Manichean will be welcomed into that church because of its vagueness on the fundamental articles of the faith, p. 121).

222 "We can say with Gregory the Great: if you do not keep the church canons and want to reverse the ordinances of the ancient (fathers), I do not know who you are". *Acte d'appel au concile général* in Première apologie, p. 7.

223 Idem, p. 4.

224 Idem, p. 3.

225 B.A. van Kleef, op. cit., p. 10.

226 A.P.R. No. 3642 (17 letters to Brigode Dubois about sending packages to Siam and Tonquin), No. 3701 (F. Lemaire in Siam, 9 letters), No. 3713 (L. Néez in Tonquin, 12 letters), No. 3802 (Journals of Tonquin).

227 Voyage en Asie avec l'histoire des Tartares (The Hague, 1735), Recueil des dynasties orientales, 6 volumes, Grammatica Linguarum Orientalium (Amsterdam, 1628), Voyage de Correal aux Indes (1722).

228 Father Terasson, an Oratorian, had been the unofficial vicar general of Bishop Caylus. Author of the Lettres ecclésiastiques sur la justice chrétienne (1733), he said aloud what Richerist leaders wrote secretly on the sacrament of penance: many just people do not come to communion because they are not in a position to confess their venial sins and to be absolved from them (p. 190). Cited by Préclin, op. cit., p. 227.

229 J.M. Neale, op. cit., p. 271.

230 Born in Culemborg on June 7, 1668, van der Croon had been parish priest at Gouda since 1714. He was elected as member of the chapter in 1720. He was a modest, gentle and pious man.

231 *Two powerful and respectable persons came and offered to open a door for me to return to France. I told them (...) that it would never be, God willing, by a door at which I should let my conscience and my honor.* Letter to his sister dated December 21, 1733, in Basil Guy, op. cit., p. 85.

232 J.M. Neale, op. cit., p. 277.

233 B.A. van Kleef, op. cit., p. 81. "The Dutchmen accepted the capitalist civilization and the traffic of money. Bishop Varlet was still living in an agricultural world." P.J. Mann, letter to the author, May 2, 1983.

[234] On July 18, 1734 he wrote to Nicolas Petitpied: "They treat me as a hired bishop (*évêque à gage*) as those who by their conduct degade the sacred character. I do not deserve to be so treated. I fear that this church will perish sooner with a bishop that without one, unless he has a rare wisdom". A.P.R. No. 3717.

[235] One who has convulsions; esp., one of a body of Jansenits in France, early in the 18th century, who went into convulsions under the influence of religious emotion. The involvement of Bishop Varlet in the affair of the convulsions and the miracles is treated by Robert Kreizer in his book <u>Miracles, Convulsions and Ecclesiastical Politics in Early 18th Century Paris</u>, Princeton University Press, 1978, p. 372-373. A text by Bishop Varlet, titled *Sur l'affaire des Convulsions* (On the affair of the convulsions) is reproduced in Part 2, p. 162-163.

[236] B.A. van Kleef, op. it., p. 80.

[237] He consecrated Hieronimus de Bock for Haarlem on September 2, 1742, and Bartholomew J. Byeveld for Deventer on January 25, 1758. More information on how the Old Catholic line of succession goes through the bishops of these two dioceses in Appendix 7.

[238] On August 11, 1873, the bishop of Deventer (H. Heykamp) consecrated Josef Hubert Reinkens, the bishop-elect of the German Old Catholics who opposed the dogma of the doctrinal infallibility and the universal jurisdiction of the Bishop of Rome (1871).

[239] To Bishop Varlet's brother-in-law Antoine Olivier, dated May 31, 1742, in Basil Guy, op. cit., p. 103.

[240] Princess Marie-Anne d'Arenberg, born in 1675, was the daughter of Philippe, duc d'Arenberg and Maria Enrichetta del Caretto. On November 20, 1707, she married François-Egon, son of Frederic-Maurice de la Tour d'Auvergne and Maria Franziska, Princess von Hohenzollern-Hechingen. According to Basil Guy (op. cit., p. 104), after the death of her husband (1710), she became interested in Jansenism and went to live in Utrecht were she died on April 24, 1708, revered by her co-religionists.

II
DEVOTION AND REFORM

The title that we give this second part shows two inseparable aspects of the personality of Varlet, clergyman. He became a reformer because he loved enough to risk big. Love for God who gives himself in Christ, by the Holy Spirit. Love also for those whom God calls into his kingdom. A term subsumes the two aspects and it is that of "missionary".

At one level, the mission is understood in its traditional sense, that is to revive abandoned church works (such as the Holy Family Mission in Cahokia); to preach the gospel to those "outside" and to incorporate them into the Church, where salvation occurs. *Only by the outpouring of the Holy Spirit do we see God's salvation. However, it is only in the Church that we have the Holy Spirit,* wrote Bishop Varlet in his <u>Annotations sur divers sujets</u>...[1]

Among his writings on mission that were preserved are letters to his family from New France (1713-1717)[2] and those sent from the Netherlands (1723) to Jean-Paul Mercier and René Thaumur de la Source, missionaries of the Illinois country.[3] We will give a general idea of them and of the letters sent to him from Canada and Louisiana (1719-1724) in Chapter I. Our interest is for what these texts reveal of Bishop Varlet's rapport to God, to Christ and to the Church.

At a second level, the mission is that of the "defender of the truth," a figure of speech borrowed from his apology. *The Truth has armed for her defense those of her children who seem the most despicable.* His work at this level is conditioned by *the obligation he feels as bishop to keep the sacred deposit of the faith.*[4] Bishop Varlet's commitment to the lordship of Jesus is accompanied by a critique of the Church.

Sacrament of salvation, she must produce the fruits of the Spirit. Pastor or layperson, we should experience different degrees of growth until we reach the full stature of Christ. *Our Lord came to lead us by degrees. He breathes to give us the Holy Spirit, as when humankind was created, to show that it is a new creation.*[5]

The *imitatio Christi* is at the center of Bishop Varlet's spirituality. It has as corollary the faithful observance of the commandments, or better, the fidelity to the truth given once for all to the saints (Jude 3). This is a leitmotif in the work of Bishop Varlet. Drawn from the Scripture, especially from St. Paul,[6] the criterium of fidelity to the truth links the devotee to a complementary aspect, that of the prophet.

We give the terms *devout* and *prophet* the meaning that Bishop Varlet gave them. The devout *has the life of the Spirit; he loves God, manifests it through prayer and takes an interest in the life of his fellow being.*[7] The prophet acts under the influence of the Holy Wisdom. He makes *a striking testimony to the Truth* against those who work *to keep her captive*. Varlet went to the aid of the "*Common Mother*" (the Church) that the alteration of doctrine degrades and he agreed *to suffer if necessary to glorify God and edify His Church.*[8]

We will show in Chapter 2, how Bishop Varlet's missionary work evolved in Holland in the prophetic sense described above, and in Chapters 3 and 4, how he worked at reforming the Church by means of polemical writings, teaching, biblical exegesis, patristics and theological expertise. Illustrative texts will be analyzed including: his

Appel au concile général (in the Première Apologie), diverse letters (to the missionaries of Tonkin, to Pope Benedict XIII, to the Bishop of Senez...), his Annotations sur divers sujets..., his Collections sur l'épître aux Romains, sur Isaie, Justin, Tertullien et saint Augustin, his Commentaire des Actes des Apôtres, his Commentaire de l'Apocalypse...

1
THE RELATIONS OF NEW FRANCE

In the years 1713 to 1718, Varlet is a young missionary in his thirties. His concerns are those of a man of his age. He shows zeal and energy, an attraction to exotism and a taste of adventure and risk, especially in his travel narratives. The tone is familiar, often enclined to provide an atmosphere. The emphasis is placed on the journey (*we left La Rochelle on March 8, 1713 and arrived in Mobile on June 6*)[9], which is described by highlighting the pathetic aspects: *The second day, after leaving Port-Louis (France), the wind became contrary, so that after being beaten by the wind, the storm still increasing and the ship taking much water, we decided to call at a port. We wished to return to Port-Louis, but when we were in sight of land, we saw the Isle-Dieu, which is a place more conducive to sinking than to anchor... The captain of the other ship shouted that we should not go there, that there was no anchoring and that we had to call at La Rochelle by night, through the Breton strait, which is very dangerous, filled with rocks. There was a very strong wind and we would have got lost because no one knew that route ...*[10]

Other aspects described include: the topography, the climate, the vegetation, the wildlife: *Where we are is to my taste, very pleasant and the air is good enough... However, summer is four months extremely hot. But what is worse is that during summer we can only eat bread ... provided we have flour from France. As for water, we have plenty. There is no meat: the colony being so small, there is not enough consumption to kill beef. Moreover, we cannot keep cattle: they get lost in the woods. We should have a dozen cows but we have not even one. It follows that we have no milk or butter or cheese. The grain is rare, we cannot have poultry. Therefore, we have no eggs. There is no hunting in the summer. Fishing does not give much. But winter is very pleasant. There are days when it is a bit cold, but others where it is very mild. We never see snow.*

We send a Savage to hunt and for three or four months, he fairly well supplied us with game, which is mainly teals, ducks, moorhens, geese and cranes... He went to hunt turkeys and deer. I do not know if he will bring some. We try to have wild ox that we will salt for the summer. That's how we live...[11]

These texts are a valuable contribution to the history of the establishment of the French in North America.[12] They are also valuable for the information they convey on the personality of Varlet. He reveals himself as a confident and passionate apostle, with a piety marked by Augustinism,[13] and completely confined in spiritual pursuits.[14] This is confirmed in the letters sent to him from Canada by Bishop St. Vallier (*you are worthy of esteem and devoted to the cause of the abandoned souls*[15]), Michel Bégon, the Intendant of New France (*you are a person who does good and whose friendship is precious*[16]), Joseph C. de la Colombière, grand vicar of Quebec (*your zeal is ardent and courageous*[17]), Charles Glandelet, superior of the Seminary of Quebec (*you have a great zeal for the missions and the talent to inspire others*[18]), Sr. Anne-Françoise Leduc, religious hospitaller of St. Joseph in Montreal (*you are a zealous and holy pastor, liked by his* missionaries[19]) and Sr. Catherine de Hautmesnil of the Congregation de Notre Dame, also in Montreal (*you are a worthy minister of the gospel[20]*).

Michel Bégon

J.C. de la Colombière

The context is different in 1723. Varlet is 45 years old. He has been a bishop for four years; has toured the world; quarreled with the highest authorities of the Church and will soon give a church organization to the Dutch O.B.C. The style of these letters, though friendly and proxemic, does not hide a certain condescension and can turn to paternalism. This is noticeable in his counsels and in the impression he gives that he can exert some influence for the missionaries among the superiors of the seminary in Paris and in Quebec.

An Example of Pastoral Exhortation
Excerpt form a letter to Father Jean-Paul Mercier, 1723

Your faithful are fewer, you say, since the arrival of the jugglers from Pimiteoui. It should not surprise you. We do not convert the infidels suddenly. It is true that it is more difficult for you and it is the only thing that worries me because you must take care of your health. But it is always a gain. There will be more children that you will send to heaven. Over time, the grace of God will improve the hearts of the fathers and mothers so they can know and love the truth. You must preach with patience but rely more on the strength of the prayers you offer to God for the conversion of these people. Thus, you would not work too hard at making them pure and fervent through a grand union with God. However, do not get attracted by the bodily mortifications that made Fr. Bergier die before the time. Be satisfied with the difficulties that are inseparably tied to your state...Take only what you can bear. You must already be pleased with the good you do by baptizing children and with the adults. You will not overcome the juggling by force but by patience, by prayer and by persevering exhortations. You have one advantage: they willingly come to you (at least if it's like in my time when the house was full of people from morning to evening).

You speak their language: you can exhort them and make them see the vanity of their juggling. The key is the catechism: gradually it will be more attended. You spend your Sundays well. The care you give these poor people in their illness is a great advantage. You win their hearts so that they like you and estimate prayer. The rest is up to God and will come in time. All the good sentiments that your letter is filled with edify me and are likely to attract God's blessing on your work ...

The letter to the other missionary, Thaumur de la Source, mentions the state of division that prevailed in the Church: *What is particularly worthy of tears and prayers, is the division that have been in the Church for ten years and is fomented by people who would find their interest in this .... Please ask God in your prayers to give peace to the Church... I do not know if I have mentioned the sad state of Persia. The barbarians have become masters of the capital. The war is on. God be praised for having made me leave before it all began.*

This division was caused by the Bull Unigenitus in 1713. Having become state law in France, it combined the repressive forces of the civil and ecclesiastical authorities. And he invoked the pretext of war to justify his return to Europe. He did not want to reveal that he had become persona non grata in the Church. But they would soon know. *A young man*, wrote Father Thomas Thiboult of the Seminary of Quebec (1723.10.13), *sent this year* (from Paris), *told Bishop St. Vallier that you are not in Persia but in Amsterdam, where you are regarded as the successor of Father Quesnel.*[21]

The rapports of Bishop Varlet with New France ceased in 1724, the year he proceeded with the consecration of Archbishop Steenoven and from there, his energies would be devoted to the establishment and consolidation of the Kerk der O.B.C. The missionaries of the Illinois had to look elsewhere for the anointing that made them want to be, at his example, more and more faithful to their vocation.

2

FROM THE CHURCH OF QUEBEC TO THE REFORM OF UTRECHT

The North American phase of Bishop Varlet illustrates the features of the devout missionary. The perspective is that of "going to those outside".

The episcopal appointment fits into this: "*It has pleased our Holy Father Pope Clement XI to call me from the end of the West to send me in the bottom of the East*".[22] However, the road to his bishopric bifurcated by Amsterdam and confronted him to a "scandal": there were inside the Church souls as abandoned as those of the infidels outside. "*This poor and desperate flock was languishing as having no shepherd.*"[23]

Clement XI

This situation would have decisive consequences for the rest of his life. To analyze it, we establish two vectors. One, associated with the administration of the sacrament of confirmation, is that of the continuity of the ministry from New France to Holland. The second, related to the suspense of the powers of orders and jurisdiction, is that of discontinuity.

Using the <u>Acte d'appel au concile général</u>, the <u>Plainte à l'Église catholique</u>, the <u>Lettre à la Congrégation de la Propagande</u>, the <u>Lettre au pape Benoît XIII</u> and the <u>Lettre au Concile de Rome</u>, we will recall the facts and show how Bishop Varlet went from the traditional acception of mission to the prophetic one: making God's will known to those inside. He contested those who use their overseeing ministry as an instrument of oppression and worked at liberating the pastors and the faithful who are its victims.

Continuity in the Ministry: Confirmations in a Church in Need

Without a bishop, the faithful of the Church of Utrecht had about 600 people to confirm. These people, because of *their poverty, their age, their infirmity or other reasons, were unable to go and receive the sacrament in neighboring dioceses.*[24] Knowing that Bishop Varlet was in Amsterdam, the members of the cathedral chapter (still existing but not recognized by Rome), on the instances of the faithful, told him of the state of necessity in which were the 300 parishes of the diocese and asked him "to give them the charity of his episcopate."[25] Recognizing that it was an "almost extreme need"[26] and based on the exhortation contained in Romans 12:13,[27] he proceeded to the rite on April 16, 21 and 23, 1719, "with all the regularity possible",[28] the local ordinary (the chapter) having given him jurisdiction to do the functions.[29]

Confirmation by Antonio Novelli, 1779

We will not bring back the subject of the dispute concerning the chapter "still existing but not recognized", that we have deliberately put between brackets, to indicate the contentious jurisdiction of the canons of Utrecht. This aspect has been treated in the Biographical sketch (Part I). What we want to emphasize is the continuity (Varlet points it out in his apology[30]) between the ministry exercised in the Church of Quebec and that of Utrecht. Let us recapitulate the arguments of Bishop Varlet. First, these functions were necessary because the souls required it.[31] Secondly, they were "consistent with the Gospel and the Holy Canons, and if he had not exercized them, he would have been "guilty of cruelty and injustice"[32] because this church was afflicted in her spiritual needs.[33] Thirdly, it is "in good faith that he followed the usual practice" because he could not imagine that the grand vicars of Utrecht were without jurisdiction.[34]

The dispute over the jurisdiction of the grand vicars being excepted (Varlet at first wanted that we except it), the event of April 1719 is nothing less than a manifestation of pastoral solicitude in the continuity of his missionary vocation. But on March 15, 1720, he was told that he had been suspended from the exercise of the episcopate since May 7, 1719. The reason: he had exercised episcopal functions in Holland, to the benefit of the refractory Catholics, and this was scandalous for the 330,000 faithfull, their vicar apostolic and the internuncio of Brussels who was in charge of the affairs of Holland.[35] For the devout missionary, satisfying spiritual needs is of prime importance. The Catholics of Utrecht, who were not "bad people, or disobedient to the Holy See",[36] were deprived of a spiritual good. Those who were offended because he helped them obtain this good (which is proper to the ministry) were "Pharisees", and the pharisaic scandal must not prevent the accomplishment of the justice.[37] Especially when it is *the Court of Rome that has brought the Church of Utrecht to that extremity, this makes the case most urgent according to the natural law and the church canons*.[38] We therefore penetrate a layer of discontinuity that the consecration of Archbishop Steenoven amplified and that Rome sanctioned in 1725 by the brief of excommunication *Qua sollicitudine*.

Discontinuity: the Advent of the Prophet Reformer

Three elements are important in the assumption of the prophetic traits by Bishop Varlet. They are: the Gospel, the Holy Canons and the Imploration of the Souls.

The first element, put forward in his opposition to the Bull Unigenitus, supports his Jansenist convictions and his missionary zeal for the abandoned souls and works.[39] The second, peculiar to his situation as a French clergy, includes Gallican aspects such as the superiority of the council over the pope and the rights and freedoms of the national churches and their episcopate.[40] The third, inspired by Father Quesnel, is in line with the democratic and presbytero-episcopal trends discussed in Part I. Trends which have led Bishop Varlet to oppose the Bull Unigenitus and to appeal to the general council. They would also lead the Dutch Kerk der O.B.C. to side later with the German Old Catholics in opposing the dogma of the infallibility of the Pope defined by the First Vatican Council (1870-1871). As we will see farther on in the following chapters, for Bishop Varlet and the Old Catholics, the infallibility of the Church comes not from the Pope who exercizes it, but from the indefectibility given to her by the Holy Spirit, through the imploration of the souls. Imploring the influence of grace, they are instructed to walk before God in humility and truth.[41] These elements interpenetrate one another to form the theological system of Bishop Varlet.

A Central Text : The Acte d'Appel au Concile Général

The <u>Acte d'appel au concile général</u> plays a key role in Bishop Varlet's work. Everything is organized and makes sense in relation to this central text. Denouncing, based on his Augustinian understanding of Christ and the Church, those who use their overseeing ministry as an instrument of oppression, the <u>Acte d'appel</u> explains the action of the reformer for the Kerk der O.B.C.

We will do a *structural analysis* of the text because we want to attain the deep meaning that underlies the language patterns and decode the frame of reference. We will use the method presented in our book <u>Approches structurales des textes</u> (Université du Québec en Outaouais, 1980).

Written in 1722 and published in 1724, as the central part of the <u>Première Apologie</u>, the *Acte d'appel* is as a canonical (legal) document[42] in which Varlet defends himself against the reasons given for his suspense: (1) not having visited the papal nuncio in Paris before departing for Persia, avoiding to subscribe to the Bull Unigenitus and to promise to enforce it in his diocese; (2) having exercised episcopal functions in Holland without the permission of the Internuncio of Brussels to the scandal of the faithful. But the canonical trait does not reflect the totality of what is communicated. This is evident if one analyzes the layers of meaning created by the enunciation process. Then appears the theme of the *prophet* and its christological articulation.[43] Seen under this light, the speech becomes an epiphenomenon of the whole work of Bishop Varlet. The author that we discover behind a canonical type of rhetoric is the interpreter of the Holy Scripture who wrote the Annotations de l'Écriture Sainte, the Annotations sur divers sujets… and the Collections sur l'épître aux Romains, sur Isaie, Justin, Tertullien et saint Augustin.[44]

The text begins on the descriptive mode (*in the middle of the divisions and scandals that have plagued the Church for 10 years because of the Bull Unigenitus*[45]) and this is indicative of its explanatory nature. Apart from the narrative elements related to the journey to Moscow[46] and the exercise of episcopal functions in Holland[47], the text is written on the descriptive mode. This includes a reflection on the ministry to the Amerindians[48], the details of his grievances against the Bull[49] and the nullity of his suspense,[50] the presentation of the Church's rules for the trial of bishops[51] (the sacred canons) that the pope should observe[52] and the improper way he was censored in Persia.[53]

The appeal against the Bull, in the first paragraph, and the allusion to the movement of the Appelants serve to create a psychological atmosphere in which he exposes his thesis (a papacy operating in continuity with the ancient canons) and the antithesis (the unjust behavior of the Court of Rome against him when he acted in accordance with the canons). This is reinforced by using the following extract from a letter by St. Bernard: *The Holy Apostolic See has this peculiarity that when it realizes that something might have been extorted by fraud and deceit, it does not hesitate to revoke it.*[54] To this are attached other aspects such as the pope acting in accordance with the established rules, Rome would remedy the abuses made in its name.[55] He then arranges a phrase of Pope Innocent I to fit his viewpoint: *In the judgment alledged to have been made against us, there was no significant charge; we were not present and nothing was alleged in our face. The pope would redress the wrongdoing of the Bishop of Isfahan, who dared pronounce against an absent an award so abrupt and inform. He would make a suitable correction so that the division which disturbs the Church be appeased and the union of fraternal friendship be restored.*[56]

This is what should be. But Bishop Varlet *has been suffering for three years without being able to obtain justice*. So, he was left with no alternative but to *make a canonical appeal to the general council against the Bull Unigenitus and the unjust persecution done to him, because of that bull.*[57]

While continuing to make use of the old canons (rules),[58] he adds developments on the particular situation of the churches in the Levant and in the Netherlands. This is done to show the importance of the bishop. *We cannot and must not pronounce rash judgements concerning the person of a bishop.*[59] The Acte d'Appel is a defense of the "old rules, freedoms and customs of the Church which are inviolable".[60] It is in total violation of the old canons that he was censored: *In the so-called jugement of the Bishop of Isfahan there were no rules or procedure, no party, no knowledge or information, nor any conditions that the Holy Fathers required for a legitimate jugement.*[61]

Map of Iran with localization of Isfahan

He appealed to the general council because he feared that "Pope Innocent XIII, prompted by the suggestions of some malignant individuals, whose bad intentions are all too familiar, would proceed in any manner, by excommunication, suspense, deposition, or some other way ..."[62] In opposing the Bull Unigenitus he shared the objective of the Appellants:" to keep unaltered the dogmas of faith, discipline and morals, the sacred rights of the episcopate and the freedoms of the Church".[63]

The situation of Bishop Varlet in relation to his speech justifies the classification of the Acte d'appel as an apology. It is the public[64] defense of his person and of the sacred rights of the episcopate. What makes it particularly interesting is that it goes beyond the subjective polemic to embrace a more elevated question, which is likely to interest the entire body of bishops and even the Church Universal. "The cause of Bishop Varlet is the cause of the episcopate".[65]

Deeper Meaning: the Frame of Reference

The systematic unity of the text is, at a deeper level, that of an opposition or dichotomy between the accomplishment of the reign of God and that of the satanic pretensions. Eugene Michaud goes in that sense when he writes: "the conduct of Rome and its agents was clearly anti-Christian in all this". Bishop Varlet reported the ills in his letter to the pope of January 1, 1723: *On one side the indiscretion of the missionaries, who were not afraid to blacken and discredit me by slander, and expose our holy ministry in disgrace and to the insults of the schismatics and the infidels, made me know that if I yielded to time, I would make myself inutile, not only then but for the rest. On the other hand, the hardness that they had to keep my income, even if it is a poor one, depriving me of any means of subsistence. Finally, seeing that the Carmelite Fathers had taken possession of my church and my house, under the vain pretext of a commitment that my predecessor had done for his debts, I was afraid to expose myself to arguments that would not fail to cause much scandal. So I had to get away with pain and throw myself in the danger, the fatigue and the expenses of a return without finding a place where it was possible to stop until in this city (of Amsterdam).*[66]

An analysis along the lines suggested by A.J. Greimas can help further deepen the meaning of this conflict.[67] The problem is posed on page 4: "arrived on the frontier of Persia, a Jesuit came to give us a message said to be a suspense against our person from the Bishop of Isfahan".[68] However, we were prepared early in the text: "In the midst of the division and scandals that have plagued the church for 10 years..."[69] Two units of meaning frame the struggle between the bishop of Babylon and the Roman Curia. They are perceived from the first pages: the allusion to the divisions and scandals caused by the Bull evokes the difficult context in which evolved Varlet and those sharing his point of view. The text is oriented towards avoiding the satanic pretensions (to configure oneself to Christ in the defense of the Truth) and its importance in the economy of the Church (fidelity to the deposit, courage and suffering for the Truth).

The semantic universe of the text is established from the opposition between Rome, divisive and source of scandals, and "the Truth who has armed for her defence those of her children who seem the most despicable".[70] These are elements taken at the surface of the text but we will now examine how their formalization leads to the deep structure of the text. Two semantic axis emerge from what we have been discussing: *Abasement* and *Pride*, which have close ties. The first axis is divided into two contradictory elements: Inferiority vs Superiority, evoking the negative aspect, i.e. the sin against the lordship of Christ. These two elements are connected to two others that are also contradictory:

The servant Church who keeps intact the deposit of faith, the rules of discipline & morals, the sacred rights of the episcopate and church liberties.	=/=	The accuser Church who violates the deposit of faith, the rules of discipline and morals, the sacred rights of the episcopate and the church liberties.

Under the semantic axis "Pride" are the following dichotomy: *Theophore*[71] vs *Accuser*.

There is a correlation between the axis *Abasement* and the axis *Pride*. The semantic universe expressing the opposition is reduced at the end of the text by progressively eliminating contrariness. This is done using the inter-textuality as a mode of representation. Varlet uses canonical formulations borrowed from the Holy Fathers in successive appropriations that come to retain one relationship: the servant Church which keeps intact the deposit of faith, the rules of discipline and morals, the sacred rights of Bishops and the church liberties.

A semantic organization type *Abasement / Elevation* covers the isotopy[72] *Theophore / Accuser*, which constitutes the universe of the Acte d'appel. This idealist order is realized in the condition of the servant Church. It is in remaining faithful to the deposit of the faith given once for all that we preserve the order of the Church and that are prevented scandals and divisions which sin against the Body of Christ.

The work of Bishop Varlet consists, essentially, in a series of ecclesiological discourses like that of the Acte d'appel. A similar analysis performed on the Lettre à la Congrégation de la Propagande and the Première lettre à son agent in Rome gave similar results. The Servant Church is opposed to that of the Court of Rome in the Lettre à la Congrégation de la Propagande and the isotopy is reduced by retaining the following message: it is in staying committed to the church canons and councils that are prevented conflicts and divisions, and that we work for the coming of the reign of God. In the Première lettre à son agent in Rome, he opposes the servant Church to the accuser Church in a valuation process that favours the object *truth* in the only ministry which fulfills the reign of God, that of the servant Church.

The pursuit of the object "good" is decisive. Disjoined himself of that object as a bishop suspended and later excommunicated, Varlet models on Christ whose *kenosis*[73] has paved the way for his exaltation by the Father.

Humiliated and persecuted for following in the footsteps of his Lord in providing the aid of his episcopate to an abandoned church, he feels justified by the grace of Him whom he intends to imitate and he denounces that Rome does not work for the wellbeing of the Church.

3

THE PURSUIT OF THE LORDSHIP OF CHRIST: THE REFORM PROGRAM

The denunciation did not produce the fruits that Bishop Varlet expected. A call to conversion, it was received as an insult to the pontificate and only contributed to make his case worse. But the theology on which it stood did not remain a dead letter, as evidenced by the advent of the Ker der O.B.C. His "prophetic" discourse, held inadmissible by the authorities of the great church, did find among the Catholic remnants of the obedience of Utrecht, a field conducive to germinate and bear fruit. This is suggested in the letter addressed to him by members of the Metropolitan Chapter on October 13, 1724, asking him to consecrate Cornelis Steenoven: *Who knows, Monsignor, if the spirit of Jesus did not send you in this country to prepare you to carry out his plans in the circumstances where we are? What merit will you not acquire in the whole Catholic Church if you raise ours, almost depressed, and that God maybe has kept free of the enslavement and scandals that prevail at present almost everywhere, to make it serve the plans He has to renew its wonders and perform miracles that have not yet been seen (Ecclesiastes 36:9).*[74]

The fact that the proclamation in the Acte d'appel has led to the formation of the Old Catholic Church presupposes a prior theological system that we will now describe. We will be using methodological tools taken from our book Approches structurales des textes (op. cit.), more specifically those related to the notion of program, i.e. the transition between two states of a subject (here it is the Church seen as a global actor). Our analysis will cover two complementary aspects: (1) the act of /doing-the-church/ or pragmatics and (2) the modalities of this praxis or competence.

Bishop Varlet's Theological System

The central program of Bishop Varlet's theological system, inspired by St. Paul's Epistle to the Romans, chapter 8, is the individual who goes from non-justice (absence of redemption) to justice by the merits of the blood of Jesus Christ. *There is no elected soul to be delivered from the hand of the destroying angel other than by the blood of the true Lamb.*[75] This is a soteriological[76] reality accessible through preaching.[77] "Receive the gospel and go preach to your people" summarizes the purpose of his Episcopal ordination.[78] To stop preaching compromises the coming of the Kingdom because faith is essential to embrace the salvation of God.

"Abraham was justified by faith: it is by faith that we become a child of God." [79] This passage which operates by faith (first grace and source of all others[80]) has for corollary the Christian who passes from not exercising to exercising charity under the action of the Holy Spirit.

There is a necessary link between the "word of faith" or Kerygma (defined as orthodoxy) and the exhortation or parenesis (orthopraxy). It appears in Bishop Varlet's refusal to accept the Bull Unigenitus. *This bull is capable of extinguishing the spirit of prayer by casting shadows on the doctrine of the Church over the necessity and power of grace that makes us do good.* [81]

The interaction of the two performances (faith and charity), under the action of the Holy Spirit, gives the Church the holiness that makes her infallible.[82] *It is reported in Leviticus 4:23-24 that the glory of the Lord appeared in the eyes of the people; that the fire that came out of the Lord consumed everything on the altar; that the people, having seen it, worshiped and praised the Lord. It is a figure of the descent of the Holy Spirit, the spiritual fire that feeds on and is lighted by the hosts of the holocausts and of the peacemakers that faith makes us put on the altar, which is the spiritual body of Jesus Christ.*[83] *The Church, spiritual body, is always led by the Holy Spirit of God. Therefore she is infallible and it is fair and reasonable to submit all our lights to her authority.*[84]

We have in these programs the topics on which stands the ecclesiology of Bishop Varlet. Let us see how it differs from the Roman position, for example on the features of the Church (apostolicity, authority, sanctity and infallibility) as defined by a Ultramontane contemporary of Bishop Varlet, Father Barrin, Jesuit. For him, only the see of Rome is apostolic and the authority of the Church remains at all times. Accordingly, holiness can only be a holiness of doctrine originated from the founders of the Church.[85] This approach, which emphasizes the authority of the living magisterium, leads directly to the infallibility of the pope. It is diametrically opposed to Bishop Varlet's perspective of the Body of Christ (borrowed from St. Paul's letter to the Romans) animated by the Holy Spirit who makes it infallibility by sanctifying it. This approach, which makes kerigma and exhortation (parenesis) structurally linked to the koinonia (Christian fellowship), cannot be satisfied with a unity of communion not based on the imperatives of faith. *Equity requires that one judges the sentiment of a church based on its confessions of faith, its creeds and the general opinion of its pastors.*[86]

For Bishop Varlet, is Catholic what results in a unity of communion built on the unity of faith. This has direct consequences on the exercise of infallibility. It has as subject the entire Church (not just the pope);[87] it relates to faith and morals[88] and the bishops are its operators in their role of faithful interpreters of the councils. Speaking of the troubles of the Church of Holland, he wrote: *During the long vacancy of the episcopal see of Utrecht, we saw several priests interfere to govern the people as pastors ... And what is more surprising is that they boasted of being protected by the one who should contribute to repress them. I mean the Minister of His Holiness. Doesn't this minister fear that the Holy Father reproached to him what St. Leo reproched to his Vicar, the Archbishop of Thessalonica, when he said: you make fall on me the blame of the excesses that you committed against the rules that you have been given.*[89]

The infallibility is linked to authority.[90] The bishops derive their authority from Jesus Christ himself[91] to judge the faith and transmit it in conformity with the canons.[92] The whole episcopate is represented in the person of the pope (primus inter pares), to whom is recognized the divine right to keep the unity of the faith and to maintain the good order of the Church.[93] He is bound by the decisions and rescripts of the councils.[94] This is the overall perspective of his two Apologies.

In principle, there should not be areas of conflict in the exercise of the jurisdiction because that of the Pope is an overdetermination of that of the bishops. There is only one overseeing function and only one goal: to conjoin the believers with eschatological[95] goods. It is a purely spiritual authority characterized by humility and charity.[96] This is what distinguishes it from the temporal power which assures the welfare of the state by the use of coercive force. Rome tends to confuse the two types of authority and pursuing worldly domination, overturns the order of dogma, discipline and morals in favor of a unity of communion not conditioned by the primacy of the unity of faith. In such a situation, the "defender of the truth" has an obligation to work at reforming the Church.[97]

Catholic Reformation

For Bishop Varlet, the overthrow of the old order of the Church has produced a state of depravity that affects the speculative and the practical plans. This leads to an "ecclesiastical hypocrisy"[98] (in the Court of Rome and among the Jesuits, allied to the domineering pretensions of the Vatican[99]) that must be combated by suppressing the greed which is the source of all ills.[100] Four areas are covered: the Church, the doctrine, the morals and the pastoral ministry.

Church Reform

The subject of the Church is addressed in the first treaty of Bishop Varlet's <u>Méthode pour étudier la théologie et l'histoire de l'Église</u> as an aspect of the general problematique of religion.[101] This is indicative of his intent to make it a "locus theologicus". Theology takes its source at the very life of the Church because the Word of God is embodied in the faith community that seeks to serve humans. Father Chenu would admit later that the doctrines of grace, incarnation and redemption are brought under a new light in that the believers experience the events of the time under the influence of the Holy Spirit.[102] The (Roman Church) Constitution <u>Gaudium Spes</u> even says that the Church "finds herself when she is lost; when she sees the joys and the hopes, the griefs and the anxieties of today's people.[103] All these features which are so characteristic of Bishop Varlet's positions are found in the orientations of the Second Vatican Council in favor of a church servant, alterocentered and non-dominating.

Nearly 250 years later, Rome recognized the merit of a criticism such as that made by Bishop Varlet and wished to renounce his ecclesiocentrism. Pope John XXIII even talked of a "theology of the signs of the times" to express the type of commitment required by the pastoral service.[104] He acknowledged that theology serves to clarify this commitment so that "the revealed Truth be always better understood and presented in a form more suitable".[105] Bishop Varlet was using that sort of arguments when he explained why he could not make his Persian diocese subscribe to the Bull Unigenitus.

The suggested framework is a sort of "new theology". However, in the early 18th century, Bishop Varlet was already defining the theological reflection as inextricably linked to a criticism of the Church challenged by the Word of God: *How is it that our fathers have found they had to set bounds to the gospel and take the word of faith in abeyance? How is it that the Word who ran with such speed in the world was stopped? With what confidence do we retain the truth of God in injustice?* [106]

This criticism has a practical intent. The Word of God received in faith must incite the Church to prepare the advent of the Kingdom.[107] This, by preaching (*how can we believe if nobody preaches*) and the exercise of charity, which is the *sweetness of the Spirit of God*.[108] Considered this way, theology has a prophetic role because its purpose is to make God's will known. It is not without reason that the prophets occupy the first place in the 13th treaty of Bishop Varlet's Méthode pour étudier la théologie ... and that the most important of his exegetical collections are devoted to Isaiah, notably chapters 40-45 (God, Lord of history and the mission of Israel towards other nations) and St. Paul's Epistle to the Romans (salvation as new life in Christ and Israel in the divine plan). It is a perspective close to Jürgen Moltman's theology of hope: the theological concepts do not run behind history but enlight it showing what lays ahead.[109] Therefore there should not be any opposition between Scripture and Tradition.

The visible Church mediates the salvation proclaimed in Scripture. It is the sacrament of salvation and as such, under the influence of grace, it must renounce selfishness to create a genuine fellowship among human beings.

Doctrinal & Moral Reform

The dogmatic teaching on the original sin and grace has to be redressed. It has become deficient because of the Roman inclination for the "pelagian" doctrine of the Jesuit Luis Molina.[110] Let us recall the Jansenist position. "The 4th canon of the Council of Trent teaches that grace excites the free will. The Jesuits asked that the canon be changed so that the motion of grace be reduced to simple illustrations that enlighten the mind." [111] "And because they had noticed that the mystery of predestination and grace were the main stumbling block of the bad Christians who wanted so much their salvation in their hands that they did not have to depend upon God for achieving it, these masters of error have made Pelagianism coarsely remedied the basis of their theology".[112]

We see that Bishop Varlet held that position when he gives the reasons why he could not endorse or oblige others to subscribe to the Bull Unigenitus. The traditional dogma has been challenged, and the merits that Christ has brought us are shaken because those who do not know the Lord have as many benefits as the believers. It follows that: (a) justice may come from the law, faith no longer being necessary, (2) the benefits that St. Paul gives the grace of baptism have vanished, and (3) grace, healing and life can be received outside the Church.[113]

The dogmatic weakening leads straight to moral laxity because orthodoxy and orthopraxy go together. This is what we read in the Nouvelles Ecclésiastiques, echoing the text of the apology: *Molinism leads to probabilism, and probabilism to the overthrowing of the rule of morals, even of the rule of faith. The necessity of faith, the certainty of the mysteries, the Law of God, the Gospel, in one word all religious and human laws have been reduced to nothing in that system of doctrine.*[114]

We must reform the morality by returning to a moral theology that is not in the wake of lax concerns as those that have dominated the scene at the Council of Trent.[115] Bishop Varlet suggests in the Apology, the procedure that could restore orthopraxy. First, we must teach that Jesus Christ died to deliver us for ever by his blood. This, to instil the spirit of adoption and love which makes us call God our Father. Secondly, to make known that without charity we cannot do the Christian actions. Thirdly, to show that it is driven by the love of justice that we are delivered from sin, not only by the fear of punishment.[116] These requirements lead straight to the pastoral reform.

Pastoral Reform

In order to fulfill their role as guardians of the faith and morals, it is important that the faithful be instructed in the mysteries of our religion.[117] Against the Bull Unigenitus which advises against it, Bishop Varlet recommends that the faithful read the bible, which "animates the hope that sustains us."[118] The biblical instruction develops the sense of prayer and contrition (not attrition resulting from simple servile fear[119]) which make the belivers approach the sacraments with respect and fear of God. This is facilitated by using the vernacular in the liturgy and by simplifying the Eucharistic rite so that the truths of faith expounded in the homily be better integrated.[120]

We cannot describe Bishop Varlet's theological system without mentioning specific modalities such as: the soteriological dimension of the Body of Christ and of the holiness of the Church; the operation of reference to Christ under the influence of the Holy Spirit; the behavior of the sanctified believers and the spiritual role of the bishop in the Church. It is to these questions of competence that we devote the next section.

Christian Competencies

In the theological system of Bishop Varlet, the performance by which the subject (operator) conjoins to the objects (goods, knowledge, values) occupies a central position. But for the transformation to occur, three modalities or conditions are needed: the subject must have the will (or desire), the know-how and the power to act. The implementation of these three modalities is the driving force of the Christian praxis.

1st Modality: the Will or Desire

Initiated in the redemptive experience of entering the justice by the merits of the blood of Jesus Christ (program A), the process is assumed in the exercise of charity (program B) and results in the Church holy and infallible (program C). The will to act is operated at the junction of programs A and B.

The fulfillment of the promises have begun with the resurrection of Christ.[121] The Holy Spirit has been poured; we live under the reign of grace and this produces in us the desire (A) to act as the Body of Christ, the Church (B). Here's how it works. A soul who, under the influence of grace, receives the Spirit of Jesus Christ, becomes oriented towards eschatological goods.[122] We pass from the material (fleshly), finite condition to that spiritual and infinite (eternal). The perspective, taken from Saint Paul,[123] is that of conversion and baptism that make us know how to act.

2nd Modality: the Know How

The modality of the /will/ comes into play in the passage (conversion) made under the influence of grace (necessary link with program C) which gives the Spirit of Jesus Christ. This gift is the adoption by God the Father through his Son.[124] Our heart is given entirely to God[125] and we prepare ourselves for the kingdom by personal cleansing and through caring for the Church. There can be no true competence to act as a Christian without the modality of *knowledge obtained through conversion. It is the revelation that God is I-AM (YHWH); that from Him we have our being and that it is by participating in his Spirit that we acquire our true meaning and dignity. Only God can fulfill the capacity of our heart.*

This is why at the beginning of his concersion, St. Augustine was convinced that the supreme happiness consists in the search for Holy Wisdom. Prior to receiving grace, the person can only sin.[126] This is a soteriologically induced passage that can be thus described: we go from egocentrism to alterocentrism through the "change of heart" that renders our ego able to see the redeeming love of God at work in Jesus.[127]

The converted soul is modeled on Christ the Servant to rise gradually to meet God.[128] This is done under the action of the Holy Spirit. It is through him that Jesus Christ speaks, bringing the nations to convert. Acting as a force of change[129], he makes us pass from the state of "vain glory and greed to that of charity[130] because he "lowers the elevation of our heart and melts its hardness.[131] This is how he "makes us see the salvation of God" and attain the beatific vision.[132]

3rd Modality: the Power

Initiated in the conversion that makes us will what God wants, our role in the actualization of the Church is first assumed at the level of the soul who feels the imperatives of the reign and is confronted by the accusing claims of Satan. In Bishop Varlet's representation, these claims are embodied in the Papal Court whose purpose of worldly hegemony takes precedence over the preservation of doctrine and morals. There is, at the center of the representation, a polemical structure. Varlet is inserted into a story that portrays him as persecuted by the Roman giant. We will not elaborate here on the pathos of the story although this aspect could be interesting to study because of Bishop Varlet's involvement in the affair of the miracles and convulsions. Our goal being to capture his contribution to the advent of Old Catholicism, we limit our analysis to the content of his discourse, especially the meaning that he gave his ordeal and how it was an incentive for reform.

A key of interpretation is given in the <u>Acte d'appel au concile général</u>: "Truth has armed for her defense ... those who seem the most despicable."[133] This figurativisation proclaims what is held by faith: the accomplishment of God's reign is done in reference to Christ, the Suffering Servant. This is an important feature for understanding Bishop Varlet's conflict with Rome. The pursuit of spiritual goods is the only purpose of the Church. God works in us, through His grace, to will and to act according to his good purpose (Phil. 2:13). A distinction that should remain clear between the "actantial" and "actorial" plans,[134] marks the accomplishment of the reign. God is the actant of his reign; the faithful and the overseers of the Church are the actors. Their vocation is to act (kerygma, koinonia and parenesis) according to the divine will. They are called to cooperate with God in the work of salvation, but must be careful not to substitute for Him. Jesus, Servant of the kingdom, must remain a constant reference. But Rome acted as a actant and as an actor. In doing so, it accused God because it took His place working towards worldly (contingent) power at the expense of the divine will which is immutable. The term "probabilist" so often used in Jansenist discourses on the Roman doctrine and morals covers this opposition (contingency vs immutability).

Persecuted because he threatens the communion of the Church (more important than the unity of the faith), the "defender of the Truth" sees his condition as a proof of the correctness of his position.[135] And the Holy Spirit who communicates grace makes him understand the meaning of his ordeal. Like Christ, our Lord, it is in taking the road of humiliation and self-forgetfulness that we attain eternal life. Consequently, the power /to-do-the-Church/ that he favours is the imitation of Jesus Christ. We must be configured to Christ in his passion to share in his glory. There is only one will: God's will, as there is only one spiritual power: the one operated in Christ and in the Church, his glorious body, until the full accomplishment of the promises.[136]

In summary, there is a fundamental drama of which God is the *Actant*: that of salvation. This drama is actorised first by Christ, then by his imitators. The challenge is not to confuse the levels. Otherwise, we are accomplices of the evil and we reverse the order of doctrine and morals, from which result conflicts and divisions that sin against the Holy Spirit and destroy charity.

The bishop is supposed to actorise in an exemplary fashion the desire that grace puts in the heart of the believers to be benevolent and beneficent as God for the world, which occurs primarily in the personal sanctification.[137] It is gathered around the bishop that the local church family is built in the love of God by configuring to Christ. The sum of these families, by the unity of their faith and their Catholic sollicitude, form the Universal Church in which the bishops are jointly responsible for the doctrine, standards of discipline and morals. One of them has by divine right, the (papal) responsibility to maintain the "communicatio in sacris" and to keep the rules and rights inherited from the Tradition and the Fathers, and that the Councils have established as inviolable because they are recognized by all as favoring the wellbeing of the Church.

4

THE CONSOLIDATION OF THE DOCTRINE

We do not want to end this Part II without giving an overview of the activities of Bishop Varlet to consolidate the doctrine that supported his action for the Church of Utrecht. This consolidation, he has done especially by teaching and writing. Between 1724 and 1742, he has produced an impressive amount of documents.[138] Some of them have been published. This is the case of the two apologies (1724 & 1727), of the letters (memoirs) to the missionaries of Tonkin (1734), to the Bishop of Montpellier (1736), to the Bishop of Senez I (1736) and II (in collaboration with Msgr. van der Croon, 1738), of the response to the Bishop of Senez (1736) and of the <u>Testament Spirituel</u> (1742). But much has remained in manuscript form. This is the case of the commentaries (exposés and petitions), reflections and critiques, demonstrations, responses, notes, work plans, autobiographical diaries, documentary collections), letters (concerning the missions of the East, the Bull Unigenitus, the Appeal to a general council and the affairs of the Church of Utrecht), miscellaneous pieces such as his protest against the election of Gerard Akkoy to the See of Haarlem and his writings on the Arabic, Ethiopian and Hebrew languages. To give an idea of the magnitude of the corpus involved, the <u>Annotations sur divers sujets</u> ..., a subset of the grouping <u>Commentaries</u>[139] alone is 20 units of notes of some 50 pages each.

We selected a set of texts from the most representative of the concerns of Bishop Varlet. Four fields of interest have been identified:

controversy, teaching, patristics and theological expertise. Since most of these writings illustrate aspects that we have developed in the preceding chapters, we will present them briefly and we will intervene only to clarify some points (names, concepts or ideas requiring explications ...). Bible interpretation could be considered as a fourth field of interest. But it will be developed in a separate chapter because of the millenarist belief that underlies it after 1725 and of its impact on Bishop Varlet's ecclesiology.

CONTROVERSY

If we were to classify the Varletian production, we would have to award the first category to controversy. All published works are in this category, as well as three quarters of the manuscript documents. This is the case of memoirs, observations, comments, refutations and a significant portion of the annotations (on the affairs of the Church, on various subjects, on the pastoral letter of Cardinal de Noailles, on the memoirs of the refusal of the bulls) and the correspondence (on the missions of the East, on the Bull Unigenitus, on the Appeal to the general council and on the affairs of the Church of Utrecht). Among controversy issues are questions of dogma, of church administration, of morals and of ecclesiastical procedure.

Questions of Dogma

The argument focuses on the doctrine of the efficacious grace which would have been undermined by the condemnation of the sentiments of Cornelis Jansen (Jansenius). Bishop Varlet addresses this question in a text that seems relevant since it goes back to when he was a seminarian at St. Magloire, 17 years before taking position in favor of the clergy of Utrecht . Taken from the <u>Testament Spirituel</u>, the excerpt is about the Formulary of Alexander VII that he regrets having endorsed in 1702, "in an age when one is dazzled". This is a confirmation of what we said in Part I, that his devout Jansenism, in line with the *Case of Conscience*, was close to the ideals of the French School of Spirituality and of the church renewal called for by the Council of Trent. This, we believe, is the meaning to be given to the "dazzle" he mentions in this text.

On the Formulary of Alexander VII

When I subscribed, in the Sorbonne in 1702, to the Formulary of the clergy[140] and to the censure of Mr. Arnauld, it was by a lack of light and bad advice that I have taken too obediently. I was aware that the Church is not infallible on recent, contested, obscure and doubtful facts, indifferent to religion, and which are the subject of criticism, not of faith. I knew therefore that the Church cannot require my belief under her own authority and that the fact of Jansenius was of this nature. Thus we could not be compelled to believe and to stop believing; that everything that could be required of individuals in this regard was that they did not rise against the decision made by Pope Alexander VII and by some bishops on this fact. And it was not questionable by the principles of the faith and by everything that had happened since the Peace concluded under Pope Clement IX, to regard the subscription to the Formulary as a sign of belief. This sentiment was then as common as convenient, and the trustees themselves declared to the candidates that the intention of the Faculty was not to ask anything more than the respectuous silence.[141] We extended this principle to the censure of Mr. Arnauld. The Faculty, it was said, did not pretend to proscribe the doctrine and the language of the Holy

Fathers. It is always possible to say that we cannot do good without the efficacious grace. The Faculty has heard the proposal of Mr. Arnauld in the sense of absolute and antecedent helplessness, or at least in the sense of a deprivation of the supernatural power in the justs. It is in this sense that we must take the censure. What the Faculty demands is that its members condemn this error and that they do not rise against the sentence on the grounds that the interpretation of Mr. Arnauld was wrongly understood.

It is in this sense and with these assurances that I signed but I recognize that I did wrong. The proposition of Mr. Arnauld regarding the right is so established in the Tradition that, as noted by M. Bossuet, Bishop of Meaux, to condemn it is to deliver all the Fathers to Jansenism. Moreover, the censure to which I subscribed also condemns the first proposition of this doctor, regarding the fact of Jansenius. Even those who undertook to subscribe acknowledged that there was no doubt that the way this proposition is stated, the Church could not require on a fact such as that of Jansenius a respectful silence. To condemn this proposition was to fix the subscription to the Formulary to signify that one believes the fact. It was as if this belief was made an indispensable duty, not only for those who signed, but for all those who knew that the propositions were condemned as extracted from Jansenius and in the meaning of the author. Moreover, regardless of this censure, the words of the Formulary marked that one believed the fact that Jansenius has not explained properly the doctrine of St. Augustine. I should not have signed the Formulary purely and simply because I do not believe this fact and that it seemed at least doubtful. The Peace of Clement IX may well allow the inferiors to sign with explanation and oblige the superiors to be satisfied with signatures that explain what this Pope has admitted with great caution, but it does not authorize someone to sign what he does not believe or simply subscribe to a formula which expresses the belief of a fact which is doubtful. Finally, nothing was more opposed to the conduct of the four bishops that this subscription that I made at the Sorbonne. These prelates had subscribed and made others subscribe with explanation and I was subscribing purely and simply. They had explained the dogma and their condemnation of the 5 propositions, saying that it was without damaging the doctrine of the efficacious grace itself. And by subscribing to the Formulary, I was agreeing at the same time with the censure that was actually undermining the need of this grace. Since it was not true that without it we can do nothing, it was not necessary for any act of Christian piety. These bishops, explaining their submission to the constitution on the point of fact, made it in such a way that the decision was not challenged. That's what I condemned with the Faculty by endorsing the censure.

I therefore retract the subscription I had the misfortune to make on wrong principles and at an age where it is not surprising that I was dazzled. I ask pardon to God and to the Church. I demand the Peace of Clement IX to which I should have conformed myself.[142] I regret that by signing purely and simply, we give pretext to destroy it and I'm joining the late Bishops of Montpellier and Senez, who appealed to the Holy See and the future council of that Peace so just and so precious, which is undermined, either by requiring pure and simple subscriptions, either by condemning the subscriptions that are conformed to the reports of the four bishops.

Nothing demonstrates better the need for the precautions taken by these wise prelates in the case of the Formulary and of the Bull Unigenitus. The decree shows what the opponents of grace have condemned under the vague and ambiguous sense of Jansenius because they made Clement XI say that the 101 propositions on grace mean what is condemned in the 5 proscribed propositions by Innocent X and Alexander VII. That alone should be enough to prevent subscribing without explanation the bulls that Clement XI explains so badly and to absolutely reject it. It also contains many other flaws that were exposed in different writings, and I was so struck first that I have always avoided giving the least sign of approval to this decree that they try in vain to reconcile with the doctrine, discipline or language of the Church.

Questions of Church Administration

Suspended from the exercise of the episcopate for having administered the sacrament of confirmation in Amsterdam in 1719, without the permission of the Internuncio of Brussels, Bishop Varlet challenges the arguments used by Rome to issue such a censure. He advocates the ordinary jurisdiction against the centralizing claims of the Vatican which reverse the order of the Church in preventing a local community to have its own ordinary. The text we chose to illustrate this aspect is taken from the <u>Première Apologie</u>.

<u>The Ordinary Jurisdiction Belongs to the Cathedral Chapter during the Vacancy of the Episcopal See</u>

We are accused of having exercized some episcopal functions in Holland, to the scandal of the Catholics, without the permission of the Internuncio of Brussels. This criticism has three parts and contains three facts. One fact is very innocent. The second is commendable because it complies with the divine and human laws, and so many obligations that we could not wash us of having omitted it. The third is absolutely false and slanderously alleged.

We did not need the permission of the Internuncio of Brussels to exercize our functions in a church where he has no ordinary jurisdiction. The Council of Trent, which reduced the powers of nuncios to more reasonable bounds, does not allow them to disturb the Ordinaries in their jurisdiction. There must be, in each diocese, a bishop who governs it. During the vacancy of the episcopal see, the jurisdiction is vested in the Cathedral Chapter.[143] These are the constant rules of the Church that it is not permitted the nuncios, or even the Pope (keeper of the holy canons), to change. If we violated those rules, we are guilty, but we're not for not having asked the Internuncio a permission it was not in his power to give as he is not the Ordinary of these provinces. We would rather have been guilty, according to St. Gregory, if we had given the pernicious example of reversing the order of the Church.¹⁴⁴ It is not more permissible for an Internuncio to disturb the jurisdiction of the bishops and their church than to defenders sent by past popes to various locations to take care of the patrimony of St. Peter. Though they were granted considerable privileges by the Holy See, Saint Gregory wanted them to refer all ecclesiastical causes to the bishops, unless some of the

Cathedral Chapter of Orleans and King Robert Le Pieux, 11ᵗʰ cent.

clergy had some controversy with his bishop. In this case, the defender could act as an arbitrator or else he would advise the parties to choose judges "te admonte sibi judices eligant". And he confirms all that by this beautiful maxim: "If we do not keep every bishop's jurisdiction where it belongs we, who have to keep and maintain the ecclesiastical order, will allow it to be overthrown".¹⁴⁵

By what right does the Internuncio of Brussels say that he exercizes in these provinces the functions of Ordinary? Is it as Vicar Apostolic? He does not say that he has this quality. Moreover, according to the rules, he cannot be Vicar Apostolic for several reasons, details of which would be too long. It is sufficient, for the present, to say that he is not a bishop. The quality of Vicar Apostolic, which gives some overseeing or jurisdiction over the bishops, must be attached to the episcopal character, otherwise the entire hierarchy is confused to the great scandal of the Church. But even in this capacity, he would not be Ordinary in these provinces. The functions of Vicar Apostolic¹⁴⁶ are not uncertain: the canons have determined that it does not depend on who *has the dignity to extend the rights to his will beyond the bounds. Above all, we must always have in mind this rule recommended by St. Gregory: you cannot do more insult to the pope than to authorize yourself to confound in his name the ecclesiastical order. The Vicars Apostolic were established to maintain the rules, not to destroy them. The first thing that St. Gregory recommends to St. Virgil of Arles in his 50th letter is: do not cause prejudice to the rights enjoyed by the Metropolitans according to the ancient custom. The letter has a great weight, not only because of the great authority of Pope St. Gregory, but also because Pope John VIII, almost 300 years later, copied it word for word in his 94th letter to Rostagne of Arles on the same subject.*

All the ordinary jurisdiction during the vacancy of the episcopal see belongs, as we have already said, to the cathedral chapter, which represents all the clergy and which has been at all time the custodian of the jurisdiction in such a case. We see that after the retreat of St. Cyprian, though the see was not vacant, the clergy of Rome, not knowing that this holy man, although he was absent, governed as if he had been present, wrote to the clergy of Carthage, warning that as taking the place of the pastor, they were obliged to watch over the flock that was in great danger. And at the end of the 7th century, the evangelical workers who were sent to these provinces jointly governed the Church until they handed over the jurisdiction in the hands of the two bishops that they chose. The clergy having extremely multiplied by the blessing that God gave to the work of his saints who planted here the faith, a chapter of the cathedral church was established to represent the clergy and be the senate of the Church.

The Chapter of Utrecht has survived until today by an uninterrupted succession. It is therefore not allowed to deprive it of the common right upheld by the Council of Trent[147] which ordered the following: the Chapter must appoint a vicar to govern the vacant Church, and if there is negligence in the chapter, it is not to a vicar apostolic, even less to a nuncio to provide for them but to the metropolitan. If the chapter of the metropolitan city is negligent, it is to the first suffragan to supply. How then could a nuncio, in violation of a right so ancient and so well established, claim to be the Ordinary of a church that has survived for so many centuries, with the constant enjoyment of her privileges, that the popes do not want them to lose? We do not want, they tell us through the mouth of Pope Hilarus, that be confused the privileges of the churches, which must always be preserved, and our ministry must fructify, not by the extent of countries, but by the acquisition of souls."[148]

We did, indeed, exercise some functions needed in the Catholic Church of Holland, but we could do and we had to. We did it with all possible regularity, not only with the agreement and permission, but the repeated instances and prayers of those who are still (as we have said) the holders of the jurisdiction of this church during the vacancy of the archiepiscopal see, namely the Chapter of the Metropolitan Church, in a word, with the permission of the Ordinary.

Questions of Morals

Although he raised against the laxist consequences attributed to the Bull Unigenitus, including *attrition*, it is on the problem of charging interests on loans (usury) that he wrote most pages. In 1733, after the death of Archbishop Barcham Wuytiers, it is under the influence of the Party of the merchants that the Chapter of Utrecht elected as successor Canon Theodore van der Croon, said to be sympathetic to usury. Bishop Varlet refused to consecrate him if he would not obtain a "deed in proper form dismissing the bad proceedings of the Chapter."[149] This put him in a conflict that has poisoned his relations with the authorities of the Church of Utrecht almost until his death.[150] This experience had made him perplexed as to the legitimacy of giving bishops to a church that cannot stand stronger on the principles opposed to usury. The following text, taken from the Testament Spirituel, is the most interesting on this issue.

The Need to Combat Usury

I beg the Archbishop of Utrecht[151] to never ordain any bishop or any priest, and even not to admit to holy orders, whoever is not declared against all usury, firm in the principles opposed to it and determined not to give the absolution to those who, lending money, stipulate that they will make more than they paid, what they want to justify in this country as a "rente rachetable des deux côtés" (an annuity callable according to the issuer or the debtor).

Usury by Albrecht Dürer

I have not forgotten what said Archbishop Barchman, being about to die: if it was an evil that the church should have no bishop, it would be an even greater if she had one that would support usury. Indeed, it is more important to help maintain throughout the Church the integrity of the faith and the purity of morals than to perpetuate the episcopate and the priesthood in a particular church.[152] If I did not take precautions regarding the two first archbishops I consecrated, it is because I did not know the church's need to be educated on this point. The more I have been informed, the more I thought we had to work to eradicate usury. And if I have seemed to some people too difficult to satisfy on this point, when it came to consecrate the last two archbishops, I rather fear that I have not been firm enough. I conjure the archbishop not to be shaken by the shouts of those who claim that we want to introduce a new formulary.

It is not here, as in the Formulary of Alexander VII, a new fact and indifferent to religion. It concerns a dogma to be undoubtedly supported and a pernicious practice to eradicate. It is in order to obtain such goods that pastors are given to the Church and it is essential to establish only those who are firmly committed to sound doctrine and powerful enough to reprimand those who deviate.

If the members of the Chapter have some gratitude for the services I have rendered by sacrificing myself for this church, I hope that they will join their worthy archbishop to extirpate the error and the abuse. When most of them professed to be committed to that principle received among the theologians, that it is not permissible to make profit from a loan made to a poor or a rich, and that one can only in the case of a gain that the loan stops, or of a damage it causes, seek just compensation in observing the conditions required by good theologians, these gentlemen probably have not wanted to surprise me by ambiguities. They therefore understood this principle as it is understood in the schools and by St. Thomas, Hesselius, Sainte-Beuve, Father Alexandre,[153] the Morale de Grenoble,[154] and by all good theologians. I ask them not to depart from this principle which is beyond doubt and belongs to the faith of the Church. The tolerance of civil laws, the temerity of some theologians who have begun to justify what the Church has always condemned, the vain pretexts of those who find a profit everywhere, except for lending to the poors, the intractability of the people, the fear of seeing them go away from their pastors are no reasons to depart from the norm received in these provinces before the revolutions. This is why I beg the members of the Chapter and all the pastors and faithful to hate usury and to distinguish themselves from the Protestants in this as in all other matters on which Calvin has innovated.

In general, one cannot be too suspicious of this license, which is the vice of this century, and which makes one deviates from the *sentiments received in the Church. The new writers that Mr. de Senez[155] has fought have made many of the excesses that Mr. de Lan[156] also noted in his twenty letters. I join Mr. de Senez to testify the horror that a good Catholic should have towards that pernicious boldness to invent and defend novelties and to exhort the good theologians to fight for the faith once left to the saints by tradition.*

Questions of Ecclesiastical Procedure

The election of Archbishop van der Croon in 1733 has not only caused Bishop Varlet doctrinal difficulties. It also included, in his view, a problem of regularity. He deals with it in a letter written July 18, 1734 to Nicolas Petitpied, a Doctor of the Sorbonne who took refuge in Holland.

Dissatisfaction with the Method of Election of an Archbishop of Utrecht

I think the Chapter differed because they expected that I would be easier. These people like to boast of vain hopes. But the other reason you ask seems only an excuse. They do not know in what disposition I am and if I approve what the Pastors and other clergy have written to the Chapter, i.e. their resolution to engage the faithful entrusted to their care to correct their contracts. I think, as I explained many times, and recently in my last letter to Mr. Dalenoort,[157] that the alleged ignorance on this point is only an excuse.

Regarding the letter of the pastors, I agree with the substance but the form has defaults that I have reported. Moreover, I do approve that the pastors engage as much as they can the faithful entrusted to their care to correct their contracts. It is the least thing they can do but it is not enough for a bishop who must be the doctor of his church. Also, I do not see how you can say that the main difficulty is removed with respect to Mr. van der Croon. Surely it would be a good thing to engage the Chapter to authorize the good practice by a decision to uproot gradually the abuse which has been introduced. But you pass over in silence the error or errors which have been published on the roofs. Mistakes so intolerable that Mr. de Montpellier has indicated to the Chapter that if the writings which contain them were penetrating in his diocese, he would be obliged to censor them by a pastoral letter. And we who are in the midst of these scandals, we treat this as a simple detail! When I have a revocation in good form of the bad deliberations, it will be a difficulty removed. Mr. Villiers[158] wrote to Mr. de la Cour[159] we might be more successful with the chapter if "I wrote something honest." I don't understand what he means because everything I wrote to the chapter was in the terms of honesty. If I have sometimes used some tough words, it is because we must speak loudly to those who are voluntary deaf, and use proper terms in dealing with people who do not understand the figurative ones.

We are embarrassed with these gentlemen. If we act with courtesy, they abuse it because they are very likely to be flattered. You can judge by the lack of success of last year's conference with the members of the Chapter. In addition, a courtesy that I made in a letter to Mr. van der Croon was quoted by Mr. Kemp[160] as an invincible argument in his favor. It is very difficult to deal with people like that. If you step out to them, they make three steps back to get away from you. It is true that in the past, I did not measure my efforts with them. I did not observe both the short and long. But what a difference between how they act today and what it was 11 or 12 years ago. They then consulted on all their efforts; they communicated all their writings; they changed all that we thought was not convenient; they followed all the advices, often with great difficulty because their lack of light prevented them from seeing the importance of them. But finally, they made it.

What happened to the measures of honesty they had? Have I become other than I was? Am I more obliged to give them a bishop now than in the past? Why do they treat me so differently? First, they began by breaking their word, then I have not seen this bishop elect since his election one year ago. He only wrote two letters and the latter had a *very loud tone. He threatened not to write me anymore and he kept his word. In my reply, I mentioned only one point of his letter to avoid an incident, but it was full of unbearable lines from one end to another. In addition, I requested to be notified of critical aspects of the case but it is only after 6 months that I received copies. They were formless and I am not sure they came from them. Finally, they find beneath them to write to me: this is their secretary who does. In short, they treat me as a hired bishop, as those called suffragans[161], who by their slavish conduct debase the sacred character. I certainly did not deserve to be so treated. If they had done well, I would have entered a case well made, but I should be informed about everything to make judgements because I must respond to God and his Church. This is necessary, especially as I have proof that they ignore the rules of the Church and do not make much of them. The items of which I request the revocation are evidence and that's what makes me fear that this Church perish sooner with a bishop than without one, unless he has a rare wisdom.*

TEACHING

If it is as polemist that Bishop Varlet was first read, respected by some and decried by others, making himself known throuhout Europe,[162] it is his role as doctor of theology[163] which consumed the greatest of his energy after 1727. Based in Rhijnwijk, where he was in charge with the archbishop, he became involved in the formation of the seminarians of the house. This is evidenced by two texts of the <u>Annotations sur divers sujets</u> ... The first text, *Nécessité d'un plan d'étude de la théologie* (The need for a plan of study of theology), outlines his pedagogy (to go from simple to complex, to understand well some basic definitions first, to vary the study, to follow a sequence in the presentation of the subjects: for the Old Testament, the Psalms, the Pentateuch, the Prophets and the other writings, for the New Testament, the Synoptics, St. John, the Acts of the Apostles, St. Paul, the other Epistles and the Book of Revelation) and provides information on the content of his courses. He gave a place of honour to the authors banned in France such as Pierre Nicole[164] and Cornelis Jansen.

The Need for a Plan of Study of Theology

I do not advise the beginners to read theological treatises before they have formed a plan of the whole body of science. A sculptor, presented with a block of marble to make a statue, does not begin to make a limb or an eye. He applies primarily to roughhew his marble to take its proportions. It is necessary to do the same with the study of theology before elaborating on the difficult questions that demand a lengthy discussion. First we must understand the definitions of Trent and Montpellier, with the instructions of Mr. Nicole. Then the memoir of the sentences, read and reread, followed by certain portions of St. Thomas, against the disadvantages of other methods.

Length produces disgust. We must vary the study by learning Hebrew, reading the Scripture and church history, first in Mr. Godeau[165], then in Mr. Fleury.[166] It is important to follow the same method for the study of Scripture. Do not read the audacious interpreters and the Protestant critics before possessing the principles of a good theology and before having acquired a taste for the good interpretation of Scripture in the ancient Fathers and ecclesiastical writers. Long texts of interpretation are tiring and disgusting. The souls may languish on a single book of the Scripture. The prodigious diversity of opinions found in the synopsis of Father Calmet[167] can confuse a reader who is not able to choose the best. The dryness of

the criticism that we get accustomed to is able to kill the spirit of prayer; corrupt the taste to the extent that we no more appreciate the best explanations of the Fathers. We want the extraordinary; we get attached to a letter that many souls, with the seductive appeal of a beautiful secular erudition, apply without discretion.

It is useful to begin by studying the Psalms. Menochius[168] and Bellarmine[169] are enough in the beginning. On the Pentateuch, Jansen; the rest of the Old Testament, Menochius; the Prophets, St. Jerome and, above all, good French authors, as Duguet. On the New Testament, that we must study at the same time as the Old Testament, first read the concord based on the treaty of Concensus by St. Augustine, with the commentary of Zacharias by St. John Chrysostom. St. Matthew, with the commentary of Jansen and of St. Jerome. The other Evangelists, with Jansen. On St. John, St. Augustine. On the Acts, St. John Chrysostom. On St. Paul, first read the authors of the 8th and 9th centuries. On the canonical Epistles and the Book of Revelation, Menochius. On the First of St. John, St. Augustine. Reserve Mr. Bossuet for a second reading of the Book of Revelation.

Bossuet

When you follow only your taste and your fantasy in the study of science, you never become learned. There must be order.[170] Similarly, in the study of religion, if we do not focus on sound principles and do not follow an order, we can only lose. The more we are witty, the more we fall. Examples: Tertullian, Origen.

The second text, *Plan d'une méthode pour étudier la théologie et l'histoire de l'Église* (Plan of a Method to Study Theology and Church History)[171], presents in 23 treaties the matter that Bishop Varlet considered necessary to teach to the students. Are to be noted: the order of distribution of the subjects (the Church and the infallibility that she exercises (not the Pope) in the councils, Treaty 1); the respective authority of the pope and the bishops under the light of tradition and canonical prescriptions) and specific aspects such as: predestination (Treaty 2),[172] probabilism in ethics (Treaty 6), the history of the constitutions on grace and the nuances between necessary, sufficient and effecacious grace, the problem of free will (Treaty 9), justification and merit (Treaty 10), the complete reparation for our sins made by Jesus Christ (Treaty 13) and the Eucharistic theology derived from it (a festive meal of the Lord's Passover, in which the sacrifice of the cross is actualized, Treaty 19)… Many of these aspects are specific to the Old Catholic positions and are as such in the text of the Declaration of Utrecht of 1889.[173]

PATRISTICS

The triumph of St. Augustine by Claudio Coello 1642-1694

The study of the Fathers is one of the main sources of references for Bishop Varlet's understanding of the mystery of the Church. After his break with Rome, his interest in Patristics went growing. He analyzed St. Justin and Tertullian, where he found a justification for his Millenarian belief (discussed in the following chapter), St. Ambrose of Milan , St. Athanasius, St. Cyril of Jerusalem, St. Eusebius, St. John Chrysostom, Theodoret, and especially St. Augustine. A significant portion of the <u>Annotations sur divers sujets</u> ... paraphrases themes borrowed from the latter. He derives from him almost all the elements of his spiritual theology. This is the case of the lines about God (His love, His attributes and the confidence that He inspires), the blindness of the mind, the affections of the heart, the spiritual battle, the conversion and the cupidity.

We reproduce below an excerpt from the *Annotations of the Confessions*, Book 1, the first seven chapters, on the representation of God.

<u>Annotations of the Confessions of St. Augustine</u>

Chapter 1   *God made us for Himself and our heart cannot be happy if it does not rest in Him. To praise and invoke God, we must recognize Him and He becomes known to us by giving us faith. It is by faith that we invoke Him.*

Chapter 2   *God Whom we invoke is in us and we in Him.*

Chapter 3   *God is immense: He fills everything and is not contained by the things He fills.*

Chapter 4   *What God is: His perfections are inexplicable. He is our life and makes it holy.*

Chapter 5   *How am I so considerable that You want me to love You and that You'll be angry if I'm not doing it...? Isn't it great enough to love You?*

Chapter 6   *The care that God takes of us from our birth is a great reason to bless, to praise and to thank Him... Our years pass but nothing passes in God. The causes of the most*

> changeable things have an immutable origin in Him, and the temporal beings deprived of reason have in Him reasons always alive and everlasting.

Chapter 7   The formation of the human beings can only be the work of God. It is a big enough reason to praise Him when we would have no others. But He did not put sin in us.

THEOLOGICAL EXPERTISE

There might be no need to establish this category because it overlaps with that of the controversy. However, there is one aspect of the contribution of Bishop Varlet that would otherwise not be covered.

After the death of Archbishop Barchman Wuytiers, the election of Msgr. van der Croon threw him into an open conflict with the Chapter of Utrecht, as mentioned previously. Disappointed by his Dutch co-religionists, he turned towards the French Convulsionists whom he saw as blessed in the miracles operated through the intercession of Deacon Pâris.

The text chosen to illustrate this point comes from a letter he wrote to Nicolas Petitpied on November 9, 1736. It focuses on the supernatural character of the convulsions, that he defended against those who viewed them as a natural disorder. This is typical of the kind of argument he used in favor of the miracles.

On the Affair of the Convulsions

I have two thoughts. The first is in relation to this statement: "Do you think the advent of the convulsions to be supernatural? Judge them as if they were natural." This is the great difficulty. The doctors claim that there is this difference between the natural and the divine supernatural that in the natural, God is not responsible for any harm because He only acts as a primary cause, according to the exigency of the case. Secondly, instead of pretending that in the divine supernatural, God takes care of everything because He is acting with particular intentions (...), they restrict themselves to saying that the Convulsionists are alienated and are not free if they are in the hands of God who acts in them miraculously and is responsible for all the harm they do...

Conversion of Carré de Montgeron[174] at the tomb of Deacon Pâris
Drawing by Jean Restout

In principle, one cannot attribute to God what would have an indissoluble connection with any disordered state in the moral order because of God's holiness. It must therefore take place in the natural order. We cannot attribute to God the derangements in the natural life because He is the prime and general cause of it.

The principle that in the natural order, God rises above the laws of nature is exactly true of the laws of physics. But it is not the same with the laws of morals because, first, if it were true that God rises above these laws, as in the order given to Abraham to sacrifice his son (whose order He did not require the execution but only the preparation) that's the place to say that in this case, the exemption should be as clear and certain as the law. Second, God is the master of the human life: He can use what He is to deprive us of our life. But it is not the same with human laws if they are absolutely immutable and it does not seem consistent with the holiness of God to dispense it in any case.

5

THE INTERPRETATION OF SCRIPTURE

The teaching of Bishop Varlet, particularly on the Church, is connected with his bible interpretation. This area, one of the most important in our opinion, is the least known part of his work. But there is one aspect of his ecclesiology (his refusal to assimilate the Church with the Kingdom) that escapes the analysis unless we take into account the foundation on which stands his exegesis, namely that the fulfillment of the Old Testament promises implies the Millennium described in the Book of Revelation, Chapter 20. The urgency to bring about the Reign of God (in the souls) takes its meaning from the "regnum of Christ on earth", when He will establish the perfect justice; restore the Jewish nation in the Alliance and destroy the "system" (Babylon in the Church), by which the elect are thrown to the Beast.

Three texts will be used. The first consists of the introduction of his <u>Commentaire des Actes des Apôtres</u> (Commentary on the Acts of the Apostles). It illustrate the "conventional" portion of his bible interpretation. The second, taken from the introduction of his <u>Commentaire de l'Apocalypse</u> (Commentary on the Book of Revelation) exposes what is characteristic of his biblical understanding: the belief in a Millennium. The third, taken from his refutation of the arguments of Pastor Basnage on the treatment of biblical figures of speech, will make us penetrate his method of interpretation: *figurism*. It was fundamentally a biblical hermeneutic which saw persecuted minorities as justified witnesses, the saved and saving remnants on whom the rejection of Christ was again enacted and who in turn would enact his triumph of reformation of the Godly community.[175]

HIS CONVENTIONAL BIBLE INTERPRETATION

COMMENTARY ON THE ACTS OF THE APOSTLES
(INTRODUCTION)

St. John Chrysostom complains that many people do not know this book or its author though it is not less useful than the Gospels. The holy dogmas are developed, especially what concerns the Holy Spirit. We see the fulfillment of the promises in Jesus Christ. The apostles changed into other men by the force of the Holy Spirit, what was predicted in John 14:12 & Matthew 10:18, 21:12: the Gospel preached to everyone (Matthew 24:14). No longer are these men shy, rude, jealous. They are superior to vain glory, greed, anger, all the passions. You see it in a union that is troubled neither by desire nor the ambition. We see them shine in all the virtues and a perfect love (John 13:35).

St. Peter preaching, Acts 2: 22-24

There are points both of dogma and morals, we would not know well without this book.

It is spoken of St. Paul more than the other apostles because this book was written by St. Luke, his disciple, who remained faithfully attached to him while the others abandoned him or left him alone, and whose writings the apostle has adopted (1 Timothy 4:11 & 2 Corinthians 8:18).

Why St. Luke, having always been with St. Paul, did not develop his story until the end of the life of the apostle? First, what he wrote was enough for those who read it diligently. Second, the Gospels were applied to what was most pressing and did not aim at writing stories. Moreover, the apostles taught many things without writing them. And what is most admirable in them is how the Holy Spirit inspired them and brought them to make their doctrine available to the ordinary people. They have said little about the divine nature of our Lord and did extend on his human nature: his death, his resurrection, his ascension, because what was crucial at that time was that we know that Jesus Christ was risen from the dead, returned to his Father in heaven, as if our Lord had specifically applied Himself to show that He came to lead us by degrees. That is why St. Paul, speaking of Jesus Christ to the Athenians (Acts 17:31), calls Him simply a man, and with good reason, because when Jesus Christ spoke of his divinity to the Jews, they were often eager to stone him and the disciples were often confused and shocked when He spoke of the sublime mysteries and said to his apostles (John 16:12): "I have many things to say but you cannot bear them now." If the apostles, who had been so long with Jesus Christ, could not bear the profound mysteries, how those who had spent their lives in the worship of idols and many other vices, and began to withdraw from that, how would they taste the sublime discovery and the Jews themselves, who had so often heard in Deuteronomy (6:4): "Listen Israel, the Lord your God is the only Lord", how they would have been outraged if they had been told initially that the One they had crucified and buried, and Whom they had not seen raised, is God equal to the Father? The apostles were therefore instructed gradually, by degrees, and the more they were lowered to be within the reach of ordinary people, the more the Holy Spirit poured grace abundantly. They benefited more from this method because in lowering themselves, they raised those who were lying down and they proved the resurrection by greater miracles than those Jesus Christ has made. The main purpose of this book is to establish the resurrection because when we believe it, the rest is easy.

HIS MILLENARIAN INTERPRETATION

The excerpt of the <u>Commentary on the Acts of the Apostles</u> presents a fairly traditional interpretation. But the tone changes a little later, when Bishop Varlet analyses the various verses of the text. Then appear the theses of the millennium, a prophetic teaching given especially in the Revival Churches[176] based on the belief that "Christ will reign on earth for a thousand years, according to passages of the Old Testament and the Book of Revelation, Chapter 20." [177]

We will identify these theses (mentioned in part in the previous pages) as Bishop Varlet presents them in his <u>Commentary on the Book of Revelation</u>, and later in the <u>Commentary on the Acts of the Apostles</u>. We will show how they form a specific system of interpretation, which differs from the allegorical exegesis[178] then in use in the Roman

Church. We will indicate the reasons for the demarcation and we will identify its impact on ecclesiology.

The Theses of the Millennium:
The Commentary on the Book of Revelation

It is against the dangers which can destroy the Church that the apostle John's prophecy strengthens and consoles the faithful. Our Lord had made appear that uninterrupted suite of dangers so that we be always prepared for it and he announced it only in general. But St. John tells us that there must be a break, a rest period he called "millennium",[179] that is to say a series of centuries, when Jesus Christ will reign in the Church and Satan will be chained, that is to say he will not be able to endanger the entire body of the Church. He may well put some parts of the Church in danger, like in Arianism,[180] but not the entire body...

In the end, Satan will be unleashed, but this time will be short. Perhaps in this time will take place what is said about the persecution of the woman (Chapter 12) ... They are wrong obviously those who want the Book of Revelation to apply to all the times of the Church since the time of peace – a time where she fights with a clear

advantage - is included entirely in the millennium and has nothing to do with the other parts of the prophecy. However, in the millennium as in all the times of the Church, there will be tares among the wheat, evil fish in the net with the good ones, and that until the Judgement Day.[181]

We find in Bishop Varlet's work the major elements of the Millenarian doctrine as established by Ralph Shallis[182] from Chapter 20 of the Book of Revelation: the imprisonment of Satan: he no more seduces the nations (v. 1-3), the reign of Christ for a thousand years (v. 4- 6), the temporary release of Satan after the millennium, his return to earth to seduce the nations again and to bring them together against God (v. 7-10), and the Judgement Day (v. 11-14).

Other aspects, also reported by Shallis, appear in the Commentary on the Acts of the Apostles. These are: the appearance of Christ that ends the persecution against the elect (which is caused by Babylon in the Church)[183] and the reign of the saints with Christ.[184]

These two aspects deserve attention. Their mention in his Commentary of the Acts of the Apostles shows the functional character of Bishop Varlet's millenarian hope. The persecution he endured with his co-religionists was prefigured in the Old Testament (Isaiah 11:65-66, Daniel 7 ...) and in St. Paul (Romans 11). It has a meaning and a purpose in the divine plan. "The promulgation of the Bull Unigenitus and the series of royal and ecclesiastical pronouncements issued in support of it were evident portents of the universal apostasy at the end of time".[185] The Last Day is near (the return of Christ)[186] and with it the spiritual regeneration of the world. "While denouncing the present evils and decrying the corruption and degeneration of the Church, (Varlet and other learned divines) became increasingly preoccupied with reviving the ancient theme of the return of the prophet Elijah, the eschatological precursor whose mysterious advent was traditionnaly interpreted as a prelude to the conversion of the Jews to the Christian faith and their restoration to their homeland, as a herald of the Last Day".[187]

An excerpt from a letter addressed to Bishop Varlet on October 3, 1726 by Philippe Boidot of Rueil (perhaps a member of the Congregation of the Priests of Calvary) tells us about the concerns that animated the Millenarians: "There will be two mysteries of iniquity, two apostasies, two Antichrists, two outstanding or general judgments before the end of the world. The first will be consumed about the Bull Unigenitus. On this occasion, Moses and Elijah will come to preach the Gospel to the Jews and they will convert. Once converted as a body, they will take the place of the body of the Gentiles fallen into unbelief and they will thus redress the losses of the Church. The Jews, scattered throughout the habitable world, will preach the Gospel to all nations. The triumph of the Church will then be universal, having been renewed and rejuvenated. She will enjoy for a long interval a period of rest and peace. After that, she will weaken and age again. Then, the second mystery of iniquity, the second apostasy will be consumed by the last Antichrist." [188]

Chassaigne, a Jansenist opposed to such an interpretation, qualifies Bishop Varlet of "figurist doctor" [189] thereby connecting him to the school of exegesis called Figurism, "a system of imagination that ruins the mind of those who practice it, teaches them nothing and makes them take, in any event, an enthusiastic tone that strikes only small minds and which is despised by reasonable people." [190] Clearly a supporter of the traditional allegorical method (which spiritualizes the prophecies concerning Israel and apply them to the Church as advocated by St. Augustine[191]), Chassaigne raises the question of the legitimacy of Figurism as a system of exegesis. This is an important issue which has ecclesiological implications and deserves consideration.

A Figurist Exegesis

The principles of figurism were developed by Jacques Joseph Duguet, former professor at Saint-Magloire (Bishop Varlet was his student around 1700), in his book <u>Règles pour l'intelligence des</u>

<u>Saintes Écritures</u> (1716). Unlike St. Augustine who, having adopted the interpretation of the Donatist Tichonius (aligned with the allegorical approach of Origen) makes the millennium starts with the first coming of Christ and sees the Church as the establishment of the Kingdom (The City of God),[192] Duguet and his followers "where interested in the eschatological aspects of Scriptures

172

and in the contemporary state of the Church." [193] The characters and events become figurative[194] of those of the Last Day,[195] hence the name *Figurism*.

This approach is not new. Philip Schaff believes it was that of the Pre-Nicene era.[196] J.D. Pentecost shares the same view: "it is impossible to find someone who lived in the apostolic and post-apostolic era, which has not believed in a real and physical return of Christ on earth to establish a literal kingdom." [197] Frederick Tatford proves the truth of this statement by quoting from Papias,[198] Justin,[199] Irenaeus,[200] Tertullian,[201] Nepos,[202] Commodanius[203] and Lactaneius.[204] This lends weight to what wrote Edward Gibbon in his <u>History of the Decline and Fall of the Roman Empire</u>: "The doctrine of the millennium was inculcated by a succession of fathers from Justin Martyr and Irenaeus, who conversed with the first disciples of the apostles, to Lactantius, the tutor of Crispus, the oldest son of Constantine. This doctrine appears to have been the opinion of all orthodox believers." [205]

But if the millennium was part of the Orthodox faith during the first three centuries, how is it that from the 4th century, the belief in an earthly reign of Christ disappeared to make way for the identification of the Church with the Kingdom? There are several causes for this transformation. Some trace it to the Gnostics.[206] However, the specialists generally agree on two reasons: the influence of the Greek thought, particularly Neoplatonicism,[207] and the merger of the Church and the State, which occurred in the 4th century, after Constantine's conversion.

It is in the East around year 250, under St. Clement of Alexandria, that the millenarian belief started to weaken.[208] "He was the first to seriously question the faith of the Early Church in a real and eartly reign of Christ on a restored Israel. He was influenced by the idealist philosophy of Plato[209] and had adopted the Greek method which interpreted the Scriptures by allegory. The teaching of St. Clement was accentuated by his student Origen (185-254). He too had been greatly influenced by the allegorical method first developed by Aristobulus (160 AD). The writings of Origen, in the first half of the 3rd century, suppressed the literal bible interpretation then in use, and replaced it with the allegorical method, which spiritualizes the Scripture.[210]

To the transformation of the exegetical concepts must be added that produced in the 4th century by the conversion of Constantine. "The fact that the Church recognized and adopted Christianity as the official religion of the empire made it impossible to identify the Antichrist with the emperor or Rome with Babylon. The application of the prophecies of Daniel and of the Book of Revelation had to be reviewed.[211] Quickly, the millennial kingdom was identified with the Christianized Roman state. St. Eusebius of Caesarea became the defender of this position in his works Life of Constantine and Ecclesiastical History. He who, in Proof of the Gospel, affirmed the return of Christ to establish the Kingdom of God on earth, now took the common view that the Kingdom of God was already established. Pope Damasus, at the Council of Rome (373), sanctioned this opinion in condemning the millenarian belief. But he opposed the idea that the Kingdom was synonymous with the empire. Having established that the Church and the Kingdom were the same, he laid the foundations on which Gregory VII would claim authority over all temporal powers.[212] St. Augustine (354-430) was the leading theologian of the Roman Church system. Defender of the positions taken at the Council of Rome, he abandoned his early pro-millenarian exegesis and adopted that allegorical of Origen, more appropriate to translate the application of the Old Testament promises to the Church as the expected earthly kingdom.[213]

St. Augustine was the main theologian of the Roman Church system in the period from the 5th century to St. Thomas of Aquinas. At this point in history, the Augustinian ecclesiology identifying the Kingdom to the Church had become the official doctrine.[214]

Most Christians accepted the teaching of St. Augustine: Satan attached to the Cross, the reign of Christ in force since the Ascension and the millennium begun with the birth of the Church. But so many things in the Church oppose the will of God. This observation led Joachim of Flores (1130-1202)[215] to reject the Augustinian interpretation and to foresee a new era, where life would be brought to a higher spiritual level. He divided history into three periods corresponding to the three persons of the Trinity and postulated that the last of the three, the Holy Spirit, would begin in 1260 and would be "the consummation of the Kingdom of God on earth".[216]

If his Jansenist convictions oblige us to associate Bishop Varlet with Augustinism with respect to grace, it is in the parentage of Joachim of Flores that he must be inserted for his ecclesiology and his biblical exegesis.

Given the relationship between non-allegorical exegesis and millenarian ecclesiology, we will now examine the theoretical positions of Bishop Varlet on scriptural interpretation. The text we have chosen to illustrate this aspect is drawn from a section of the <u>Annotations sur divers sujets</u>, where he dismisses passages from the <u>Histoire des ouvrages des savants</u> of Pastor Basnage on the Holy Eucharist. Do we take the meaning of the Words of Institution: "this is my Body, this is my Blood", literally or figuratively? [217]

<u>Theoretical Positions on Scriptural Interpretation</u>

When we present a reasoning to a reader, he can judge it and it is easier to attest the facts and the words reported. It is different when we read a story: the reader is more at ease. However, as he stands less on his gards, it is easier to surprise him. The preparation to the figurative meaning is necessary since it is a meaning other than the natural one.

Our use of the metaphor must be reasonable and understandable. It is as common as we like, it must be reasonable. This is not the abundance but the nature of the metaphors that demand caution. However violent they are, they should not be unintelligible. In addition, there is a difference between the speech of a book, of a title, of a preface and the ordinary one which does not allow figures as bold, especially when speaking with ordinary people, who want an explanation of the terms rather extraordinary.

As to the rule that it is the apposition[218] between the subject and the predicate of a proposition that helps unravel the metaphorical sense from the literal, it is neither the main nor the only one. The apposition needs not be complete but alike, as if the attribute is the image of the subject. Thus, a valuable diamond, rare, resistant, can be the image of a great prince. But the apposition is not enough. If someone says showing an oak: "this is Alexander", the apposition is correct but the speech is senseless and we may even find it outrageous. We will not be inclined to suspect a metaphor or attempt to discover one. There is no reasonable person, hearing this speech, who will conclude that this tree was transubstantiated [219] into Alexander. Those who say there is no need to consider if the subject we are talking about is a human or a sign confuse the metaphor with the other figures of speech. We do not transfer the name of a thing to another if it is not the sign of it, if it does not have a property suitable to the other, unless the rapport is common, as the laurel which is a sign of victory.

The frequent use of the metaphors should produce two effects. One is to keep the mind far from the idea of literal meaning, not only whenever the subject and the predicate of the proposal is compatible, but when there is a necessity, even if it is not sensitive nor obvious. The other is that this use of the figurative style must help to penetrate the true meaning of the metaphor and do a better use of it. As inconsistent as the subject and the predicate may be, the reader will not leave the literal sense, and if falsehood is suspected, he will consider the proposition absurd, unless he sees a connection between the subject and the predicate. A connection established by the nature of the thing that produces a likeness, or by the usage, or by a particular invention. The frequent use of the metaphors does not dispose the mind to penetrate their true meaning unless it is of a common use and that it is not difficult to see the connection.

THE DOCTRINE BEHIND THE EXEGESIS

We have considered most of the elements of the Millenarian doctrine upon which is built the Christian hope of Bishop Varlet. We must now organize it into a coherent ensemble. To do this, we will rely on two books: <u>Le Règne de 1,000 ans sur la terre</u> already mentioned in the references and the little book of Pierre Despagne, <u>Le Millennium et le règne messianique</u>. The first, scholarly, describes the doctrine; gives a historical account of it and presents its biblical foundations. The second, that shows the actuality of the system, applies it to our time, using many of the themes developed by Bishop Varlet about the Church. We find it interesting in this regard.

Two aspects are important in this doctrine: the rejection of the Roman Church ecclesiology centered on the institution (the Kingdom identified with the Church) and its replacement by a spiritualist ideology that makes the Church the place of the Spirit (God reigning in the souls) between the Ascension and the fulfillment of the promises (Christ's return in glory to establish the Kingdom on earth), with the Resurrection[220] as starting point.[221] This view, expressed in the <u>Commentary on the Acts of the Apostles</u> and in the <u>Commentary on the Book of Revelation</u>, presents similarities with the ecclesiology of the Reformation. Like Calvin and Luther, Bishop Varlet has of the Kingdom an essentially spiritual idea: it is "God's reign in the hearts of the redeemed".[222] Like them also, he identifies the Kingdom with the invisible Church. However, the parallel stops there because "the reformers held the non-millenarian view of the Roman Catholic Church." [223] For Bishop Varlet, the Kingdom is not only a concept: it must be actualized. "The reign of Christ will be visible."[224]

In this respect, he distinguishes himself as much from the Reformation as from Roman Catholicism to stand on a biblicist tradition as that represented by Johann Albrecht Bengel of Stuttgart.[225] Like him, he rejects the approach which spiritualizes the prophecies because "it twists the meaning of Scripture and goes against history. It undermines the authority and inspiration of the Bible and the veracity of the divine promises to the extent of rejecting the redemptive plan that God has accomplished in favour of Israel." [226]

It is this precomprehension that Chassaigne denounced in terms similar to those used even today by the non-millenarians. Eric Sauer summarizes the argument: "The teaching about the millenial reign is often extravagant and unscientific. It joins many other exaggerations which are often childish fantasies. We must guard against such excesses. The secular quarters, especially certain sects and fanatic movements abuse of it." [227]

Rene Taveneaux did the same denunciation when he said that figurism was closely associated with the Convulsions of the Cemetery of St. Medard.[228] Louis Targny also tried to discredit the Jansenists of Holland, making them pass for "dangerous illuminated living in the expectation of a new kingdom and committed to the destruction of the existing world." [229]

179

What Targny said raises two points that are still at the heart of millenarian beliefs: "the personal and visible reign of Christ is meaningless unless it involves both the end of a system and the introduction of a new order on this same land." [230] A system must disappear (that of the greed associated with the empire of the Beast)[231] so that be established the other (that of perfect charity[232] under the imperation of Christ, King of the real world). This was foretold by the prophets of the Old Testament for the fulfillment of the promises: *As long as the kingdoms of Judah and Israel have survived,* wrote Bishop Varlet, *the promises made to Abraham, David and Solomon were sufficient, as well as the prophecy of Jacob. But when these kingdoms began to be shaken from all sides and ready to fall, surrounded by implacable enemies, who wanted their destruction, God has sent prophets to reveal His intentions regarding the accomplishment of the promises.* [233]

For Bishop Varlet, the Bible forms a continuous history, progressive and dispensational attesting the great theme of the person of Jesus Christ and his redemptive work, for the day when He shall reign over all flesh." [234] It is in the light of the prophecies that he interprets the facts about the First Coming: *The Passion foretold in Psalms 68:26 & 108: 8, the Resurrection in Daniel 7 and Isaiah 4, the Ascension in Psalm 46:6, the Pentecost in Leviticus 23:21 and Psalm 18:4-5.* [235]

It is the Holy Spirit (poured into the Church at Pentecost[236]) who spoke through the prophets".[237] And the fulfillment of the prophecies in the past confirms that those to come will be realized in a similar fashion, because the Holy Spirit continues to announce what is to come according to the same prophetic word: "The infusion of the Holy Spirit for the zeal of the elect was predicted in Psalm 17 [238] and the return of Christ (when He "shall make them sit on thrones") as predicted by St. Matthew (19:28) and St. John (14:28)." [239] This statement is indicative of Bishop Varlet's belief in the fulfillment of the promises according to the millenarian view. As noted earlier, this view is expressed in his commentaries on the Acts of the Apostles and on the Book of Revelation. We summarize it below as it appears in biblicist speeches on the millennium with references to the work of Bishop Varlet.

The Fulfillment of the Promises: Millenarian View

There is initially the resurrection of the elect [240] and the rapture of the Church. They go to meet the Lord in the air.[241] This is followed by a tribulation and the trial of the nations.[242] Then, Christ comes to earth for a reign of a thousand years with his saints.[243] He enchains the Antichrist[244] and renders him powerless. Israel converts[245] and spreads the knowledge of God and of his salvation to all nations.[246] After the millennium, Satan is released for a short time,[247] then comes the resurrection of the wicked, the Last Judgement[248] and eternity.

Implications on the Representation of the Church

To highlight the implications of such a view on the representation of the Church, we must resolve some difficulties, which stem from the ambiguity of the discourse of Bishop Varlet. This ambiguity is due to two factors. The first is that, contrary to the Biblicist millenarian tradition, the Church is not raptured. The text only mentions the resurrection of the elect. The second regards Israel. Again, there seems to be a difference with Biblicist millenarianism. Bishop Varlet does not say that the restoration of the chosen people must make the Church disappear. The theme of the rapture is replaced by that of the deliverance: David in Psalm 118: 84, speaking in the name of the Church in the Old Alliance, asks God how long it will take for the deliverance to occur.[249] The same phenomenon of transfer /Church-Israel/ applies to the Holy Spirit. Given at Pentecost as a fulfillment of the prophecy of Psalm 17,[250] he has the same functionality, in the Post-Paschal apostolic zeal[251] as in the prophets of the Old Testament.[252] This sort of *neo-testamentarization* of the Old Testament, typical of figurism, has Augustinian bearing.[253] Indeed, St. Augustine tends to eliminate the difference in status between the faithful of the Old Testament and those of the New. The patriarchs are already of the New Testament.[254] This is true of another aspect. During the earthly kingdom of Christ, the Church being in the world (she has not been raptured), some parts are still at risk despite the chaining up of Satan.[255] This is similar to St. Augustine's teaching: Satan, despite his chaining (started during the earthly ministry of Christ), has a power on the wicked in default of having it on the believers.[256]

There is, in Bishop Varlet's ecclesiology, interpenetration of two traditions: that of St. Augustine and that, biblicist, of the millennium. His vision of the Church has in common with the Millenarians the refusal to identify the Church with the Kingdom but it incorporates the

Augustinian ecclesiology for what relates to the reign of God in the souls. The second tradition glimpses the first (tied to the fulfillment of the promises) and the two superimpose as suggested by the use of the parable of the wheat and the tares, and of the bad fish in the net with the good, to illustrate the life of the Church before and during the millennium, until the Jugement.[257]

Christ reigning will take Babylon "out of the Church,"[258] and bring justice to the elect who have suffered the persecution of the Beast (the Jansenists in particular). Purged through the election of grace, the rest of Israel, the Church, will become the elected people by the addition of the Jewish nation converted at the view of the King Messiah.

TO SUM UP...

Bishop Varlet left a theological sum that could lead to extensive research. There are elements of mystical theology in his work. But what most characterizes his speech is his doctrinal interpretation of the mysteries of God and of the Christian behavior. The dogmatic and moral components of his work are the most important aspects.

His doctrine is linked to the great moments of his life: the parish ministry, the evangelization of the Amerindians, his duties as Vicar General of the Bishop of Quebec, his Episcopal nomination for Persia, his position in favor of the rights of the Chapter of Utrecht, the intrigues surrounding the succession of the archbishops and the problem of usury, to the solution of which he has invested much energy in the last years of his life. As a consequence, he had on the theology of salvation and ecclesiology, penetrating positions which contrast strongly with those of the official Church of his time.

Two events played a decisive role in the development of his theology: his suspense in 1719 and his excommunication in 1725. These were the two major events of his life, events of which he has sought the meaning in the Holy Scripture in particular. But the persecution he suffered did not prevent him from expressing his gratitude to God he loved above all: *Considering before God that my disabilities and the various accidents which have happened to me in recent years warn me to think only of eternity and to prepare myself to appear before the Supreme Judge of the living and the dead, who is at the same time my*

Redeemer and my Savior, I am humbled and I prostrate in spirit as deeply as I can, before God, to give thanks for His blessings and to ask through the merits of Jesus Christ and the intercession of the blessed angels and all the saints, especially the Blessed Virgin Mary, the forgiveness of my sins and the glory which I am confident that He has predestined me before all centuries.[259]

This action of grace flows between the lines of his work, especially in the manuscript documents which testify to his meditations. His ordeals have not diminished his thanksgiving but amplified it. Instead of being a source of degradation, it became the motive of abundant blessings, because it allowed him to understand that only humility makes possible the gratitude. In his miserable refugee situation in the Netherlands, he discovered the great truth of his condition: without God, he was nothing. It is God who recalls the exile and his trust is even greater than his misery is deep. It is in humility that human beings happen to release in them the self which is different from that which seeks its own glory. The injured has the propensity to seek after the common good, this form of charity which is participation in the love of God. At the heart of his meditation, is the fear of God, this awareness of the misery that "prepares charity."[260] In pondering his own misery, Bishop Varlet captures that it is that of every human being. So, he forgives the human wickedness that prevents him from enjoying communion with the See of Rome, the center of Catholic unity. We understand that this orientation predisposed him particularly to the common life in the houses of Schonauwen and Rijnwijk. It is in the brotherly compassion that he passes from the truth of his misery to that of God who is love. Love that he recognized under the guise of Christ the servant. The imitation of Jesus is the lens through which he expounded his doctrine of grace and of the Church. As Jesus came to make us live under grace by the examples He gave us, we must imitate him in the Holy Spirit, "by going through various degrees of growth".[261]

The Church, spiritual reality, is for Bishop Varlet the place where divine grace is given by the Holy Spirit. Because of this, she is first and foremost a society of holiness and charity. *"The spiritual fire which is the Holy Spirit, he wrote, lives on and is lighted up by the hosts of the sacrifices, of the peace makers and of expiation that faith makes us put on the spiritual altar, which is the Body of Christ."* [262] Although he does not spare the references to the extensive Catholicism, it is the local community of the seekers of God that concerns him most because God communicates his holiness to them primarily. So even if he lived and died in the communion of the Church of Utrecht, he was persuaded to have remained a member of the Universal Church.

Community of those who are united with Christ in the Holy Spirit, the Church is also an organization: it has a legislation and a hierarchy. Bishop Varlet was an expert in canon law. He often referred to it. It is as a canonist that he did the apology of his conduct in the affairs of the Church of Utrecht. The numerous quotations he borrowed from the Fathers show that he has read them and was inspired by them. If he opposed the centralization of power in the person of the pope, it is because of his spiritual conception of the Church. The bishop, in his view, is one who chooses to imitate Christ in an exemplary fashion. In serving his brothers and sisters in the diocesan church, he experiences the universal church communion in episcopal collegiality. This teaching he found in the Church Fathers and in the canons of the ecumenical councils.

Where Rome wants to increase the powers of the cardinals and of the legates, Bishop Varlet, as a reformer, insists on the poverty and the simplicity that should animate the servants of God. On behalf of those principles he espoused the cause of the Church of Utrecht (O.B.C.).

Everything depends on the Christological topics *Abasement / Elevation*. Model of the Christian behaviour, it conditions that of the Church whose purpose is to serve and not be served. It is on this understanding that is grafted his canonical argument. It operates as a demonstration whose premise, taken from Jude 3 (the truth once for all given to God's people), generates a representation of the Catholicism as defined by St. Vincent of Lerins (What everywhere, what always, and what by all has been believed, that is truly and properly Catholic).[263] The emphasis is put on preserving the deposit of the faith in fidelity to the old order of the Church. In this way, are prevented the conflicts and divisions that sin against the Body of Christ and is made possible the advent of the Kingdom of God.

Three superimposed layers form the discourse of Bishop Varlet: a biblical understanding of Christ which is strongly influenced by the mystery of the kenosis (self-renunciation of the Lord's deity), the

Church as the iconic place of this understanding and a legal know-how that defends it by a meliorative reference to the old order. This is, in its essential articulations, the theology of Bishop Varlet at the origin of Old Catholicism.

Notes

1. <u>Recueil alphabétique des annotations sur divers sujets d'ordre historique, théologique et moral,</u> op. cit., p. 14 & 17.

2. This corpus is made of nine letters and extracts from letters sent to his mother and his brother Jean-Achille. They are reproduced in our book <u>Dominique-Marie Varlet. Lettres du Canada et de la Louisiane, 1713-1724</u>, PUQ, p. 35-50.

3. Grouped with the <u>Journaux du Tonquin</u> (A.P.R. 3802), these letters are reproduced in our book, op. cit., p. 49

4. <u>Première Apologie</u>, p. 1.

5. <u>Recueil alphabétique des annotations</u>..., p. 6 & 13.

6. Commentary on Romans 6:17 (though at a time you were slaves to sin, you have obeyed with all your heart the truths found in the teaching you received) in <u>Collections sur l'épître aux Romains, sur Isaïe, Justin, Tertullien et saint Augustin</u>, A.P.R. No.3768.

7. <u>Recueil alphabétique des annotations</u>..., p. 201.

8. <u>Première Apologie</u>, p. 1-2.

9. Letter to his brother, from Mobile, dated January 5, 1714, in <u>Lettres du Canada et de la Louisiane</u>, P.U.Q., p. 39-40.

10. Loc. cit.

11. Idem, p. 40-41.

12. Maximin Deloche, op. cit., p. 41.

13. Idem, p. 42.

14. Loc. cit.

15. Letter of July 20 1719, in Lettres du Canada et de la Louisiane, P.U.Q., p. 60.

16. Letter of November 10, 1720, op. cit., p. 64.

17. Letter of November 8, 1719, op. cit., p. 64.

18. Letter of September 27, 1719, op. cit., p. 65.

19. Letter of September 5, 1719, op. cit., p. 60-61.

20	Letter of April 23, 1719, op. cit., p. 61-63.
21	Op. cit., p. 73.
22	To Pope Benedict XIII on August 4, 1724, in <u>Première Apologie</u>, p. 93-98.
23	D.M. Varlet, *Acte d'appel* in <u>Première Apologie</u>, p. 24.
24	To Pope Benedict XIII, op. cit., p. 27-30.
25	These facts are reported in the Acte d'Appel (Première Apologie) and in letters to the Congregation of Propaganda (1722.02.19), to Pope Benedict XIII (1724.08.04, 1725.03.23) and the Council of Rome (1725.03.23).
26	Ace d'appel à l'Église catholique, in <u>Première Apologie</u>, p. 24.
27	Romans 12:13: *Share with God's people who are in need.*
28	Acte d'appel…, op. cit., p. 24.
29	The ordinary means the diocesan synod (faithful and canons of the cathedral chapter) when the Episcopal see is vacant. This synodalism inspired by Father Quesnel is at the origin of his conflict with Rome. He explains himself on this in his Protestation (et appel) au futur concile général (<u>Deuxième Apologie</u>, chapter 8: what is a cathedral chapter, p. 188-194, chapter 9: a church keeps her rights even though she does not enjoy complete freedom to hold public services, p. 217-228; the Church of Utrecht is not destroyed de facto nor de jure, p. 234-260; necessity is above the law, p. 294-305).
30	This continuity is defended in the following letters accompanying the <u>Première Apologie</u>: to the Congregation of Propaganda, to Pope Benedict XIII and to the Council of Rome.
31	Acte d'appel…, op. cit., p. 24.
32	*Plainte à l'Église catholique* in <u>Première Apologie</u>, p. 16.
33	To Pope Benedict XIII, op. cit.
34	To the Congregation of Propaganda, March 19, 1722 in <u>Première Apologie</u> (Première plainte à l'Église catholique), p. 37-40.
35	The details of these objections can be found in the book <u>Histoire abrégée de l'Église métropolitaine d'Utrecht</u> by Gabriel du Pac de Bellegarde, J.A. van Woestenberg, Utrecht, 1852, p. 300-301. C.B. Moss (op. cit.) and J.M Neale (op. cit.) also make mention of them.
36	To his agent in Rome, April 30, 1723 in <u>Première Apologie</u>, p. 81-82.

37 Acte d'appel..., Première Apologie, p. 25.

38 Acte d'appel, op. cit., p. 24.

39 The pressing duty of charity did not permit us to refuse the help of our ministry to souls who implored it in a state of necessity that might be called extreme. Première Apologie, p. 24.

40 G. du Pac Bellegarde (op. cit., p. 301) says, about the Gallican based course of action taken by Bishop Varlet: "Could he, as a French bishop, recognize the jurisdiction of the nuncio in Paris swearing in his hands that he accepted the Bull Unigenitus and would make it accepted, when there was in those days, a so vivid and striking claim in France, from the two powers, and on which the laws of the sovereign imposed a rigorous silence?

41 Imitation of Christ by Thomas A.Kempis, Chapter III.

42 We have read that Apology with a singular pleasure. We have noticed a lot of evidences which show that the censure which have been brought against you is directly contrary to the Holy Canons. Collette, regent of De Valk College (Collège du Faucon), Louvain, to Bishop Varlet, February 6, 1725, A.P.R. No. 3652

43 On the Christological articulation, see our article *L'articulation christologique comme forme de la thématique ecclésiologique dans trois textes de Dominique-Marie Varlet aux origines du vieux-catholicisme*, I.K.Z., 1990, Vol. 80, No. 389., p. 40-58.

44 A.P.R. No. 3800, 3798-3799 and 3768.

45 Acte d'appel, op. cit., p. 1.

46 Idem, p. 4 ff.

47 Idem, p. 20 ff.

48 Idem, p. 2.

49 Idem, p. 6 ff.

50 Idem, p. 7 ff.

51 Idem, p. 27 ff.

52 Idem, p. 31 ff.

53 Idem, p. 37 ff.

54 St. Bernard, Epistle 180.

55	Acte d'appel, op. cit., p. 4.
56	Acte d'appel, p. 6. The reference is taken from Palladium, Dialogus de Vita S. J. Chrysost. p. 23.
57	Idem.
58	Bishop Varlet makes a great use of the intertextuality in his text, particularly in the section that begins on page 27 and deals with the Church's rules for the trial of bishops. Are cited: St. Cyprian (Epistle 55), Pope Nicholas I (Epistles 8, 9 & 22), St. Gregory (Epistles 30 & 37), Pope Adrian I (c. Hadriani 1), Pope Zozimus (Epistle 7), Pope Celestine 1 (Epist. at Illiric.), Pope Leo I (Epistle 87), Pope Hilarus (Epistle 4), Pope Gelasius I (Epistles 4 & 9), Pope Agapetus (Epistle 6), Pope Martin I (De addit. Partic. Filioque), Pope Leo IV (Apud Grat. 25), Pope Adrian II (Epistle 34), Pope John VIII (Epistle 231), Pope Benedict VIII (Letter to the Council of Limoges), Pope Gregory VII (Epistle 5), Pope Innocent III (Epistle 104), St. Augustine (Psal. Contra part. Donati, letter F).
59	Acte d'appel, p. 27. Citation taken from St. Gregory, Epistle 30.
60	Première Apologie, p. 34.
61	Idem, p. 46.
62	Idem, p. 53.
63	Première Apologie, p. 52.
64	It is the characteristic attributed to apologetic writings in Trésor de la langue française, Tome III, Centre National de la recherche scientifique, Paris.
65	Eugène Michaud, op. cit., p. 477-503.
66	Quoted by Eugène Michaud, op. cit., p. 501.
67	A.J. Greimas (Du Sens, Le Seuil, Paris) hypothesizes that the meaning depends on a deep semantic organization that is independent of the surface of the text.
68	Première Apologie, p. 4.
69	Idem, p. 1.
70	Loc. cit.
71	A theophore is a vehicle of God.
72	Two continuous functions from one space to another.

73 The term *kenosis* comes from the Greek word for the doctrine of Christ's self-emptying in His incarnation. The kenosis was a self-renunciation, not an emptying Himself of deity nor an exchange of deity for humanity. Plilippians 2:7 tells us that Jesus "emptied Himself, taking the form of a bond-servant, and being made in the likeness of men."
http://www.gotquestions.org/kenosis.html

74 Deuxième Apologie, p. 479-482.

75 Acte d'appel, p. 16.

76 Soteriology is the portion of Christian theology treating the saving work of Christ.

77 Acte d'appel, p. 16.

78 Letter to a Parisian correspondent on March 10, 1725.

79 Recueil alphabétique des annotations..., p. 39.

80 Acte d'appel, p. 16.

81 Idem.

82 See Appendix 4: The Holy Trinity in Bishop Varlet's theology.

83 Commentary on the Acts of the Apostles (2:6) in Recueil alphabétique...,p. 14.

84 Lettre aux missionnaires du Tonquin, op. cit., p. 138.

85 The thesis of Barrin, defended in April 1735, sparked a controversy in the Nouvelles Ecclésiastiques: years 1735 (p. 105-106) and 1736 (p. 157).

86 Recueil alphabétique des annotations..., p. 112.

87 *The Church is infallible, but the pope not being so, it is to confide in a man against the defence of God to blind onself with all that comes from him*. Lettre aux missionnaires du Tonquin, op. cit., p. 138-139.

88 It is by maintaining the purity of the Christian faith and morals that we provide adequate remedies to the present evils and to the longings of the faithful. Letter to the Council of Rome, March 23, 1725, in Lettres..., p. 77.

89 Letter to the Council of Rome, op. cit., p. 85. The question of the rules is treated in the Apology: the pope is the custodian of the holy canons and must be the first to observed them (Première Apologie, Chapter IX). It is supporting the interests of the Holy See to defend the cause of the bishops (Deuxième Protestation et Appel, p. 32).

90   It is through his challenge of the notion of authority among the Protestants that Bishop Varlet exposes his own. "The (Anglicans) define the catechism as a brief but adequate exposition of the principles of Christianity published by authority. The authority, according to their principles, is misplaced here. They would do better to say that each one is judge. This authority is rejected absolutely by Mr. Élie Saurin (Preface, p. 20). He says that our catechisms engage the faithful to open their eyes and to weigh our evidences with all the severity that they are capable. But since they are usually incapable, they do not always discern the evidences that weight from those that are slight. Having thus warned about the fatal consequences of the blind submission, they give up a fair and informed submission to the Church to compel their followers adroitly to all their opinions ... In the Catholic Church, we are not subject to this drawback. Recueil alphabétique..., p. 54-55.

91   *Jesus Christ, through the mouth of the consecrating bishop, says: receive the gospel and go to preach it to the people entrusted to you. This ministry would be unnecessary if the authority that Jesus Christ gave for the edification of his people became despicable.* Letter to Pope Innocent XIII in Lettres..., p. 54.

92   *The bishops are the natural judges of heresy and heretics. Their vigilance is necessary to correct the irregularities of their flock and especially their clergy.* Recueil alphabétique..., p. 222-223. *When the churches are governed by courageous bishops, they do not usually abandon the faith.* Idem, p. 222. *This government is done in reference to the canons that the pope must maintain, enforce and observe himself.* Idem, p. 116. *We should judge the affairs of the Church by the canons.* Loc cit.

93   *I have reason to persuade me that so many prelates, being assembled by a pontife zealous for the glory of God, for purity of doctrine and the observance of the sacred canons, Jesus Christ will be among them.* Letter to Pope Benedict XIII on March 1723, on the occasion of the Council of Rome, in Lettres..., p. 72.

94   *God forbids,* wrote St. Gregory (Epistle 37), *that I infringe the statutes of the ancients in whatever church. I would do injustice to myself if I broke the law of my brothers. What dishonors them dishonors me for my honor is inseparable of the whole Church and of the preservation of the rights of my brothers,* Acte d'appel, p. 32.

95   Eschatology is a doctrine related to the ultimate destiny of the soul and of the whole created order.

96   *A zeal that seeks God and a sincere charity that does not seek its own interest and does not use piety as a means of enriching themselves, these are the faithful disciples of Jesus Christ. They do not preach themselves and are not ashamed of the cross of the Savior.* Plainte à l'Église catholique, op. cit., p. 18.

97   *Rome is not conducive to reforms and when she wants to do them, she does not succeed.* Recueil alphabétique..., p. 168.

[98] Acte d'appel, op. cit., p. 25.

[99] Recueil alphabétique..., p. 168.

[100] Idem, p. 16, 170-171.

[101] A.P.R. No. 3768.

[102] The theology at the Saulchoir in <u>La Parole de Dieu I. La foi dans l'intelligence</u>, Paris, 1964, p. 259.

[103] Constitution Gaudium & Spes, I.

[104] M.D. Chenu, Les signes des temps, Réflexions théologiques, in <u>Vatican II, l'Église dans le monde de ce temps</u>, Paris, 1967, p. 205-225. See also Signes des temps, in Concilium 25 (1967), p. 125-132.

[105] Loc. cit.

[106] Letter to Pope Benedict XIII, August 4, 1724, in <u>Lettres</u>..., p. 61.

[107] <u>Recueil alphabétique</u>..., p. 34.

[108] Paraphrase on Acts 2:1 in <u>Recueil alphabétique</u>..., p. 12.

[109] J. Moltmann, <u>Theology of Hope: On the Ground and the Implications of a Christian Eschatology</u>, SCM Press, London, 1967.

[110] Molinism minimizes the effects of the original sin. After the fault, the humans remain unchanged in their nature: they are only deprived of the supernatural gifts. God compensates for this loss by giving the help of the actual grace that their will is free to accept or reject. R. Taveneaux, <u>Jansénisme et politique</u>, Armand Collin, Paris, 1965, p. 8. The Jansenists, who taught the corruption of nature caused by the sin of Adam and its transmission as a habit to all generations (op. cit., p. 9) saw in the positions of Molina similarities with those of the British monk Pelagius, who denied the existence of the original sin (in *Pro libero arbitro*) and that St. Augustine denounced in his *De gestis Pelagii*. <u>Documents of the Christian Church</u>, Oxford University Press.

[111] <u>Nouvelles Ecclésiastiques</u>, 1762, p. 2.

[112] Idem, 1763, p. 2.

[113] Acte d'appel, op. cit., p. 15-16.

[114] Nouvelles Ecclésiastiques, 1762, p. 3.

[115] *The influence of the Jesuits was predominant at Rome and the Counter-Reformation was largely under their control.* Claude B. Moss, op. cit., p. 28.

[116] Acte d'appel, op. cit., p. 15-16.

[117] In the sense of the liturgical changes favorable to the laity. É. Préclin, op. cit., p. 179.

[118] Acte d'appel, op. cit., p. 14.

[119] Loc. cit.

[120] The <u>Nouvelles Ecclésiastiques</u> (May 7, 1756) reported that a priest of Thouars, Father Moreau, did not administer the sacraments without explaining the ceremonies and without translating in French what was said in Latin.

[121] Commentary on the Acts of the Apostles, op. cit., p. 17.

[122] The love of God prefers the divine will to his, <u>Recueil alphabétique</u>, p. 27. The goal is to love God and to have him as ultimate end., Letter to the Bishop of Senez in <u>Lettres</u>..., p. 147.

[123] Acte d'appel, op. cit., p. 16.

[124] Idem, p. 17.

[125] Loc. cit.

[126] Recueil alphabétique..., p. 102 & 104.

[127] Idem, p. 114.

[128] Prologue of the Commentary on the Acts of the Apotles, op. cit., p. 6, and Commentary on the Book of Revelation, op. cit., p. 10.

[129] Prologue of the Commentary on the Acts of the Apostles, p. 6.

[130] Loc. cit.

[131] Idem, p. 12.

[132] Idem, p. 17.

[133] Acte d'appel, op. cit., p. 1.

[134] <u>Actant</u> is a term introduced by A.J. Greimas. It was borrowed from the work of the syntactician Lucien Tesnière, where it refers to a linguistic notion corresponding to an abstract, semantic category similar to the concept of deep-structure case or role. The actant is a constant or invariant role

maintained by characters in the narrative deep structure. It is opposed to the actor or variable role that the character assumes in the unfolding of the story on the surface level. Each actant is claimed to be the opposite of another such as Subject versus (vs) Object.

[135] Acte d'appel, op. cit., p. 1.

[136] Commentary on the Acts of the Apostles, op. cit., p. 9.

[137] His ideas on the spiritual role of the bishop in connection with the rules of Christian conduct are expressed in his Remarques sur le Traité contre l'usure (A.P.R. 3760), in his Écrit concernant les prétentions du chapitre d'Utrecht (A.P.R. 3761), in his Mémoire sur l'établissement d'un évêque de Haarlem (A.P.R. 3763) and in his Acte de protestation contre l'élection de Gérard Akkoy (A.P.R. 3766).

[138] In regular contact with the main French Jansenists, Varlet had an abundant literary production, entirely devoted to the theological, moral or disciplinary problems of Jansenism. R. Taveneaux, Jansénisme et prêt à intérêt, p. 217.

[139] Are classified as commentaries the writings which are a statement or query, a reflection or a critique, demonstrating the falsity of what another has said, responding to a question or request, made of annotations on texts, in the form of a project, describing the facts of his life, collected and classified in a documentary purpose.

[140] At the urging of several bishops, and at the personal insistence of King Louis XIV, Pope Alexander VII sent to France the apostolic constitution *Regiminis Apostolici* (dated February 15, 1664) which required all French Catholics to subscribe to the following *formulary*: I, (Name), submitting to the apostolic constitutions of the sovereign pontiffs, Innocent X and Alexander VII, published May 31, 1653 and October 16, 1656, sincerely repudiate the five propositions extracted from the book of Jansenius entitled *Augustinus*, and I condemn them upon oath in the very sense expressed by that author, as the Apostolic See has condemned them by the two above mentioned Constitutions. The five propositions are reproduced in Appendix 1.

[141] This is a concern related to the sacrament of penance. See note 76 (Part 1) regarding the *Case of Conscience*.

[142] A truce of 35 years followed the promulgation of the brief of Clement IX on January 14, 1669, granting the distinction between the right and fact of Cornelis Jansen in the case of the Formulary of Alexander VII. The brief was followed in 1704 by a second Jansenism, political, gallican and parliamentary, which had very little to do with Cornelis Jansen.

[143] The cathedral chapter is synonymous for Bishop Varlet of diocesan synod. In his letter to the Council of Rome on March 23, 1725 (Lettres, BAnQ, p. 85), he speaks of Msgr. Cornelis Steenoven as "the one that the wishes of the

clergy and the people have placed on the archiepiscopal see." He wrote in the <u>Acte d'appel</u> (op. cit., p. 23) that the chapter serves to "represent the clergy and the senate of the Church".

[144] Council of Trent, session 6, reference c 5.

[145] St. Gregory, Epitle 32.

[146] *The functions of vicar apostolic as described by St. Gregory are to ease the disputes that may arise between the bishops. If it is a case where the presence of other bishops is necessary, he must assemble the appropriate number, that is to say 12, to discuss the matter with fairness and integrity as the canons prescribe. If it is an affair that concerns the faith or a question which is difficult and requires the Holy See's decision, he will report to the Pope after careful consideration of the truth (in a council of 12 bishops). He also arranges to assemble the bishops from time to time to confer with them on the needs of the churches. St. Gregory, Epistle 53 to St. Virgil of Arles.*

[147] Session 24, de res. C. 16.

[148] Hilarus, Epitle 4.

[149] Letter to Nicolas Petitpied, July 28, 1734, in Lettres, BAnQ, p. 103.

[150] This conflict is developed in R. Taveneaux, <u>Jansénisme et prêt à intérêt</u>: p. 59 ff (the first clashes of the clergy of Utrecht with the French Jansenists), p. 67 ff (the decline of the French influence) and p. 139 ff (the crisis of the Church of Utrecht: the Dutch party <u>vs</u> the French party).

[151] The petition is addressed to Msgr. Peter Meindaerts, consecrated archbishop on October 18, 1739. A member of the Dutch party, he marked the end of the French Jansenist influence in the Church of Utrecht.

[152] This phrase evokes the tragedy that has been for Bishop Varlet the victory of the Dutch party. He was, therefore, obliged to take from the Church of Utrecht the same distance taken a few years earlier towards Rome. In his eyes, there was no more in the O.B.C. this link, essential for him, between orthodoxy and orthopraxy.

[153] Father Noel Alexandre (1639-1724) was professor at Saint-Magloire. When he was a simple monk, Pope Benedict XIII regarded him as his master... After having spoken against the Bull Unigenitus, he formulated before the letter, on April 5, 1714, the doctrines of the <u>Témoignage de la Vérité</u> (by Father Vivien de la Borde): "it is hoped that after His Holiness, who is willing to give peace to the Church, will have assured (by a proper explanation) the safety of the truth of the doctrine and of the purity of the discipline, his constitution will be confirmed by the consent of all the faithful, so that the Lord makes known that what comes from the first see is from him." E. Préclin, op. cit., p. 53-54.

154 The *Morale de Grenoble* evokes the figure of Cardinal Le Camus, a Richerist prelate (Préclin, p. 85) who had influence on Bishop St. Vallier of Quebec, under whom Bishop Varlet served as vicar general. Guy Plante (op. cit.) has highlighted the moral rigor of Bishop St. Vallier, who was regarded as Jansenist by some Jesuits of New France.

155 We have an idea of his correspondance with the Bishop of Senez in <u>Lettres</u>... (BAnQ): p. 147 (against the Molinists because of our obligation to love God and to have Him as final end), p. 148 (the need for the bishops to preach mainly repentance), p. 149 (importance that they give a good example because they are the "angels of the Church who fights on the earth").

156 François-Hyacinthe de Lan, doctor of the Sorbonne, was among those who on August 2, 1749, signed the <u>Délibéré des docteurs de la Faculté de Paris contre les prêts de commerce</u>. The letters that Bishop Varlet has exchanged with him are part of the Archives of Port Royal (A.P.R. 4092).

157 Willem Frederik van Dalenoort, a member of the Chapter of Utrecht, was parish priest at The Hague.

158 Louis Paris Vaquier de Villiers, former canon of Lectoure, was administrator of the houses at Rijnwijk and Schonauwen.

159 De la Cour was the pseudonym used by Jacques Jubé, former parish priest at Asnières.

160 Willibrord Kemp was parish priest at Utrecht and a member of the cathedral chapter.

161 Bishop Varlet was appointed suffragan on June 16, 1727 and this title has never been withdrawn. However, his role did not have the same importance after the death of Archbishop Barchman Wuytiers, when the O.B.C. had adopted the views of the Dutch Jansenist party favorable to usury.

162 P. Hurtubise, op. cit., p. 32.

163 Eugene Michaud, op. cit., p. 502.

164 Pierre Nicole (1625–1695) was one of the most distinguished of the French Jansenists. For some years he was a master in the "petite école" at Port Royal and had the honour of teaching Greek to young Jean Racine. But his chief duty was to act, in collaboration with Antoine Arnauld, as general editor of the controversial literature put forth by the Jansenists. He had a large share in collecting the materials for Pascal's <u>Provincial Letters</u> (1656) and is co-author of the very successful <u>Port-Royal Logic</u> (1662), based on a Cartesian reading of Aristotelian logic. In 1664 he himself began a series of letters, *Les Imaginaires*, intended to show that the heretical opinions commonly ascribed to the Jansenists really existed only in the imagination of the Jesuits. http://en.wikipedia.org/wiki/Pierre_Nicole

165 Antoine Godeau, a Jansenist moralist, was famous for his Tableaux de la pénitence. On his Jansenist tendencies, see A. Cognet, Antoine Godeau, évêque de Grasse et Vence, Paris, 1900, p. 177 and 307-349.

166 Fleury, Claude, abbé (1640-1723). Historian and teacher. His weightiest work is the *Histoire ecclésiastique* (1691 onwards, 36 vols., of which 20 by Fleury). It was placed on the Index because of its Gallican tendencies. Other didactic writings include the *Catéchisme historique* (1679), *Les Mœurs des Israélites* (1681), and *Les Mœurs des chrétiens* (1682). Fleury's important *Traité du choix et de la méthode des études* (1683) lays stress on the value of sound reasoning. Advocate of the grand sublimity of ancient Greek and, above all, Hebrew poetry (*Discours sur la poésie des Hébreux*), he is one of the most impressive of the *anciens* [see Querelle des Anciens et Des Modernes].

167 Dom Augustin Calmet, a Benedictine monk of Saint-Vanne (an active Jansenist center), aimed to bring the Holy Scriptures in the hands of the faithful. This is the origin of his Commentaire littéral sur tous les livres de l'Ancien et du Nouveau Testament. E. Mangenot wrote an article on him in the Dictionnaire de la bible of Vigouroux, Tome II, col. 72-76.

168 Giovanni Stefano Menochio (Menochius), 1575-1655, was an Italian Jesuit biblical scholar. His magnum opus was *Brevis Explicatio Sensus Literalis Sacræ Scripturæ optimus quibusque Auctoribus per Epitomen Collecta*, 3 vols.

169 Robert Bellarmine (in Italian: Roberto Bellarmino) (1542–1621) was one of the most important cardinals of the Counter-Reformation. He was the first Jesuit to teach at the university, where the subject of his course was the *Summa* of Thomas Aquinas. He also made extensive studies in the Fathers and medieval theologians, which gave him the material for his book *"De scriptoribus ecclesiasticis"* (Rome, 1613).
http://en.wikipedia.org/wiki/Robert_Bellarmine

170 St. Augustine, De Ordine, Vol. II.

171 The Plan is reproduced in Appendix 5.

172 Not to be confused with the certainty of salvation. He sees the uncertainty of salvation as "useful and beneficial because if we knew the end of our life, we could become negligent". Recueil alphabétique…, p. 128.

173 We will discuss in Part 3, the continuity between the theology of Bishop Varlet and the Old Catholic positions. We can already mention some obvious similarities: adherence to the rule of faith laid down by St. Vincent of Lerins (art. 1 of the Declaration of Utrecht), rejection of papal infallibility (art. 2), repudiation of the Bull Unigenitus and renewal of the protests of the Church of Holland (art. 4) and fidelity to the ancient Catholic doctrine concerning the Sacrament of the Altar (art. 6). The text of the Declaration of Utrecht is reproduced in Appendix 6.

[174] Carré de Montgeron was a magistrate at the Parlement de Paris. He experienced conversion at the tomb of deacon Pâris on September 7, 1731 and became an apologist for the convulsionists, notably in his book La Vérité des miracles.

[175] Dale K. Van Kley, The Religious Origins of the French Revolution: From Calvin to the Civil Constitution,1560-1791, New Haven: Yale University Press, 1996. Reviewed by James Livesey (Trinity College Dublin), August 1997: http://www.h-net.org/reviews/showrev.php?id=1235

[176] Revival in a Christian context generally refers to a period of spiritual renewal in the life of the Church. The key factor in revival is the restoration of the Church to a vital and fervent relationship with God after a period of decline. http://en.wikipedia.org/wiki/Revivalism

[177] André Lamorte, L'autorité de la bible et l'exégèse allégorique, in Le Règne de 1000 ans sur la terre, p. 13.

[178] In allegorical exegesis the sacred text is treated as a symbol or allegory of spiritual truths. The literal, historical sense, plays a relatively minor role, and the aim of the exegete is to elicit the moral, theological or mystical meaning which each passage is presumed to contain.

[179] Although the word *millennium* does not appear in Revelation 20, Bishop Varlet believed what St. John wrote describes it.

[180] Arianism originates in the teachings of Arius in the early fourth century, which stated Christ was not of the same substance ὁμοουσιας (*homoousios*) as God the Father, but of a similar substance ὁμοιουσιας (*homoiousios*). Supported by nontrinitarian Christian churches. http://en.wiktionary.org/wiki/Arianism

[181] Commentary on the Acts of the Apostles, op. cit., p. 33-34.

[182] R. Shallis, *Mon ami millénariste* in Le Règne de 1000 ans sur la terre, p. 30.

[183] Commentary on the Acts of the Apostles, op. cit., p. 11.

[184] Idem., p. 10.

[185] Robert Kreiser, Miracles, Convulsions and Ecclesiastical Politics in Early Egitheenth-Century Paris, Princeton University Press, Princeton, 1978, p. 246-247.

[186] R. Taveneaux (Jansénisme et prêt à intérêt, p. 63, note 56) places the heyday of the doctrine in the 1730s: "for the month of September 1733 was expected the return of Elijah, prefiguration of the coming of Christ and of the destruction of Babylon".

187	R. Kreiser, op. cit., p. 247. The leaders of this doctrine were: Alex Desessarts (<u>De l'avènement d'Élie</u>/Concerning the coming of Elijah, 2 volumes), with whom Bishop Varlet corresponded (A.P.R. 3663), and Jacques-Joseph Duguet (Quatorze vérités sur la conversion des Juifs/Fourteen truths about the conversion of the Jews in <u>Règles pour l'intelligence des Écritures Saintes</u>/ Rules for understanding the Holy Scriptures, 1716), another correspondent (A.P.R. 3667) who taught Holy Scripture to him at Saint Magloire.
188	Quoted by B.A. van Kleef, op. cit., p. 61.
189	Excerpt of a letter dated August 7, 1727 quoted by van Kleef, op. cit.
190	B.A. van Kleef, op. cit. Eric Sauer (op. cit., p. 46 ff) refutes this accusation and indicates that the thesis of the millenial reign is defended by scholars such as: Esward Greswell of Corpus Christi College, Oxford, and Henry Alford, Dean of Canterbury.
191	Referring to the Gospel passages where the strong man is bound by a stronger than him (Matt. 3:27 par.), the anti-millenarians agree with St. Augustine, that this is an image of Christ who has virtually ended the power of Satan whom he saw fall from heaven like lightning. The defeat of Satan would be an accomplished fact. As for the Church, it would be, in fact and currently, the presence and reign of Christ here on earth. The anti-amillenarians believe in the return of Jesus in glory, but only to introduce the redeemed in the heavenly kingdom. A. Lamorte, op. cit., p. 14.
192	Frederick A. Tatford, *Réponse au livre Le Grand dénouement/Answser to the book Revelation, The Grand Finale*, in <u>Le Règne de 1000 ans sur la terre</u>, p. 151-152.
193	R. Kreiser, op. cit., p. 246-247.
194	R. Taveneaux, Jansénisme et politique, p. 213.
195	R. Kreiser, op. cit., p. 247.
196	P. Schaff, *History of the Christian Church* in <u>Le Règne de 1000 ans sur la terre</u>, p. 146.
197	J.D. Pentecots, *The Prophetic Witness*, in Le Règne de 1000 ans..., p. 146. R. Kreiser (op. cit., p. 249) states that the eschatological views of the Figurists were oriented towards brigning the Church back to the pure faith and the simple virtue of the apostolic age.
198	"There will be a period of 1,000 years after the resurrection of the dead and then the reign of Christ will be established."
199	<u>Dialogue with Trypho</u>, Chapter LXXX.
200	<u>Adversus haereses</u>, Book 5, Chapter 32.

201   Against Marcion: "The thousand years will take place after the resurrection and the city built by God".

202   Cornelius Nepos , c.100 BC-c.25 BC, Roman historian. He was an intimate friend of Cicero and Catullus. He wrote a refutation of the allegorists.

203   Commodanius (200-245) was a bishop in Northern Africa.

204   Lactaneius was a Christian apologist of the beginning of the fourth century.

205   Cited in Le Règne de 1000 ans sur la terre, p. 148-149. An anonymous work of 1724: La Tradition des Saints Pères sur la conversion des Juifs goes in this direction.

206   The Gnostics believed in the future disappearance of the physical body, materiality existing only for disciplinary purposes. R. Shallis, op. cit., p. 25; F.A. Tatford, op. cit., p. 149-50.

207   R. Shallis, op. cit., p.26.

208   Eric Sauer, op. cit., p. 48.

209   Salvation could only consist of the liberation of the soul (the only pure and real) from its physical prison (the evil and the illusory body) and its resorption in God, the essential soul.

210   F.A. Tatford, op. cit., p. 149.

211   Idem, p. 150. Tatford wrote the book Daniel and His Prophecy. Studies in the Prophecy of Daniel, June 1980, Klock & Klock Christian Pub.

212   Idem, p. 151.

213   Idem, p. 152.

214   F.A. Tatford, op. cit., p. 152.

215   Joachim of Flores was born of the minor nobility in Sicily. In the mid-1160's he went on pilgrimage to Jerusalem where he became converted to a deeper understanding of mystical Christianity. After a few years as a hermit on Mt. Etna, he returned to Italy and joined the Benedictines. His visions began around 1183 and soon after he was summoned to Rome by Pope Lucius III and encouraged to record his visions and his theories. From this recognition, Joachim became a star, the most authoritative spokesman of his age on the imminent last days. He felt that his knowledge and visions imposed a heavy sense of obligation to spread the news of the impending apocalypse. In the next 18 years, he would be consulted by four Popes, as well as Kings, Queens and Emperors. In spite of this acceptance during his life, after his death in

1202, the Church condemned his views and his writings. Since that time, Joachim has been treated as a saint and as a heretic, but his view of the End of the World retained its popularity in esoteric circles down to the 20th century. http://www.sangraal.com/library/gsa13.html

[216]   F.A. Tatford, op. cit., p. 153.

[217]   Recueil alphabétique des annotations…, p. 85-89.

[218]   The apposition is a grammatical construction in which two elements, normally noun phrases are placed side by side, with one element serving to define or modify the other. When this device is used, the two elements are said to be *in apposition*. For example in the phrase "*my friend Alice*" the name "Alice" is in apposition to "my friend". http://wiki.answers.com/Q/What is apposition

[219]   From *transubstantiation*, the official Catholic concept referring to the change that takes place during the sacrament of the Eucharist. This change involves substances of bread and wine being turned miraculously into the substance of Christ himself. The underlying essence of these elements is changed, and they retain only the appearance, taste, and texture of bread and wine. Catholic doctrine holds that the Godhead is indivisible, so every particle or drop thus changed is wholly identical in substance with the divinity, body, and blood of the Savior.
http://christianity.about.com/od/glossary/g/transubstantiat.htm

[220]   The resurrection is for Bishop Varlet fulfilling the prophecies of Daniel 7 and Isaiah 4. Recueil alphabétique…, p., 10.

[221]   Pierre Despagne, Le Millenium et le règne messianique, Cosne-sur-Loire (France), 1980, p. 10.

[222]   F.A. Tatford, op. cit., p. 153.

[223]   Loc. cit.

[224]   Commentary on the Acts of the Apostles, op. cit., p. 11.

[225]   J.A. Bengel (1687-1752) was a German Lutheran theologian and biblical scholar who was a pioneer in the Critical exegesis of the New Testament. His principles of interpretation were to import nothing into Scripture, but to draw out of it everything that it really contained, in conformity with grammatico-historical rules not to be hampered by dogmatical considerations; and not to be influenced by the symbolical books.
http://en.wikipedia.org/wiki/Johann_Albrecht_Bengel

[226]   Pierre Despagne, op. cit., p. 13.

[227]   Eric Sauer, op. cit., p. 46.

[228]   R. Taveneaux, Jansénisme et prêt à intérêt, p. 63, note 56.

[229] L. Targny, Mémoire sur l'état present des réfugiés en Hollande... and Mémoire sur le projet janséniste. Cited by R. Taveneaux, op. cit., p. 62-63.

[230] P. Despagne, op. cit., p. 9. The same view is expressed by R. Kreiser (op. cit., p. 249): the figurists were laying the foundations for a work of reform that involved the establishment of a new dispensation which affected a total religious renewal of the Church.

[231] Recueil alphabétique des annotations..., p. 170-171.

[232] Idem, p. 17.

[233] Idem, p. 33.

[234] P. Despagne, op. cit., p. 14. According to R. Kreiser (op. cit., p. 249), the figurism is associated with a redemptive mission in the Church.

[235] Recueil alphabétique..., p. 10-17.

[236] Fulfillment of the prophecy of Joel: Bishop Varlet, Recueil alphabétique..., p. 17.

[237] Idem, p. 11.

[238] Idem, p. 13.

[239] Idem, p. 11.

[240] Idem, p. 10.

[241] Loc. cit.

[242] Loc. cit.

[243] Idem, p. 11, 33-34.

[244] Idem, p. 33-34.

[245] Recueil alphabétique..., p. 9.

[246] Loc. cit.

[247] Idem, p. 34.

[248] Loc. cit.

[249] Idem, p. 8.

[250] Idem, p. 13.

251 Loc. cit.

252 Idem, p. 11

253 The Old Testament prefigures the Church. R. Taveneaux, op. cit., p. 231.

254 St. Augustine, Contra duas epistolas Pelagianorum, III, iv.11.

255 D.M. Varlet, Recueil alphabétique des annotations..., p. 33-34.

256 We paraphrase an excerpt of St. Augustine's City of God cited by F.A. Tatford, op. cit., p. 151.

257 D.M. Varlet, op. cit., p. 34.

258 Idem, p. 35.

259 D.M. Varlet, *Testament spiritual*, in Nouvelles Ecclésiastiques, Paris, July 1742.

260 Commentary on the Acts of the Apostles (2:42), op. cit., p. 12.

261 D.M. Varlet, op. cit., p. 13.

262 Idem, p. 14.

263 In his work Commonitorium against Heresies written in 434.

III
BISHOP VARLET AND OLD CATHOLICISM

Robert Kreiser, in his book Miracles, Convulsions, and Ecclesiastical Politics in Early Eighteenth-century Paris,[1] provides a summary of the Gallicano-Jansenist opposition to the Bull Unigenitus which is interesting in relation to our subject. He summarizes it by the words *alternative ecclesiology*[2] and defines it as a "shared attitude of mind with an attendant concern for spiritual reform".[3] Bishop Varlet is inserted in it[4] and his contribution in favour of the Chapter of Utrecht is mentioned as an aspect of this "spiritual revival" of which the miracles were seen as the divine legitimation.[5]

Kreiser's purpose is to analyze the Convulsionist Movement. But what he says of the alternative ecclesiology supports the problematique of our book. So, we will summarize his findings and use them as a framework for assessing the contribution of Bishop Varlet to the advent of Old Catholicism.

1

THE GALLICANO-JANSENIST ALTERNATIVE: ITS ORGANIZATION INTO AN INDEPENDENT CHURCH

The doctrinal and ecclesiological strife, that followed the promulgation of the Bull Unigenitus, generated a loss of confidence in the authority of the clerical establishment.[6] The institution, already contested by philosophers who saw it as antisocial and dysfunctional, was challenged from within by non-conformist Catholics, who questioned its rigid hierarchy and advocated a new model of community based on old Christian ideals of brotherhood and freed from the constraints of the establishment. An egalitarian society of brothers and sisters in free association.[7]

With the distrust of the hierarchy came a sense of spiritual discontent,[8] as if the church establishment could be an obstacle to salvation.[9] The Church was perceived as sclerotic[10] and in need of spiritual renewal and redemption.[11] These concepts are in line with figurism, this system of interpretation, which invited to struggle against the forces of evil (incarnated in the clerical establishment); advocated the purification of the Church and her return to the faith and simplicity of primitive Christianity, as well as the importance of being messengers of redemption.[12]

The redemptive mission that was seen as legitimated from above in the miracles, contains the key aspects of the alternative ecclesiogy: denunciation of the principle that the divine is accessed exclusively through the priests (in favor of the autonomy of conscience, of the primacy of internal individual dispositions and of the efficacy of grace which predestinates to salvation) and exaltation of the laity (rendered competent to make the Church by appropriating the truths of the faith contained in the Scripture) and of the second order (hitherto held aloof from the ecclesiastical polity).[13]

The model of the sacerdotal church, acting as exclusive mediator between God and humans was replaced by that of the participatory congregation of believers.[14] But this spiritual liberation had no schismatical intention. The non-conformists were united by a common attitude of mind, without corporate existence and independent of all authorities, royal, papal or episcopal.[15] This explains that in the case of the convulsions and miracles, a wide variety of events were seen, from the penitential severity of Deacon Pâris to ritual behaviors perceived as extravagant, including assertions of being reincarnated prophets.[16]

Bishop Varlet and Alternative Catholicism

There is between Bishop Varlet and the Gallicano-Jansenist alternative catholicism a clear ideological resemblance. It is shown in his reform program, which contains most of the elements mentioned above: a critique of the hierarchical institution (which may impede salvation), the redemptive mission (part of the figurist doctrine) and the revival (encouraged by reading the Scripture) with, as a result, the passage from being subjected to the cupidity of the church establishment to enjoying the *Communio Sanctorum*.

The Bishop of Babylon did not invent a doctrine. He appropriated the components of an existing ecclesiological universe.[17] His work reveals him in that sense. He was the clever compiler of the <u>Recueil alphabétique des annotations sur divers sujets d'ordre historique, théologique et moral</u>. He assimilated the first masters of Jansenism (Arnauld, Nicole ...), Pasquier Quesnel, the figurist exegetes (Duguet, d'Étemare..) and the laicist authors such as Vivien de la Borde (le Témoignage de la Vérité). He maintained a correspondence with leading figures of the movement as Le Gros and Petitpied, asking for their advices. His originality lies in the skill with which he summarized what he had borrowed from others and his involvement, hitherto unprecedented, in the milieus of the alternative ecclesiology, for organizing into a church a defence of the Truth that was lacking in corporate existence, had never formed a cohesive or tightly organized church order, or subscribed to a uniform or coherent set of beliefs.[18] It is as a synthesizer and an organizer that Bishop Varlet has marked the history[19] and laid the cornerstone of the ecclesiastical structure from which came the Old Catholic Church.

The new order that was sought by the French non-conformist Catholics of the time, but whose inability to exist strongly[20] had led to the pathos of the convulsions, Bishop Varlet made it happen in the Netherlands equipping the Metropolitan Chapter of Utrecht with the power to be fully the Church (the episcopate) from which these people were deprived. This is the major factor to be taken into account to understand the meaning and scope of Bishop Varlet's contribution.[21] It did not escape the attention of the Roman Catholics: "It was he who really established the Church of Utrecht".[22] It did not escaped either, at the time, the attention of the temporal allies of the papacy as indicated in the following event reported by Claude B. Moss. "The Bishop of Babylon (upon whom the possibility of consecrating Barchman Wuytiers depended) was staying with the parish priest, Pastoor Verheul, at Helder, at the entrance to Zuyder Zee. He was told that a lady warmly attached to the other party had basted that he would not trouble the country any longer. A few days later he was invited to dinner by the captain of an unknown ship. On his refusal, the ship set sail, and he had no doubt that there had been a plot to kidnap him." [23]

Bishop Varlet was the operator by which the clergy and parishes of the Chapter of Utrecht (stakeholders in the work of defense of the Truth) have passed from a state of demobilization (being powerless) to that of Kerk der O.B.C., having possession of the necessary means to survive and grow. Where the Jansenist party in France sanked into the pathos of dolorism and convulsionism under persecution, the Dutch Jansenists, endowed by Bishop Varlet with the power of being fully the Church, became a life force for alternative Catholicism as shown by the subsequent addition of anti-infaillibilist and national groups in Germany and elsewehere in Europe and North America.

In the subsequent chapters, we will show how the Old Catholic Movement was formed from the Church of Utrecht, the beneficiary of the instrument of cohesion that is the Apostolic Succession inherited from Bishop Varlet.[24] Also, relying on a set of texts (statements, synodal acts, pastoral letters of bishops and writings of theologians), we will demonstrate that the Old Catholic Church has inherited a body of doctrine based on the alternative ecclesiology advocated by the Bishop of Babylon.[25]

2
THE INSTRUMENTALITY OF THE APOSTOLIC SUCCESSION

The reform introduced in Holland in the first half of the 18th century was to play a crucial role in the history of the Church. In the following centuries, other resistance groups have made protests similar to that of the Kerk der O.B.C. and turned to the See of Utrecht to insert their ministry in the apostolic succession inherited from Bishop Varlet.[26]

Three aspects are to be considered in this development: (1) the advent of the German *altkatholizismus* which led to the formation of the Utrecht Union of Old Catholic Churches, (2) the addition of national groups and (3) the intercommunion with the Anglicans.

From the Kerk der O.B.C. to the Utrecht Union of Old Catholic Churches

The Church of Utrecht has first been designated as the Kerk der Oud-Bisshopelijke Clerezij (O.B.C.). She adopted the name Oud-Katholieke Kerk van Nederland after the Convention of September 24, 1889,[27] which gave birth to the Utrecht Union of Old Catholic Churches. The convention was signed with the partner churches of Germany and Switzerland, organized in the wake of the "alkatholische" protest[28] against the papal dogmas of 1870.[29]

The Altkatholische Protest

Ignaz von Döllinger

Ignaz von Döllinger was the main promoter of the protest against the papal dogmas. Holder of the Chair of Church History in Munich, he distinguished himself by his scholarly works on patristics, the Reformation, the history of the papacy, and his political and religious activity in Bavaria and at Frankfurt, and his contemporaries considered him a leading Catholic theologian. Germany was in that period twenty years ahead of other countries in the field of history[30] and its theology was deeply influenced by it, hence the formation of the Munich School of History of which Döllinger was the head. Among his associates were Johann Möhler, this historian of dogma who did the "living synthesis of early Christianity and the Church of his time",[31] and Charles Hefele who in 1835 published his History of the Christian Councils.

Refusing to accept the papal dogmas, Döllinger was excommunicated on April 17, 1871 by the archbishop of Munich. Some days later, his disciple and friend, Prof. Dr. Friedrich had the same fate. They were followed in the opposition by other professors in Bonn: the exegete Reusch, the philosophers and historians Knoodt, Hilgers and Langen. Their colleagues in Breslau, Professors Baltzer and Reinkens did the same. Also in Munich, lay historians as Adolf von Cornelius, Moritz Ritter, Max Lossen, Felix Stieve and August von Druffel separated from the Roman obedience.[32] Josef H. Reinkens soon became important among the dissenters. He was an effective leader and organized parishes that took the name *Altkatholischen* (Old Catholic) to indicate their loyalty to the Church before Vatican I. Otto von Bismarck, the minister of the King of Prussia, gave his support to the dissidents and called for the establishment of a German National Catholic Church. He nationalized the clergy and entrusted the parishes to Old Catholic priests. This project did not last and the bishops regained the control of the parishes.

Josef H. Reinkens

On June 14, 1873, a delegation of 77 dissident priests and laymen assembled in Cologne, proceeded with the election of a bishop. The priest Josef H. Reinkens was elected and the Kerk der O.B.C. was approached to confer on him the episcopate. Msgr. Hermann Heykamp, Bishop of Deventer, proceeded with the consecration on August 11. The new bishop took part, on April 8, 1875, in the consecration of a new archbishop of Utrecht, Johannes Heykamp, with the Bishop of Haarlem. The cohesion between the German and Dutch churches was effected by the instrumentality of the apostolic succession inherited from Bishop Varlet.

Archbishop J. Heykamp

From Germany to Switzerland

One important aspect of the Catholic reform in Germany was the involvement of the laity. This was a new phenomenon since, during the Vatican Council, the laity had been completely excluded. Johann Friedrich von Schulte, who was a member of the ecclesiastical tribunal in Prague at the opening of the council, had sent a demand for the admission of lay delegates, but it remained unanswered.[33] In Switzerland, the opposition to the papal dogmas was made by laypeople. The reasons were not historical but political.[34] Because of the importance of the laity in the German reform,[35] Old Catholic sympathies were quickly felt in some Swiss cantons.

The opposition to the Roman centralism has a long history in Switzerland. The Council of Basel has left its mark.[36] The influence of Wessenberg was still felt in the North[37] and in 1849, a theologian of Fribourg, Johann Baptist von Hirscher, advocated reforms similar to those undertaken by the German Old Catholics. Two major meetings were held on April 29 and on May 1, 1871, in Solothurn and in Berne. The decrees of the Vatican were dismissed and a demand was made that the constitution of the country be revised in order to defend citizens against the clerical demands and to protect the dissident priests. A committee was formed and three representatives were sent to the Old Catholic Congress held September 22-24 in Munich: landamann Augustin Keller, Law Professor Walter Munzinger and Senator Fridolin Anderwert.[38] Parishes were soon organized. The church of St. Peter and St. Paul in Berne passed to the Old Catholics as well as the church of the Dominicans in Basel.

On June 14, 1876 was held the second Synod of the Church of Switzerland (called *Christian Catholic*). There were 161 delegates, including 46 priests. Father Eduard Herzog was elected bishop

and his consecration took place in the parish church of Rheinfelden on September 19. It is Bishop Joseph H. Reinkens who presided the ceremony, again sealing the church *cohesion* by the instrumentality of the episcopate inherited from Bishop Varlet.

Bishop Herzog

From Switzerland to the U.S.A. and Canada

On June 7, 1885 in Berne, Bishop Herzog ordained the Reverend Rene Vilatte for missionary work among the Franco-Americans.[39] With Jean-Baptiste Gauthier of Montreal, also ordained by Bishop Herzog,[40] he founded several parishes under the aegis of the Society of the Precious Blood.

René Vilatte

Jean B. Gauthier

The work is continued in Canada under the name *Christian Catholic*.[41] It is a constituency of the International Council of Community Churches, a member communion of the World Council of Churches.[42]

In 1897, Polish dissidents in the United States joined the Utrecht Union and Msgr. Herzog consecrated a bishop for them on November 21, in the person of the priest Anton Kozlowski of Chicago.[43] He was succeeded by Father Franciszek Hodur, leader of another group of Polish dissidents in Scranton, Pennsylvania. Archbishop Gerard Gul conferred the episcopate on him at Utrecht on September 29, 1907.

Bishop Kozlowski (4th) with Msgr. Herzog (2nd) and co-consecrators, Archbishop Gul (1st) & Bishop Weber of Germany (3rd)

English & Polish Mariavite Dioceses

Other developments took place in England, under the leadership of Father Arnold H. Mathew[44] whom Archbishop Gul consecrated at Utrecht on April 28, 1908. On October 5, 1909, Msgr. Mathew consecrated with Msgr. Gul the leader of the Polish Old Catholic Mariavites,[45] Jan Michał Kowalski. The following year, on Sept. 4, Archbishop Gul co-consecrated with him Father Roman Jakub Próchniewski[46] who was to become second Ordinary.

Bishop Mathew   Bishop Kowalski   Bishop Prochniewski

At the end of 1909, the Utrecht Union included churches in the Netherlands (dioceses of Deventer, Haarlem and Utrecht), Germany (one diocese based in Bonn), Switzerland (one diocese based in Berne), the United Kingdom (one diocese based in London),[47] the Polish National Catholic Church (P.N.C.C.) based in Scranton, Pennsylvania, U.S.A.[48] and the Mariavite Church based in Plock, Poland.[49]

Croatian, Czech, Austrian & Slovakian Dioceses

The Utrecht Union undergone a new expansion in 1924. Msgr. Franciscus Kenninck, then Archbishop of Utrecht, consecrated Father Marko Kalogera for the Croats (then part of Yugoslavia)[50] on February 25, 1924 and Father Alois Pascheck for the Czechs (then part of Czechoslovakia)[51] on September 24. The following year, Father

Adalbert Schindelaar was consecrated for Austria by Msgr. Kenninck and other bishops, including Msgr. Adolph Küry of Switzerland. [52]

The split of Czechoslovakia into two separate countries in 1993 caused the division of the church as well. The Old Catholic Church of Slovakia was organized and became the youngest member of the Utrecht Union in 2000.[53]

Old Catholic Parishes in Italy, France, Denmark and Sweden

There are areas in which Old Catholics have not developed into dioceses. They are given episcopal oversight by delegates of the Bishops Conference of the Utrecht Union. They are bishops of other dioceses who are commissioned to exercise episcopal oversight in these areas. This includes parishes in Italy, France, Denmark and Sweden.

The Intercommunion with the Anglicans

Early in the Old Catholic movement, the Anglicans had not hidden their sympathy for such a reform.[54] Already in 1873, barely a month after the German Church had obtained her first bishop, representatives of the Church of England participated in the Old Catholic Congress held in Constance.[55] The following year, the dialogue was established on a formal basis. The union conferences began and they would continue until 1931.[56]

In 1878 the Lambeth Conference had recognized the resemblance between Old Catholic and Anglican principles: "It is with happiness, said the bishops, that we welcome any attempt at reform made on the model of the Ancient Church." [57]

Ten years later, the same Lambeth Conference allowed the Anglican priests to give communion to the members of the Old Catholic Church[58] and in 1897 encouraged the continuation of union negotiations. The only obstacle stood in the refusal by the Mother Church of Utrecht, to recognize the validity of the Anglican Orders. It disappeared in 1925 when the commission charged to study the issue submitted a favorable report to the Archbishop of Utrecht, Msgr. Franciscus Kenninck.[59]

In 1930, an official delegation represented the Old Catholic Church at the 7th Lambeth Conference and the possibility of union was discussed. The following year, representatives of the two communions met in Bonn on July 2 and reached a comprehensive agreement that led to a joint statement called the Bonn Agreement. The text, approved by the authorities of both communions, included the following three points:

1. Each Communion recognizes the catholicity and independence of the other and maintains its own.

2. Each Communion agrees to admit members of the other Communion to participate in the Sacraments.

3. Full Communion does not require from either Communion the acceptance of all doctrinal opinion, sacramental devotion or liturgical practice characteristic of the other, but implies that each believes the other to hold all the essentials of the Christian faith.

In the Bonn alliance were united a church who lived through the Reformation of the 16th century and another church that, in a different way, had carried out her own reform.[60]

3

THE INSTRUMENTALITY OF A BODY OF DOCTRINE

The cohesion that led to the Utrecht Union and later to the intercommunion with the Anglicans, was achieved via the "church order" bequeathed by Bishop Varlet to the Kerk der O.B.C.[61] But this parentage, as functional as it was, does not alone explain the "corporate existence" of the Old Catholic Church. The inclusion in the apostolic succession is accompanied by the adherence to a body of doctrine. This is evidenced by the fact that the constitution of 1889[62] is accompanied by a doctrinal statement. However, this statement did not emerge from the cohesion: it was developed progressively through the inter-influences between the Kerk der O.B.C. and its Altkatholich partner. This is what Claude B. Moss shows in his analysis of the Old Catholic Church using the Gallicano-Jansenist ecclesiology as integrative principle.[63]

We will illustrate it in two ways. First, we will discuss the theological synthesis which was formalized in the *Acta et Decreta secundae Synodi Ultrajectensis* of 1764 and we will compare it to the reform program of Bishop Varlet. Second, relying on the minutes of the Old Catholic Congress of Munich (20-24 September 1871), which established the principles of the altkatholizismus, on the speech delivered by Father Josef H. Reinkens on September 20, 1872, at the Congress of Cologne, and on his first pastoral letter as bishop, on August 11, 1873, we will show that the German-Dutch coming together was made by means of a doctrinal cohesion that completed the instrumentality of the apostolic succession.

The Synod of Utrecht of 1763

We have, in the inaugural address delivered by Archbishop Peter Meindaerts on September 13, 1763, the principles that have governed the thinking and work of the various committees of the Synod of Utrecht: "The fabricators of errors have left nothing untouched, they have left nothing unattempted, to overthrwow the genuine sense of Holy Scripture, to impugn the sacred mysteries of the Christian religion, and to destroy all ecclesiastical discipline and every rule of morals, by sophism and equivocation".[64]

The problematique is expressed in the terms formulated by Bishop Varlet in his reform program. They regard the faith (the content of the Revelation and the sacred mysteries which express it) and the rules of discipline and morals (that Rome has tainted with sophism and equivocation). We will examine the reports of the different committees to get an idea of the concerns of the synod and access the theology which has been codified.

The Concerns of the Synod

With the exception of two aspects (the obedience to civil authority and the discipline of the Eucharist and of baptism, confirmation, penance and marriage) on which we will not insist, the efforts of the synod were to refute errors relating to faith, morals and spirituality. Were condemned:

(A) the thesis of Pierre Le Clerc, particularly those regarding the propositions of Cornelis Jansen and the infallibility of the Church;

(B) the book Histoire du peuple de Dieu of the Jesuit Isaac J. Berruyer (assuming the presence of two persons in our Lord Jesus Christ) and of Jean Hardouin, his master (convicted of blasphemy against the doctrines of the Holy Trinity, of the Incarnation and of grace);

(C) the Attritionist books L'Esprit de Jésus Christ et de l'Église sur la fréquente communion (by Jean Pichon, S.J.) and Onderwys voor de Erste Communie that destroy the argument of satisfaction as an essential part of repentance and reduce the sacrament of penance to a cure of sin acting *ex opere operato*;[65]

(D) the Probabilistic works of Hermann Busembaum,[66] Claude La Croix,[67] Nicolai Mazzotta[68] and François Neumayer.[69]

We will explain briefly the issues discussed by the various committees and we will reproduce excerpts from the reports submitted to the approval of the Synod.

Against Pierre Le Clerc

Pierre Le Clerc, a French sub-deacon living in Amsterdam,[70] had expressed views that the authorities of the Church of Utrecht found likely to jeopardize the rapprochement with Rome they wanted. These views were on the propositions attributed to Cornelis Jansen, the schism of the Greeks, the infallibility of the Church, the creed of Pope Pius IV, the equality of bishops and priests, indulgences and excommunication. We will not elaborate on all these points. The majority of them were treated in a manner favorable to the papacy, to the prejudice of Bishop Varlet's positions.[71] We will focus on the theories regarding the propositions of Jansen and the infallibility of the Church which confirm the persistence of the Jansenist tradition and are directly related with the rest of the condemnations made by the synod.

On the Propositions of Cornelis Jansen

The dispute concerns the question of right and the question of fact regarding Jansen. Le Clerc said that the five propositions attributed to the Bishop of Ypres contained the Catholic faith on grace.[72] The first committee, which had been mandated to study the case of Le Clerc, rejected this opinion on behalf of the continuity of the Dutch discourse on this. The question was not to assert the orthodoxy of Jansen, but to maintain that the propositions are not in his book <u>Augustinus</u>. The interest of the committee's report is that it is a reminder of the Augustinian doctrine: "The holy Synod declares that the doctrine of grace efficacious *per se* and *ab intrinsic*, and of gratuitous predestination to glory without any prevision of merits, handed down by St. Augustine and St. Thomas, is consonant with the Holy Scripture, the decrees of the pontiffs and councils, and the sayings of the Fathers."[73]

On the Infallibility of the Church

Le Clerc affirmed that the Church could claim to infallibility only when it is gathered in an ecumenical council. To this, the committee replied: "The Church is not less infallible in all things which the body of its pastors, though dispersed, sets forth as to be believed concerning the faith and morals, that in those which are thus set forth by them in a general council assembled." [74]

Against Jesuit Fathers Berruyer and Hardouin

It was the task of the second committee to decide on the Histoire du peuple de Dieu by Father Berruyer (book challenged even among the Roman Catholics[75]) and the ideas of his mentor, Father Hardouin, who relativized the Scripture and the Tradition against those who made them the rule of faith. Using as pretext the censure against them by the bishops of Soissons, Lyons and Vienne,[76] and by the doctors of Sorbonne, they reaffirmed four points considered essential by Bishop Varlet: 1. universal redemption, 2. justification by faith alone, 3. grace necessary to produce good works, and 4. need to comply with God's will and translate it into charity in order to combat lust.

- *Universal Redemption*

Jesus Christ, through the sacrifice He made himself once for all, has obtained full reparation for the sins of the humans, the original sin as well as their other transgressions. "Being the suffering and death of the incarnate God, they are of infinite virtue and price." [77] And this, not only "of those who were born after His incarnation, but of those also who had preceded His advent".[78] In other words, He shed his blood for all humankind.

- *Justification by Faith Alone*

Neither natural law nor that of Moses can justify us before God, but only the faith in Jesus Christ, our only mediator between him and humans. "By His blood and merits all the righteous, whether of the Old or the New Testament, received remission of sins, the true adoption, and the grace requisite to fulfill the divine commandments." [79]

The Necessity of Grace to Produce Good Works

Not only grace is what allows us to pursue what is good and progress in justice, but it is also what allows us to keep doing good. It is not based in the exhortations and examples, but "in inspiratione dilectionis qua cognita sancto amore faciamus." [80] God works in us to will and to act according to his good purpose (Phil. 2:13). And "the predestination of the Saints to glory is entirely gratuitous, and before provision of merits".[81]

Against Lust, the conformity to God's Will and its Expression in Charity

There is a immutable law requiring that we obey the divine will, of which depends all the natural order, and that we avoid anything that might undermine it. "Wathever is willfully done against this invariable rule of morals, whether by ignorance, whether by inadvertence and forgetfulness, or whether by an erroneous conscience, lies under sin".[82] Lust, which comes from sin and leads to it, and all its movements, are bad and irregular, and the Christian life consists "in its eradication, and the endeavour with our whole strength to fulfill the law of charity, by which we are bound to love God with our whole mind, with our whole heart, with our whole power, and to refer all our actions to Him as to their ultimate end".[83]

On the Rule of Faith

The Word of God, written in the Holy Scripture, which was transmitted by tradition, in an uninterrupted succession, is the rule of faith. And the holy Catholic and Apostolic Church is its "infallible interpreter and incorrupted guardian." [84]

Against Two Attritionist Works

In the light of the prescriptions of former Archbishop van Neercassel (in his book <u>Amor Penitens)</u> and of the teachings of Antoine Arnauld on the "Frequent Communion", the members of the Third Committee assessed the book entitled <u>L'Esprit de Jésus Christ sur la fréquente communion</u> published in 1745 by Father Pichon, and a manual used by the Jesuits in Holland (although condemned by Rome in 1703) to prepare the children for their first communion (the <u>Onderwys voor Erste Communion</u>). They rejected them because they were not presenting contrition as a prerequisite for receiving Holy Communion. "Satisfaction, an integral and essential part of the sacrament of penance was eliminated from the Jesuit theology". [85]

The committee, which adhered to the doctrine formulated by van Neercassel and Charles Borromeo (in his Instructions for Confessors), recommended the adoption of the following standards for the reception of the sacraments:

(a) In addition to faith and hope, one must have the salutary fear expressed by a beginning of love above all.

(b) To access the sacraments, it is necessary that our sins have been pardoned and that we be renewed from within, to the image of Him who created us just and holy.

(c) Sinners must pass by degrees from the love for the creatures to the love of God, which implies a change of heart and life.[86]

Against Probabilism

The Fourth Committee's task was to identify the errors of the casuists,[87] including those on probabilism. Its report condemned the works of Busembaum, La Croix, Mazotta and Neumayer, based on the principles formulated by Bishop Varlet and the Jansenists: "The external law, naturally implanted in all, can only be matter of ignorance from the blindness and corruptions of the heart. This ignorance can never excuse from sin." [88]

The Positions of the Synod: Similarities and Differences with Those of Bishop Varlet

The questions discussed at the synod and the content of the committee reports reveal a significant continuity with Bishop Varlet's positions in regard to the first two modalities of the competence in his reform program.

The synod insisted on the conversion, which corresponds to the modality of the will. Under the effect of grace, the soul is longing for the eschatological goods and the person passes from the carnal to the spiritual, from finiteness to infinity. This consequently calls for the other modality: the know-how. When grace enters a soul, it transmits the Spirit of Jesus Christ. It is a radical gift (divine adoption) that has a radical exigency: to give one's heart wholly to God. This results in a personal cleansing that leads to charity. The /knowledge/ begins with the revelation that it is God who gives the being, and that the dignity of the humans comes from their participation in the divine nature.[89] Feelings of humility follow: greed gives way to newness of life, which is essential to recognize that in Jesus Servant is at work the redeeming love of the Father. Christ is taken as a model and under the action of the Holy Spirit, the believer gradually rises to meet Him who comes. Force of change, the Spirit transforms greed into charity, thus allowing to see salvation.

The continuity is broken on the power to do the church. For Bishop Varlet, this modality, imperative upon conversion, is enacted in the soul that feels the urgency to make the reign of God come. But the attempt to conjoin the believers with the spiritual goods runs into the accusing claims of Satan: the worldly objectives of hegemony of the Church establishment vs the defense of doctrinal truth and morals. This polemical structure, reminiscent of the temptation of Jesus in the desert (Matt. 4:1-11), the Christological hymn in Phil. 2 and the conflict between the woman and the dragon (Rev. 12)[90] has a kerygmatic intent: God's plan is fulfilled in the 'Ebed Yahweh', the Suffering Servant announced by Isaiah.[91] The leaders and the faithful of the Church should manifest in word and deed, that they have been made willing and able to obey God's purpose if they want to reach the goal of the church life: to enter the Kingdom (not identified with the institution).

The synod has not maintained in its entirety Bishop Varlet's reform program as shown in the relativization of the grievances against the papacy. This poses the problem of the meaning of the Jansenist positions (always asserted in 1763) and of their links (strongly influenced by the Bishop of Babylon) with the functionality of the Church. To see more clearly into this, we will recall Bishop Varlet's perspective and we will compare it with that of the Synod.

The Perspective of Bishop Varlet and That Defended by the Synod

The discourse of Bishop Varlet, as we have seen, is built on three central soteriological performances: (a) the passage from perdition to salvation by the merits of the Blood of Jesus Christ (2) that of non-translating to translating into action (charity) that salvation by the operation of the Holy Spirit, and (3) the passage from the fallibility to the infallibility of the Church resulting from the spiritualization of the believers. It is on this last program, which is a necessary consequence of the first two, that he articulates his pragmatics, centered on the exercise of infallibility. He defines it as resulting from a unity of communion built on the unity of the faith; specifies its main subject (the Church) and its operators (the bishops, interpreters of the councils) and indicates its objects (faith and morals).[92] By so doing, he presents a conception of the authority in the Church, that becomes the epicenter of his whole system. The bishop, as operator (facilitator) of the performance of infallibility, has the essential and full power (which comes directly from Jesus Christ) to judge the faith and transmit it in conformity with the canons. With his colleagues, he forms a body (the College of Bishops) which is epiphenomenoned[93] by the pope.

Called by divine right to maintain the unity of faith and the good order in the Church, the pope is no less bound than the bishops by the decisions and rescripts of the councils. Therefore his jurisdiction should not, in principle, undermine that of the bishops since it is the same function of stewardship of God's mysteries for the conjunction of the faithful to eschatological goods[94] in the time between the first and the second manifestation of Jesus Christ. It is a purely spiritual authority characterized by humility and charity, and it is distinct from the temporal power, which assures the welfare of the state by means of the coercive force. Rome which identifies the Church with the Kingdom confuses the two levels of authority. Pursuing worldly goals contrary to the spirit of the Gospel, Rome reverses the order of the doctrine, discipline and morals. This reversal, which results from the influence of the Beast (Rev. 20), has produced a state of depravity,[95] which expresses on both speculative and practical plans. We must defend the truth by reforming the Church.

At the outset, the approach tallies with that of Bishop Varlet establishing three central performances, also of soteriological type: (1) the entry into the justice by the sacrifice of Christ,[96] (2) the law of charity (which translates salvation into action)[97] and (3) the infallibility of the Church.[98] But there is a demarcation on the third performance. Instead of depending on the action of the Holy Spirit operating the sanctification of believers, the infallibility is related to the living magisterium of the body of pastors,[99] under the control of a pope having "not only a primacy of honour but also an ecclesiastical power and authority." [100] Therefore, the restriction expressed by the synod ("It is not jure divino but simply jure ecclesiastico that the Bishop of Rome is St. Peter's successor" [101]) does not change the fact that the epicenter of Bishop Varlet's system, his conception of the authority of the Church and in the Church, is completely modified. The Jansenist issue becomes a matter of individual Christian competence: the possibility to make the propositions of Jansen correspond to Catholic orthodoxy is rejected. Greed is denounced as an obstacle to personal sanctification, but not the ecclesiastical system that keeps its attributes of "power" in the exercise of authority.

The interest of the synod for the issues related to the sacrament of penance is in line with the reforms of the Council of Trent (the Instructions of Charles Borromeo are recommended along with the Amor Penitens of van Neercassel) and the theses of Jansen (the problem is suspended pending a decision of authority) only evoke the classic devotion of the Fréquente Communion. There is no more of that "prophetic" impulse which made Archbishops Steenoven and Wuytiers await a divine confirmation of the autonomist "gesture" of Bishop Varlet.[102] In 1763, the Church of Utrecht aspires to a reunion with Rome and no longer claims to the functional Jansenism that pushed Bishop Varlet to denounce that the Church rest on imperatives of "system" to the detriment of those of faith.

But the altkatholische protest against the papal dogmas of 1870 was to bring the Kerk der O.B.C. back to the alternative ecclesiology defended by Bishop Varlet. Bishop Josef H. Reinkens held in this regard positions similar to those of the Bishop of Babylon.

The Arguments at the Origin of the Altkatholizismus: Similarities with Bishop Varlet's View

The acts of the Congress of Munich (1871) affirm the absence of "dogmatic disagreements" between the German Old Catholics and the O.B.C. of Utrecht. The persistence of the Jansenist Tradition is clear in the allusion to the Jesuits "who teach and practice a system of morals which is wrong and corrupt".[103] Josef Reinkens developed the idea in his speech to the Congress of Cologne (1872) and in his pastoral letter of 1873. Appeared the great themes of the resistance of Bishop Varlet and of the Chapter of Utrecht: justification by faith, need not distort the Word of God in defiance of Scripture and Tradition, divine adoption as a way of salvation, grace that makes us pass from darkness to full light and the importance to make God reign in the souls so that the life in (and the fruits of) the Holy Spirit, being exhibited in us, there can be a renewal of Christianism brought back to its original simplicity.[104] It is by the "living union with Christ and before the Cross of Calvary" that Prof. Reinkens see the advent of the Old Catholic movement against "the ultramontane clergy who thinks that the unity has a price per se, when it is based on errors.[105] The opposition to the constitution Pastor Aeternus (1870) has the same premise as the struggle of Bishop Varlet against the Bull Unigenitus (1713): the unity of the faith (believed everywhere, always and by all), not the communion at the expense of the reversal of the rules of dogma and morals.

The first bishop of Germany is, of course, in line with the Synod of Utrecht when he says that the Old Catholicism (that aims at "renewing Christianity") will only be achieved by "a living union with Christ" (as taught by the Jansenists).[106] He is also evidently in line with Bishop Varlet when he affirms that we must defend the unity of the faith against Vatican I, which reverses the rules of doctrine and morals in favor of the unity of the "system" (a unity based on error). It is as if the specificity claimed by the Bishop of Babylon in 1724 (the mix of Jansenist devotion and Gallican claim) but abandoned by the Kerk der O.B.C. in 1763, had resurfaced in Germany, in the *altkatholische* resistance to the papal dogmas.[107]

Even before he took his stand against the constitution *Pastor Aeternus*, the Gallican influence was evident in Döllinger. Already in 1825, had appeared in Rattisbone a German translation of the Histoire des variations des Églises protestantes by Bossuet and he had a copy in his library.[108] Victor Conzemius, quoting the Bishop of Meaux, shows the analogy with the Gallican position: "the Catholic truth is a divine work and was perfect from the start. Known directly by the apostles, it has spread through the Church, without undergoing any change." [109]

But if Döllinger was a sympathizer of Gallicanism, he was not a Jansenist. He had not found necessary to report the existence of the Church of Utrecht in his book The Church and the Churches, where he reviewed the denominations of the worlds. We can presume that from 1871 to 1889 (the year of the Convention of Utrecht), there were inter-influences between the O.B.C. and that of the altkatholizismus. One would have inspired the other with the Jansenist spirituality expressed at the Synod of Utrecht (1763). The other would have given back to the first its Gallican claim that vain hopes of being reunited with Rome had made the O.B.C. Kerk hide under a bushel. It is this Gallicano-Jansenist interpenetration which is reflected in the Declaration of Utrecht that we will now analyse.

The Declaration of Utrecht

This text, written on September 24, 1889, by the bishops of Germany, Holland and Switzerland, describes in eight articles the "church principles" which govern the life of the Old Catholic Churches. The first 5 articles, inspired by Gallicano-Jansenism, present the rule of faith[110]: "Id teneamus, quod ubique, quod semper, quod ab omnibus creditum est / What has been believed always, everywhere and by everyone" (Art. 1); reject the decrees of the Vatican opposed to it (the Bull Unigenitus, the dogma of the Immaculate Conception of Mary of 1854, the Syllabus of Errors of 1864 and the Papal Dogmas of 1870 (Art. 2 to 4); renew the protests of the Church of Utrecht against Rome (Art. 4); and reject the disciplinary decisions of the Council of Trent, retaining only the dogmatic decisions that "are consistent with the doctrines of the Ancient Church" (Art. 5). The 6th article, the most developed, describes the "ancient Catholic dogma of the Holy Sacrament of the Altar".[111] The 7th article expresses the wish that come an agreement on the differences arising from schisms based on the beliefs of the Undivided Church. Finally, the 8th article, particularly close to the concerns of Bishop Varlet, advocates an unwavering commitment to Jesus Christ and the rejection of the ambitions of the hierarchy and of the errors introduced by speculation[112] as a remedy to the disbelief and the religious indifference, two evils of the time.

Work of balance and precision, the Declaration of Utrecht proved that the instrumentality of the Apostolic Succession has been coupled with that of a body of doctrine since the time it was inherited from Bishop Varlet by the Kerk der O.B.C. This gives reason to Claude B. Moss, who inserts the Old Catholic movement in the church alternative derived from the Gallicano-Jansenist ecclesiology. But some say that influences opposed to those of the reformers have infiltrated the Old Catholic Church and that she is now removed from the sources and principles she claimed in 1889.[113] Msgr. Urs Küry, third bishop of the Swiss Church, spoke of these opposing influences, he called "liberal rationalism", in a pastoral letter of 1972: *Perspectives d'avenir pour notre église après cent ans d'existence autonome*.[114] There are two types of liberalism, he wrote: the *rationalist or naturalist*, which does not include divine revelation, but sees in Christianity a moral force to promote human culture, and the *supernaturalist* attached to the revelation, the confession of faith, the order of ministry and the cultural life of the Church. This is the first, he said, heir of the Enlightenment, which is seen as contrary to the spirit of the fathers of altkatholizismus.[115] According to him, it quickly disappeared to make way for a higher Catholic fidelity.[116] We will check the validity of this assertion and, consequently, of the doctrinal continuity with the synthesis made by Bishop Varlet.[117] Synthesis that establishes the authority and infallibility of the Church on the Spirit of Jesus Christ, communicated to the believers through the operation of grace. To achieve this, we will examine the theological discourse during the first 100 years of the Utrecht Union, particularly that found in the Revue Internationale de Théologie / R.I.T. (now known as the <u>International Kirchliche Zeitschrift</u> / I.K.Z.), whose first releases date from 1893.

The Theological Discourse in the First 100 years of the Utrecht Union, 1889-1989

We will consider four periods[118] in our analysis: the Eugene Michaud period (1893-1913), the Rudolf Keussen period (1914-1940), the period that Professor Werner Küppers inaugurated around 1940 with his colleagues Urs Küry and Ernst Gaugler, and that of professors Herwig Aldenhoven, Peter Amiet and Kurt Stalder, who were members of the Christian (Old) Catholic Faculty when we did our doctorate in Berne.

Eugène Michaud sees the Church as a "society of believers incorporated in Christ through faith and baptism". Its mandate is to "keep intact, without addition or subtraction, the deposit of the teachings and the means of salvation established by Christ."[119] Although imperfect, that society is "infallible" when it transmits what comes from the "Incarnated Word who is infallible."[120]

Professor Keussen interprets the same tradition when he reproaches the Roman Church for claiming the dignity and authority of the Saint (Christ) she represents." [121] The whole-kindness of God can be expressed in the personality of a saint but not in a visible institution as shown in "the Inquisition and the autodafés."[122] To be legitimate, the pretense of the Church to the authority and dignity of the Lord must demonstrate that "the Spirit of Jesus is alive in the fullness of the moral and religious substance in her representatives."[123] The holiness is for Keussen an ideal to be achieved but his determination to prove that the Church did not make divine love grow in humankind makes him minimize the action of the Holy Spirit who, for Bishop Varlet, sanctifies the faithful and transmits them the infallibility of Christ who lives in us by grace.

Professor Küppers is closer to Bishop Varlet. Of the four notes of the Church it is holiness that he develops mainly, attributing its historical and visible continuity in the subsistence and development of an ecclesial reality founded in Jesus Christ.[124] The concern, echoed by Bishop Urs Küry in a pastoral letter of 1965, shows that it has been characteristic of this phase, called *theological renewal*, that began in the 1940s.[125]

Here is an excerpt that has for theme the catholicity of the Church. "We can, with Tertullian, define the Church as a body of the three divine persons, a earthly vessel in which and through which God the Father sends the Son and the Holy Spirit, and secondly the Son and the Holy Spirit sent by Him, to communicate to the faithful the fullness of life, which is grace and truth. Better, the Church is essentially that life, the totality and fullness of the divine life of the Holy Trinity. This gift of life makes the Church the "communion of saints" professed in the Apostles' Creed. According to the oriental language of symbol, the church is doubly a *Communio Sanctorum*, a communion of saints. First in the sense of the people sanctified by the grace of God and made participating in the new and eternal life. Then in the sense of a fellowship in holy things, instituted by Christ and the apostles, and through which God communicates his grace."[126]

We have summarized the concerns and the theological context in which spoke the professors of the Faculty of Berne in the 1980s. We cannot better evoke the affinity with Bishop Varlet than mention this sentence by Kurt Stalder: "In Jesus Christ, the Church is thus created a basic soteriological, pneumatological, eschatological and anthropological reality in this world." [127]

The soteriology, central in Bishop Varlet's theology,[128] is at the core of Peter Amiet's reflection on the Church, the Body of Christ (in its local and universal reality),[129] in that of Herwig Aldenhoven on the understanding the Old Catholic Churches have of themselves[130] and also in that of Kurt Stalder who sees it as the foundation of ecclesiology.[131] It is the Holy Spirit who makes salvation seen in the Church,[132] communicating to the believers the grace that can make them change in reference to Christ. Stressing the pneumatological component of the Old Catholic ecclesiology, Peter Amiet cites this phrase of Döllinger: " A time will come… in which the Petrine and Pauline churches will develop themselves further to Johannine or, as one said in the Middle Ages, an age of the Holy Spirit will follow the church periods of the Father and the Son." [133]

He recalls, against those who wonder if the prophetic role of the theologian in relation to the magisterium had been considered by the provost of Munich and his protesting colleagues,[134] the principle already defined by Bishop Varlet that the authority of the Church comes, not from the living magisterium,[135] but from the Holy Spirit who animates and sanctifies the Church. An approach that emphasizes the "koinonia", that is to say, a unity of communion[136] built on faith.[137] Instead of ignoring the prophetic role of the theologian, the Old Catholic doctors, attentive to the action of the Spirit, make it one of their concerns. The Church, place of salvation, is convened and interpellated by the Word of God that calls to repentance. In concentrating her theological reflection on ecclesiology the Church avoids falling into navel-gazing[138] and thus becomes capable of acting as "the salt of the earth". [139]

The opinion expressed in Roman Catholic circles that the Old Catholic theology ignores the prophetic dimension, comes from the fact that the movement has maintained the Gallican positions summarized in the Catholic criterion of St. Vincent of Lerins.[140] Positions said to be static, as if fidelity to the revealed deposit forbade any thought on its subject.[141] Msgr. Leo Gauthier, former Bishop of Switzerland and former Secretary of the Old Catholic Bishops Conference, wrote on the question: "St. Vincent held the conviction that Bossuet expressed later with eclat: the Catholic truth that came from God was made perfect at first glance.[142] There is a main intellectual and spiritual option that the philosopher Josef Pieper has well analyzed in his book <u>Uberlieferung, Begriff und Anspruch</u> (Münich, 1970). The option is this: the antiquity of a sacred tradition is not a matter of time but of priority of the divine revelation. For the Christian faith, it means the fullness of the divine revelation came with Christ in the fullness of time (Gal. 4:4) and was entrusted to the apostles under the action of the Holy Spirit. It does not mean that there is no progress of faith. There is an intelligence and an expression always more fruitful and appropriate of the tradition, or better, of the original revelation. But no new dogmas as in the Roman Catholic Church." [143]

The important role of the Holy Spirit in the economy of the Church, so pronounced in Bishop Varlet's <u>Commentary on the Acts of the Apostles</u>, is among the priorities of the Old Catholic reflection as shown in the works of Aldenhoven and Stalder.[144] And pneumatology is related to eschatology, the third term of Stalder's statement on the Church as a reality of this world: *In the Holy Spirit, Christians confess Jesus as Lord* (1 Cor. 12:3). *He is from the Father who sent Him to them in the power of the Holy Spirit* (Luke 1:35 & 3:22) *and the Son draws us to the Father* (John 6:44) *in the Holy Spirit. And the Spirit of truth, who proceeds from the Father, testifies of the Son* (John 15:26). *The Holy Spirit directs us in the whole truth* (John 16:13). *And this truth is Christ* (John 14:6) *who is with us to the end of the world.*[145]

The Church is "in this world".[146] It is an "anthropological reality".[147] Christ offers salvation to the people of the world, inviting them to convert and to enjoy the goods of the kingdom (eschatology): "*The knowledge of salvation*, wrote Amiet, *gives meaning and direction to our lives and brings healing to our body and soul. We want to build a society with all the people so that being united in a community, we may have a good and true life where it is possible to grow in love and freedom.*" [148] *It is to form this community in which the Son of God becomes the first of many brothers and sisters* (Romans 8:19 & 29:35-39) *that Christ sends his disciples to proclaim the Gospel.*

By their missionary work, they build the Body of Christ in various locations uniting the isolated members to the local church and making them experience the Trinitarian life of the community." [149]

If the contours are somewhat lacking in clarity with Michaud (who does not keep the Augustinian aspect of the Communio Sanctorum[150] dear to Bishop Varlet in its treatment of infallibility) and with Keussen (who inserts the question of the Church authority in the problematique of conformity to the Spirit of Jesus Christ, but without believing much in its realization), the tradition around 1940 was consolidated in the soretiological, pneumatological, eschatological and anthropological dimensions[151] that that were charactric in the beginning (the Dutch O.B.C. phase). The salvation obtained from redemption is laid as the foundation of ecclesiology.[152] The role of the Holy Spirit is emphasized as the transmitter of grace between the Ascension and Parousia, realizing in this way in various places the one Body of Christ. The Holy Spirit makes God reign in the souls and transmits, through the ministers and witnesses of the Word and Love, the knowledge of salvation that gives meaning and direction to our lives.

The affinity is clear between the positions of Bishop Varlet on the Church and those defended by the Old Catholics. This has contributed to the formation of the Utrecht Union with the instrumentality of the apostolic succession that he transmitted to the Kerk der O.B.C.

The Last Twenty Years, 1990-2010

Changes have characterized the last twenty years of the Old Catholic Church. First came the opening of the three orders of ministries for women in 1996-97,[153] then the acceptance and liturgical celebration of same-sex unions in 2006.[154] Lastly, the *communicatio in sacris* has been extended to certain Protestant communities.[155]

These are, according to the majority of bishops and synods, answers to the needs of the time,[156] which are of a disciplinary nature[157] and do not alter the doctrinal cohesion that led to the formation of the Union of Utrecht and cements it.

It is not our purpose to discuss whether these changes are only disciplinary or if there was a falling away from the core of the faith as claimed by the P.N.C.C. and the Slovakian Old Catholic Church, both separated from the Utrecht Union.[158] Some would argue that the core of the faith has more to do with the Divinity of Christ, the accuracy and authority of the Bible, that Jesus is the way to salvation, etc.[159] In other words, essential teaching as that of Bishop Varlet on justification by the Blood of Christ;[160] on the necessity and power of grace, on the role of the Holy Spirit who gives the Church her holiness and infallibility...[161]

In an open letter to P.N.C.C. clergy and laity, Prime Bishop Robert Nemkovich pointed out that (...) the character of the Utrecht Union (has been altered) to such an extent that it is no longer the same communion that Bishop Franciszek Hodur joined as a result of his consecration in 1907.[162]

The Utrecht Union is now a purely European body[163] and a realignment of the Old Catholics seems necessary, at least in North America. The P.N.C.C. is listed under the *Free and Independent Churches* of the World Council of Churches with the International Council of Community Churches which has within its membership a number of communities derived from the Old Catholic movement, including the Christian Catholics in Canada, and others from the English Old Roman Catholic tradition.[164] They are significantly present in North America[165] and have their origin in the *Declaration of Autonomy and Independence* issued by Bishop Arnold H. Mathew in 1910.[166] It has similarities with the P.N.C.C. position, including denounciation of a falling away from Catholic orthodoxy supposedly inspired by the Anglicans.[167]

Notes

1. R. Kreiser, Miracles, Convulsions and Ecclesiastical Politics..., op. cit.
2. Idem, p. 397.
3. Idem, p. 4.
4. Idem, p. 79. Similar point of view in Douglas B. Palmer's Ph.D. (History) dissertation <u>The Republic of Grace: International Jansenism in the Age of Enlightenment and Revolutions</u>, Ohio State University, 2004, p. 5.
5. In January 1727, Amsterdam was the scene of the sudden cure of a 45 years old woman named Agatha Leenders-Stouthandel. The event occurred after she had received the Eucharist from the hands of Archbishop Barchman-Wuytiers. The miracle stood for its supporters as a divine legitimation of the prelate's elevation. R. Kreiser, op. cit., p. 79. The event is also reported by: J.M. Neale (op. cit., p. 273), J. Carreyre (L'Église d'Utrecht, op. cit., columns 2,401-407) and P.J. Mann (op. cit., p. 48).
6. R. Kreiser, op. cit., p. 395.
7. Idem, p. 396.
8. Idem, p. 395.
9. Idem, p. 397.
10. Idem, p. 395.
11. Idem, p. 396.
12. Idem, p. 249.
13. R. Kreiser, op. cit., p. 397.
14. Loc. cit.
15. Op. cit., p. 3.
16. Pierre Vaillant, a priest of the Diocese of Troyes and a convinced adept of the figurists, began asserting his claim to be the prophet Elijah's true reincarnation.
17. Kreiser (op. cit., p. 14) calls this universe "Gallicano-Jansenism" or Second Jansenism and he assigns to it statements concerning the nature of the Church (defined as the entire body of the faithful), as well as notions and reforming tendencies which were foreign, even antithetical to the spirit of the established hierarchical Church and regarded as subversive of traditional ecclesiastical authority.
18. R. Kreiser, op. cit., p. 9.

[19] P. Hurtubise (op. cit., p. 32) speaking of the Jansenism which led Varlet to become schismatic, said that it served to make him known to all Europe. His contribution to the establishment of the Church of Utrecht has earned him inclusion in the <u>Dictionnaire critique de biographie et d'histoire</u> (Jal, Paris. 1867, p. 726-729), in the <u>Biographies universelles anciennes et modernes</u> (Michaud, Paris, Tome 42, p. 649) in the <u>Dictionnaire de théologie catholique</u> (Vol. 15, col. 2535-2536) and in the <u>Grand Dictionnaire</u> by Moreri (Tome X, p. 481).

[20] This is because of the imposition of the Bull Unigenitus as a law of the Church and State and the establishment of religious conformity throughout the kingdom. R. Kreiser, op. cit., p. 241.

[21] Bishop Varlet « affected the whole fortune of the Church of Utrecht, was the means of animating her dropping spirit, of providing her with the episcopal succession, and of perpetuating her to the present day." J.M. Neale, op. cit., p. 241.

[22] J. Carreyre, op. cit., col. 2401.

[23] C.B. Moss, op. cit., p. 125-126.

[24] There is no doubt that the interest of the Church of Utrecht in the eyes of many dissenting Catholics was the fact that she received from Bishop Varlet an apostolic succession unquestionably valid. This has not escaped criticism, as shown in an article by Ch. M. in the <u>Revue Catholique</u> (tome 8, Louvain, 1872) titled *Le jansénisme en Hollande*: The Church of Utrecht, one thought so little about it that Professor Döllinger did not even mentioned it in his book <u>The Church and the Churches</u> (Hurst & Blackett Pub., London, 1862)) where he reviews all the denominations of both worlds. Suddenly, the conciliar turmoil, the intrigues of the (German) Old Catholics and the presence of some Jansenists in their conventicles have brought the attention to this church almost forgotten "(p. 19-20). The Dutch Church valued the apostolic lineage inherited from Bishop Varlet. B.A. van Kleef (op. cit., p. 19-20) commenting on his ceremony of consecration on February 19, 1719, considered it necessary to add a development on his line of succession that it traces back to Cardinal Antonio Barberini, the nephew of Pope Urban VIII. See the Old Catholic Episcopal Succession in Appendix 7.

[25] Bishop Varlet ensured that the principles on which he had established his action in favor of the Church of Utrecht be not altered. R. Taveneaux (*Le Jansénisme en Lorraine*, p. 540, note 19). Some of these principles, we will see in the next chapter, have been formally codified at the Synod of Utrecht in 1763.

[26] The Episcopal paternity of Bishop Varlet is mentioned in several studies, including: Raoul Dederen (*Un Réformateur catholique au 19e siècle, Eugene Michaud*, Droz, Geneva, 1963, p. 183), Claude B. Moss (op. cit., P. 119-120), Urs Küry (*Précis d'histoire de l'Église*, Allschwil, 1968, p. 27), J.M. Neale (op.

cit., P. 241)... In general works such as: John A. Hardon (*Religions of the World*, Vol. 2, New York, 1968, p. 207). In articles and books on issues relating to the Church of Utrecht: Louis Cognet (*Le Jansénisme*, Presses Universitaires de France, 1975, p. 105), J. Carreyre (Utrecht, in *Dictionnaire de théologie catholique* XV, p. 2402), E.O. Groman (*An Old Catholic History*, in God's Field, August 1978, p. 4), R. Ackermann (*Un partenaire peu connu du dialogue oecuménique: l'Église vieille-catholique* in La Croix, July 16, 1979), Kees Middlehoff (*Les vieux-catholiques souhaitent jouer les intermédiaires entre les Églises*, Informations catholiques internationales, No. 424, 1973, p. 10), E. Allemang (*L'Église janséniste d'Utrecht* in Annuaire pontifical catholique, 1912, p. 441). Finally, in publications from independent churches and ministries that claim Bishop Varlet as the originator of their apostolic succession: Bernard M. Williams, *A Summary of the History, Faith, Discipline and Aims of the Old Roman Catholic Church in Great Britain*, 1924, p. 19, J. Trela, *A History of the North American Old Roman Catholic Church*, Scranton, 1979, p. 2), K. Pruter, *The Old Catholic Church. A History and Chronology*, 1996, p. 20, A.W. Cockerman, *The Apostolic Succession in the Liberal Catholic Church*, St. Alban Press, London, 1980, p. 9, Dean Bekken, *Table of Apostolic Succession of the Liberal Catholic Church International*, St. Alban Press, 2001, p. 1-2, John Kersey, The Apostolic Succession in the Liberal Rite, ed. by The Liberal Rite, Enfield (England), 2007.

[27] The Utrecht Union is a union of churches and their bishops who are determined to maintain and pass on the faith, worship, and essential structure of the undivided Church. On September 24, 1889, at Utrecht this determination was recorded in three documents that form the *Convention of Utrecht*: the "Declaration", the "Agreement", and the "Regulations". By their uniting to form a Bishops' Conference, which other bishops joined later, the full communion of the Churches represented by them found its expression. The text of the *Declaration of Utrecht*, fundamental for Old Catholic doctrine, is reproduced in Appendix 6.

[28] An analysis of this protest is found in Charles Muller's book Esquisse historique du mouvement vieux-catholique dans les pays de langue allemande, Schautz Publisher, Geneva, 1897.

[29] In the dogmatic constitution *Pastor Aeternus* issued by the First Vatican Council, July 18, 1870, was defined the universal jurisdiction of the pope on all the faithful taken individually and collectively, and also his infallibility when he speaks ex cathedra , i.e. when as chief pastor of the Church he defines a doctrine on faith or morals.

[30] John Acton, *German School of History*, in Historical Essays and Studies, London, 1907, p. 344.

[31] Idem, p. 248.

[32] The protest movement is well documented in the book of J.F. von Schulte, Der Altkatholizismus, Giessen, 1887, p. 123 ff.

[33] J.F. von Schulte, op. cit., p. 14-16.

[34] Charles Muller (op. cit., p. 45) speaks of the "casual and political character of the Catholic reform in the Bernese Jura. He is of the opinion that "politics might have been detrimental to the Old Catholic Church of Switzerland. It supposedly introjected in the movement a spirit contrary to that of the reformers, liberal rationalism.

[35] J.F. von Schulte, op. cit., p. 65.

[36] Herwig Aldenhoven, *Das Konzil von Basel in alkatholischer Sicht*, Theologische Zeitschrift, Vol. 38, 1982, p. 359-366.

[37] Ignaz Heinrich von Wessenberg was administrator of the diocese of Constance in the early 19th century. Reformer, he tried to raise the level of the clergy; tried to expunge the liturgy of abusive practices; prohibited the recitation of the rosary during Mass; published prayer books and hymnals and opposed to the frequency of confessions and the exaggeration of Marian piety. He also considered abolishing clergy compulsory celibacy and advocated synods. His reforms aroused a keen interest among the clergy of South Germany and Switzerland. Urs Küry, op. cit., p. 31.

[38] C.B. Moss, op. cit., p. 245.

[39] Of Belgian and French Canadian origins. The work was supported by Episcopalian Bishop John H. Brown of Fond du Lac who acted as Episcopal Visitor (1885-1888).

[40] On October 28, 1889 at Berne.

[41] The Christian Catholic Church (CCC) comes from a reform originating in the French Canadian parish of St. Anne (Kankakee), Illinois, U.S.A. in the middle of the 19th century. Michel Drolet, Moise Langelier, Joseph Martin, Louis Mercier, Abraham Pelletier, Anselme Robillard and the priest Charles Chiniquy (1809-1899) directed the first society, registered at the Court of Kankakee September 13, 1859. In 1885, parishes were founded among the French-speaking colonists of Wisconsin, by the Reverend Vilatte sent from St. Anne, IL, by Father Chiniquy. The ministry was extended to the Canadian provinces of Ontario and Quebec. The liturgy and doctrine of the church have been strongly influenced by the Swiss Christian (Old) Catholics and close rapports existed in the 1880s and 1980s with their bishop and faculty of theology. Its centre is in Ottawa-Gatineau. More details on the CCC can be found in our book Msgr. Rene Vilatte, Community Organizer of Religion, Apocryphile Press, Berkeley, 2006.

[42] After the passing of Episcopal Bishop J.H. Brown, the work was organized into an Incorporated Synod under the Reverend Vilatte elected as Bishop (Oxford Concise Dictionary of the Christian Church, 2006, p. 421). This was opposed by the Old Catholic Bishops of the Utrecht Union who did not want to put an

⁴² *Old Catholic Episcopate side by side with that of the Anglican Church in America.* Published in <u>Le Catholique Français</u>, Paris, October 1890. *You refuse to give our work a bishop while you had yourself the assistance of Bishop Dominique Varlet who lost his seat to give you a bishop* wrote the Rev. Vilatte to Archbishop Johannes Heykamp of Utrecht. C.R.C.: P 103, S4, D37/8. The synod had him consecrated in 1892 by an Independent Catholic Church in Sri Lanka, attached to the Syriac Patriarchate of Antioch.

⁴³ Bishop Herzog was assisted by Archbishop Gerard Gul of Utrecht and Bishop Theodor Weber of Germany.

⁴⁴ Arnold Harris Mathew was born at Montpellier in France in 1852. He was baptised as a Catholic, trained to be an Anglican priest, but was nevertheless ordained into the Roman Catholic Church in 1877. He later joined the Church of England in 1892 and was curate at Holy Trinity Church in London before joining the Old Catholic Movement.

⁴⁵ The name "Mariavite" comes from Latin words: *Mariae vitam (imitans)* – '(following/ imitating) the life of Mary'. The community was founded in 1906 in Warsaw by Father Kowalski, then diocesan priest and Sister Feliksa Kozłowska of the Third Order of Franciscans. It developed out of the community of sisters founded by the latter in Plock in 1887 and the community of secular priests organized at her instigation in 1893. Both groups adopted the Franciscan rule and aimed at religious, moral and social renewal of clergy and people. They joined the Utrecht Union through the efforts of Russian Orthodox General Alexander Kireev. The church has now some 25,000 believers in Poland, under Prime Bishop Michał Ludwik Jabłoński and 5,000 in France, under Bishop André Le Bec. An independent faction of some 3,000 members is led from Felicianow by Bishop Maria Beatrycze Szulgowicz. There is a Mariavite Community in the U.S.A. led by Bishop Robert R. Zaborowski and centered in Wyandotte, Michigan.

⁴⁶ Msgr. Prochniewski gave a bishop to the Old Catholic Church of Hungary, in the person of Budapest parish priest Tomasz J. Czernohorski-Fehérváry (1917-1984). The consecration took place at Plock, Poland, on November 11, 1945. Exiled to Montreal for political reasons in 1965, Bishop Fehervary organized a parish that was built around a group of immigrants of Austro-Hungarian heritage who, like him, came to Canada in 1965, following the failure of the Hungarian revolt. He was Episcopal Visitor of the Christian Catholics in Quebec till our predecessor, Msgr. O'Neill Côté (1939-1986), ordained priest and mitred by him, became Ordinary.

⁴⁷ On December 29, 1910, Bishop Mathew separated his jurisdiction from the Utrecht Union by a Declaration of Autonomy which was published in <u>The Guardian</u> on January 6, 1911. He disagreed with certain practices and disciplines that he felt deviated from Catholic tradition. Bishop Mathew's activities gave birth to the Liberal Catholic Church (LCC) and the more conservative Old Roman Catholic Churches (ORCC), which are autocephalous

churches holding to a Roman Catholic worship style, while rejecting the dogmas of the First Vatican Council. Churches and ministries of these two traditions exist in significant numbers in North America due to the missionary activities of Bishops Francis Rudolf de Landas Berghe de Rache (ORCC) and James Ingall Wedgwood (LCC), consecrated in England, one in 1913, the other in 1916.

[48] In 2003 the church withdrew from the Utrecht Union due to Utrecht's acceptance of the ordination of women and open attitude towards homosexuality, both of which the P.N.C.C. rejects. The Old Catholic Church in Poland, created as a missionary diocese of the P.N.C.C. but independent since the 1950s, is still a member church of the Utrecht Union.

[49] In 1924, the Mariavite Church was excluded of the Utrecht Union because of certain reforms considered heterodox by the Old Catholic Bishops Conference, including the ordination of women. In 1972, links were renewed with the Utrecht Union and on August 8, 1997, the Archbishop of Utrecht presided at the consecration of Presiding Bishop Tymotheusz Kowalski at Plock (Poland) assisted by other Old Catholic Bishops.

[50] A national church movement among the Croats (1924) has resulted in the establishment of the Old Catholic Church of Croatia. Although it is a member church of the Utrecht Union, it no longer has a functioning diocesan organization. The responsibility for the remaining parishes lies with the Bishops Conference, who carry out their jurisdiction by way of a delegate.

[51] The Old Catholic Church as a movement of Christians who had not accepted the dogma of the First Vatican Council came to being in the territory of the present Czech Republic after 1870.
http://www.ekumenickarada.cz/erceng/starokat.html

[52] There was opposition in Austria to the definition of the infallibility and the universal primacy of jurisdiction of the pope as a dogma in 1870. The Old Catholic Church of Austria became an established church in 1877, through the recognition by the Austrian imperial government, although the authorities did not permit the consecration of a bishop before 1925. But already in 1890, the episcopal administrator of the church, Amandus Czech, had joined the Utrecht Union.

[53] "The bishop-elect of the Slovak church, Fr. Augustin Bacinsky, broke with the Utrecht Union in early 2004 after expressing disaffection with its modernist direction." L.J. Orzell, *"Disunion of Utrecht. Old Catholics Fall Out over New Doctrines',* in Touchstone, Chicago, *May 2004*. He was consecrated by three bishops of a union of churches related to the Brasilian Catholic Apostolic Church on February 8, 2004.

[54] Raoul Dederen, op. cit., p. 207.

[55] C.B. Moss, op. ct., p. 257.

56 On the difficulties of the dialogue with the faction *Low Church*, see the article by M.F.G. Parmentier, *Evangelical Anglicans and Old Catholics in 1931*, <u>Kracht in Zwakheid van een klein Wereldkerk</u>, Oud-Katholieke Seminarie, Amersfoort, 1982, p. 125-144. An Anglican participant, Dr. Graham-Brown, used the <u>Old Catholic Missal & Ritual</u> of the English Old Catholics, the ritual of ordination, to show the different conception about the priesthood and the Eucharist, between the Church of England and the Old Catholic Church. The discussion focused on the word *propitiation* associated with the sacrifice offered by the priest at the altar. *The English word "expiatory" was found to be more appropriate… This objection having been removed, Graham-Brown felt able to sign the Bonn Agreement*, op. cit., p. 137.

57 Cited by Hyacinthe Loyson in <u>La Réforme catholique et l'Église anglicane</u>, Paris, 1879, p. 10.

58 R. Dederen, op. cit., p. 221, note 73.

59 The Archbishop of Utrecht informed by letter the Archbishop of Canterbury (*Reverendissimo Domino Archiepiscopo Cantuariensi Salutem in Domini*) on June 2, 1925. It was published in I.K.Z., Berne, April 1925, p. 65.

60 Ruth Rouse & Stephen C. Neill, <u>A History of the Ecumenical Movement (1517-1948)</u>, London, 1954, p. 470.

61 Regarding the intercommunion with the Anglicans, C.B. Moss wrote (op. cit., p. 349): (in the consecration of bishops) care was taken that the Old Catholic bishop should lay his hand on the head of the candidate and pronounce the words of consecration. The Church of Rome upheld the ancient tradition that at least three Bishops were required to consecrate a Bishop. This tradition was confirmed and ordered to be observed universally by the Council of Nicaea in 325, and this custom has been carefully observed in the Church of England since the Reformation. In this way, if one of the lines of succession were invalid, the other two lines would supply the necessary validity. Thus every Bishop who joins in the laying on of hands is a co-consecrator who passes on his own line of succession to the Bishop he assists in consecrating. For this reason the Episcopal Church asked Bishop De Landas Berghes de Rache (consecrated by Bishop Mathew) to assist in the consecration of Hiram Richard Hulse, their Missionary Bishop for Cuba, on January 12, 1915. http://www.christianepiscopal.ca/orders.html

62 This is a 6-point text on the ecclesiological foundations of the Utrecht Union.

63 C.B. Moss, op. cit., p. vi.

64 J.M. Neale, op. cit., p. 296.

65 J.M. Neale, op. cit., p. 309.

66 Medulla theologiae moralis.

67   Theologia moralis, 1729.

68   Theologia moralis P. Nicolai Mazzotta: in quatuor tomos distributa atque omnem rem moralem absolutissime complectens ...

69   Discours de panégyriques et de morale, and Morale du Nouveau Testament.

70   On Le Clerc, his theology and his relations with the Church of Utrecht, see the article by Archbishop Franciscus Kenninck, *Le Clerc und Pinel im Urteil der Utrechter Kirche*, I.K.Z., April-June 1949, p. 69-93.

71   To make the decrees of the synod as possible acceptable to Rome, they tempered the teaching of the Gallican theologians. J. Neale, op. cit., p. 302. This included the millenarian belief of Bishop Varlet, which lessened the importance of the empirical Church for the earthly Kingdom to come.

72   J.M. Neale, op. cit., p. 300.

73   *Acta et Decreta secundae Synodi Ultrajectensis*, Utrecht, 1764. Cited by J.M. Neale, op. cit., p. 300.

74   Cited by J.M. Neale, op. cit., p. 304.

75   The first part of the book was censured in 1733 by Bishop Colbert of Montpellier.

76   J.M. Neale, op. cit., p. 304-305.

77   Idem, p. 307.

78   Loc. cit.

79   J.M. Neale, op. cit., p. 307.

80   St. Augustine, Lib. IV, cont. 2 Epist. Pelag. 11, cited by J.M. Neale, op. cit., p. 308.

81   Loc. cit.

82   J.M. Neale, op. cit., p. 308.

83   Loc. cit.

84   Loc. cit.

85   J.M. Neale, op. cit., p. 309.

86   Idem, p. 313. As we have noted, it is a point on which insisted Bishop Varlet.

[87] Someone who argues over fine details; a quibbler or sophist. en.wiktionary.org/wiki/casuist

[88] J.M. Neale, op. cit, p. 316.

[89] D.M. Varlet, Recueil alphabétique..., p. 204.

[90] S.A. Theriault, *La femme et le dragon. Analyse structurale du chapitre 12 de l'Apocalypse*, The Canadian Journal of Research in Semiotics, 1979, Vol. 7, No. 2.

[91] D.M. Varlet, Collections sur l'épître aux Romains, sur Isaie, Justin, Tertullien et saint Augustin, A.P.R. 3768.

[92] These are the programs (A, B...) of the performance described in Part II.

[93] A phenomenon that occurs with and seems to result from another. http://www.yourdictionary.com/epiphenomenon

[94] God reigning in the souls.

[95] A greedy self-righteousness.

[96] *Jesus Christ, by His own unmerited offerings and death made satisfaction for all the sins of the sons of Adam.* 8th decree in Acta et Decreta cited by J.M. Neale, op. cit., p. 307.

[97] This law is expressed as love of God against the evils of greed. 8th decree in Acta et Decreta, op. cit., p. 308.

[98] This infallibility, as for Bishop Varlet, concerns *all things set forth as to be believed regarding faith and morals*. 4th decree in Acta et Decreta, op. cit., p. 304.

[99] Fourth report of the 1st Committee. Cited by J.M. Neale, op. cit., p. 303.

[100] Third report of the 1st Committee, op. cit.

[101] Idem.

[102] *The Church of Utrecht was waiting for the day of its liberation which, as written by the followers of the great Port-Royalist, would happen when Israel would be returned to the homeland of the patriarchs Abraham, Isaac and Jacob.* E. Lagerwey, *Utrecht, centre d'unité*, op. cit., p. 68.

[103] C. Muller, op. cit., p. 24.

[104] Bishop J.H. Reinkens, Pastoral Letter of August 11, 1872 in R.I.T, Jan.- March 1901, p. 1-6.

[105] Allocution of Bishop Reinkens to the Congress of Cologne on September 20, 1872. Cited by C. Muller, op. cit., p. 28.

[106] Justification by faith alone, divine adoption, triumph of God's reign in the souls under the action of grace.

[107] *The Altkatholische opposition was from the beginning, not only against the infallibility of the pope's doctrinal decisions, although this has been put forward by the opponents, but equally against the dogma teaching that the pope has, by divine right, the fullness of the ordinary jurisdiction over all the pastors and faithful, as a whole and individually.* Herwig Aldenhoven, Der ekklesiologische Selbstverständnis der Altkatholischen Kirchen, op. cit., p. 402-403.

[108] V. Conzemius, *Aspects ecclésiologiques de Döllinger et du vieux-catholicisme* in <u>Revue des sciences religieuses</u>, Nos. 2-3-4, 1960, p. 260, note 51.

[109] V. Conzemius, op. cit., p. 160-161.

[110] Taken from St. Vincent of Lerins but already formulated by Bossuet.

[111] Memory and representation of the unique sacrifice of Christ, performed as a sacred meal, in which believers receive the Body and Blood of Christ and are in mutual communion.

[112] Introduction of new dogmas motivated by reasons of worldly power.

[113] Among the first authors from outside the church to raise the issue are: J. Carreyre (op. cit., col. 2430, 2443), V. Conzemius (op. cit., p. 267, 269, 271, 275), Ch. M. (op. cit., p. 85), A. Malet (op. cit., p. 251 & 271) and C. Muller (op. cit., p. 45, 55-58). From inside the church, ten years after Bishop Küry, the problem was mentioned by others, including Liliane Krämer in the article *Appelés à vivre dans la plénitude* published in <u>Présence catholique-chrétienne</u>, October 1982, p. 84.

[114] The pastoral letter was published in the book <u>Chemins vers la vérité</u>, Labor & Fides, Geneva, 1980, p. 254-256.

[115] Urs Küry, op. cit., p. 255.

[116] Idem, p. 256.

[117] To the extent that there is Varletian continuity in the words of Bishop Reinkens, we can infer that there was fidelity to the Gallicano-Jansenist ecclesiology of early Dutch O.B.C.

[118] The first three periods are those established by Victor Conzemius (op. cit., p. 276).

[119] R.I.T., Vol. 15, 1907, p. 37.

[120] Idem, p. 290.

[121] R. Keussen, *Der Katholizismus und seine Ideale*, I.K.Z., 1924, p. 92.

[122] R. Keussen, op. cit.

[123] Idem.

[124] Urs Küry, *Christus und die Kirche in der theologischen Lehre*, I.K.Z., Vol. 46, 1957, p. 35-66.

[125] Urs Küry in <u>Chemins vers la vérité</u>, p. 256.

[126] Urs Küry, op. cit., p. 138.

[127] Kurt Stalder, *Ekklesiologie und Rechtsstruktur der Utrechter Union der altkatholischen Bishöfe*, <u>Kracht in Zwakheid van een kleine Wereldkerk: De Oud-Katholieke Unie van Utrecht</u>, Amersfoort, 1982, p. 266.

[128] The central performance of Bishop Varlet's theological program is as follows: by the merits of the Blood of Jesus Christ, we pass from perdition to salvation, from injustice to justice.

[129] Peter Amiet, *Ortskirche – Universalkirche, Amt un Bezeugung der Wahrheit*, IKZ, January-March 1982, p. 33-34. It is the experience of salvation within the Church which is accentuated by Professor Amiet and his colleagues Aldenhoven and Stalder. See the note 144 on the issue of the Filioque, p. 266.

[130] Herwig Aldnhoven, op. cit., p. 401-430.

[131] Kurt Stalder, op. cit., p. 114.

[132] *Outside the Church, whose soul is the Spirit, we cannot see the salvation of God*, said Bishop Varlet.

[133] P. Amiet, *Zum altkatholischen Kirchenverständnis*, <u>Okumenische Rundschau</u>, June 1981, p. 48. Döllinger resumes the vaticination of Joachim of Flores, the spiritual millennarist whose influence on the ecclesiology of Bishop Varlet was mentioned. But if he quoted the Prevost of Munich, Prof. Amiet did not assume his phenomenology.

[134] Yves Congar, <u>Vraie et fausse réforme dans l'Église</u>, Paris, 1950, p. 526.

[135] A system, as shown in the papal dogmas, that puts the ecclesiology in the wake of new canonical norms arising from the claims of universal jurisdiction of the Bishop of Rome. H. Aldenhoven, op. cit., p. 403. In this way, the authority of the thinking-function, according to Professor Keussen (op. cit., p. 92), can be maintained only as a legal entity.

[136] The Holy Spirit is nourished by that communion. D.M. Varlet, <u>Recueil alphabétique</u>..., p. 14. Professors Aldenhoven, Amiet and Stalder emphasize this aspect of "koinonia" in favor of salvation experienced in the Church (its intra-church character).

[137] The experience of faith builts the Body of Christ. D.M. Varlet, op. cit.

[138] Bishop Varlet spoke of the *pharisaism* (hypocrisy) born of greed.

[139] H. Aldenhoven, op. cit., p. 402.

[140] Id teneamus quod ubique, quod semper, quod ab omnibus creditum est; hoc est enim vere proprieque catholicum.

[141] V. Conzmius, op. cit., p. 262.

[142] Léon Gauthier, *Actualité de saint Vincent de Lérins* in <u>Kracht in Zwakheid van een kleine Wereldkerk</u>, Amersfoort, 1982, p. 104-105..

[143] K. Stalder, Ekklesiologie..., op. cit., p. 104-105.

[144] The rapport of the outpouring of the Holy Spirit with the life of the Church. H. Aldenhoven, *Geist Gottes – Geist Christi*, Verlag Otto Lembeck, Frankfurt, 1981, <u>Beiblatt zur ökumenischen Rundschau</u>, No. 39, p. 134-143. The Filioque in the Old Catholic Churches (...) and the Ecclesiastical opinions. <u>Beiblatt zur ökumenischen Rundschau</u>, op. cit., p. 89-99. It must be stated that unlike Bishop Varlet, the pneumatology of the Union of Utrecht does not accept the "Filioque procedit". There is a difference of perspective: The Holy Spirit is not so much the Spirit of Jesus Christ as that of the Father who makes Jesus recognized as Lord. For Bishop Varlet's position on the Filioque, see Appendix 5, note 76.

[145] P. Amiet, *Ortskirche – Universalkirche*..., op. cit., p. 35.

[146] K. Stalder, *Ekklesiologie und Rechtsstruktur*....., p. 11.

[147] Loc. cit.

[148] P. Amiet, op. cit., p. 34.

[149] Idem, p. 35. See also, in Appendix 4, Bishop Varlet's Trinitarian view of ecclesiology.

[150] Imperfect, the Church has her infallibility from the Word infallible, R.I.T., Vol. 15, 1907, p. 290. But Michaud does not explicitly link the sanctification of the believers with the Holy Spirit and the infallibility of the Church from which she has her authority.

[151] These various objects, which circulate in the ecclesiological system of Bishop Varlet, were present at the Synod of Utrecht in 1763.

152   It was not until the 19th century that the question of ecclesiology in relation to the pneumatic aspect of ecclesiology has gained importance in the Roman Catholic theology. The concerns of Bishop Varlet and the Old Catholics seem, in this respect ahead of their time. L'Ecclésiologie au 19e siècle, Unam Sanctam, Paris, 1960.

153   The first woman was ordained priest in Germany in 1996. Freedom of choice was left to member churches of the Utrecht Union in 1997.

154   It is a rite of blessing and not the celebration of a marriage which stays specific to the man-woman relationship in the light of the theology of creation. H. Rein, *Report of the (Swiss Church) Commission Church & Homosexuality*, Supplement No. 4, Présence catholique-chrétienne, Switzerland, Vol. 98, No. 6, July-August 2006.

155   German Old Catholics have entered into an intercommunion agreement with Lutherans and all West European Old Catholic churches now follow the practice of open communion.... West European Old Catholic representatives also attend, as observers, mettings of the Poorvo Communion, a group of several Anglican and North European Lutheran churches... It is likely that the Bishops Conference will establish a formal relation, whether with the Porvoo group as a whole or with individual member churches (e.g. Sweden). Laurence J. Orzell, *Disunion of Utrecht. Old Catholics Fall Out over New Doctrines*, Touchstone, Chicago, May 2004.

156   The social changes of the last 40 years: evolution that has endorsed the equality between men and women, scientific understanding that we do not choose our sexual orientation. J.C. Mokry in Présence catholique-chrétienne, April 2000, p. 11 and July-August 2006, p. 3; H. Rein, *Report of the Commission Church & Homosexuality*, op. cit. The approval of this report shows the openness of our church to listen to the problems of today's world and the evolution of society. Irene Savoy, *L'ouverture d'esprit de notre église*, Présence catholique-chrétienne, July-August 2006, p. 5.

157   Regarding the ordination of women, already in 1990 the German Old Catholic Church's synod had declared that it was a matter of discipline rather than of doctrine.

158   Though the principal cause of the split was the admission of women to the priesthood by several of the Old Catholic churches, wrote Laurence J. Orzell (op. cit.), the decision reflected longstanding tensions between the "progressive" majority and the P.N.C.C. over other issues, such as homosexuality and ecumenism... On April 28, 2008, the bishops of the P.N.C.C. wrote in a document called Declaration of Scranton:"*We reject the contemporary innovations promulgated by the Anglican Communion and the Old Catholic Churches of the Union of Utrecht. We also regard these innovations as being in defiance of the Holy Scriptures and in contradiction to*

the Tradition of the first centuries, namely: the ordination of women to the Holy Priesthood, the consecration of women to the Episcopate and the blessing of same-sex unions." As for the Slovakian Church, we can read on their website: (*In 2003) the Utrecht Union arrived at a critical point, when because of new attitude which was in conflict with authentic Catholic doctrine, the biggest church, the Polish National Catholic Church in USA and Canada separated from the Utrecht Union. The Old Catholic Church in Slovakia decided in a special synod in 2004 to separate from it and joined the World Council of National Catholic Churches.* www.slovenski-katolici.sk

[159] Hoffman von Fallersleben, Gesammelte Werke, edited by Heinrich Gerstenberg (Berlin, 1892), 6: 54; cf. A. Eekhof, De Zinspreuk In Necessariis Unitas, In Non Necessariis Libertas, In Utrisque Caritas: Eenheid in het Noodige, Vrijheid in het Niet Noodige, in Beide de Liefde: Oorsprong, Beteekenis en Verbreiding (Leiden: A.W. Sijthhoff's Uitgevermaatschappij, 1931), 77-8.

[160] Act of Appeal to the General Council, op. cit., p. 16.

[161] Commentary on the Acts of the Apostles, op. cit., p. 14.

[162] L.J. Orzell, op. cit.

[163] Idem.

[164] http://de.wikipedia.org/wiki/Liste_christlicher_Konfessionen

[165] Bishop Rudolf de Landas Berghe de Rache arrived in the U.S.A. in November 1914. He ordained and consecrated priestly pioneers including William Francis Brothers (1887-1979) and Carmel H. Carfora (1878-1958) from whom came a network of communities, along the design of primitive christianity. http://en.allexperts.com/e/o/ol/old_catholic_church.htm

[166] Published in The Guardian on January 6, 1911.

[167] *The Holy Sacraments,* wrote Bishop Mathew, *should be administered only to those who are members of the Holy Catholic Church, not only by Baptism, but by the profession of the Catholic Faith in its integrity, by repudiation of all heresies, by rejection of any bond of union, and refusal of actual communion, with all persons and sects professing unorthodox beliefs... Unhappily, we find persons who are not Catholics (...) are now admitted (...) to receive Holy Communion in all Old Catholic places of worship on the continent. Moreover, clergymen of the Anglican Communion (...) have been permitted to celebrate the "Service for the Administration of the Holy Communion" from the* Book of Common Prayer, *at the Old Catholic Altars... "West European Old Catholic leaders (...),* wrote L.J. Orzell (op. cit), *have come under liberal Anglican influence as a result of their full communion with the Church of England under the terms of the Bonn Agreement (1931)."* A similar view is expressed in Alan

M. Cole's book The Old Catholic Phenomenon (Avon Books, London, 1997): "Anglicanism and Old Catholicism are now fallen or falling away from the Catholic Faith." Also in the *Declaration of Scranton (P.N.C.C.)* of April 28, 2008: "We reject the contemporary innovations promulgated by the Anglican Communion and the Old Catholic Churches of the Union of Utrecht (that we regard) as being in defiance of the Holy Scriptures and in contradiction to the Tradition of the first centuries."

CONCLUSION

The administration of the sacrament of confirmation in a church deprived of a bishop in April 1719 was the occasion and the starting point of the adventure that was going to make Bishop Varlet pass to history. Everything originates in this pastoral event: the consolidation of his Jansenist and Gallican convictions, his determination to liberate the "truth of God" from the injustice and the assurance that the visible, institutional church, is not the Kingdom announced in the prophecies of the Old Testament. There would have been no consecration in 1724, nor the establishment of the Kerk der O.B.C. without the tragic finding that the reign of God in the soul could be thwarted by the very person who acknowledges himself as having the ultimate responsibility of shepherding the flock of Jesus Christ, that is to say, the Pope. The opposition made in the Première Apologie,[1] between the realization of justice by the ministry and its hindrance by the hypocrisy of Rome is in this regard of primary importance. It is the central isotopy on which is built the theological understanding of Bishop Varlet's action in favor of the Chapter of Utrecht.

The term "justice", we have shown, homologates the whole domain of the competence to be the Church. The Jansenist convictions give the mode and the aspects of the operation. Modal is the Redemption that justifies the humans before God, making them beneficiaries of the grace that makes them see the salvation in the Holy Spirit. Is aspectual the Christian praxis resulting from divine adoption. Bishop Varlet summarizes the problematique with the idea of "faith translated into action". What we have expressed with the terms orthodoxy and orthopraxis. The link between the two is so necessary that the absence of one presumes the non-existence of the other. An example of this is the dispute over probabilism. We see that the aspectual dimension of the conflict rests with the Vatican. A conflict that is expressed in a series of two opposites: supremacy of Scripture vs. living magisterium, attrition vs. contrition, Synodalism vs. Vaticanism ...

Bishop Varlet's thesis can be summarized as follows: Rome precludes that faith translates into action. To the primacy of the Kingdom of God, it opposes that, temporal, of the greedy institution. This he explains to Benedict XIII when he writes that the Word, who ran with speed in the world, was stopped,[2] calling to mind the argument of the anti-Roman magisterium used by the opponents to the Bull Unigenitus. We approach this way the issue of the antithesis of justice: pharisaism. The homologation of this second term operates in making the Gallican claim identical to the "defense of the truth" (another way of expressing the problem of the competence to be the Church). This operation has for postulate the difference between the Church and the Kingdom.

Renewing with the pre-Nicene ecclesiology and the spiritualist intuitions of Joachim of Flores, Bishop Varlet re-reads the Book of Revelation and feels authorized by Scripture to advocate the establishment of the Kingdom through Christ, who will end the injustice (Babylon) which is in the Church. The persecution perpetrated against the elect is the proof that we should not rely on the ecclesiastical power (epiphenomenon of the influence of the Beast (Rev. 12), but on Christ who alone has the capability to release his saints. Meanwhile, we must hold on the wisdom contained in the rescripts of the councils to guide us in being the true Church. This is what we read in the Apology. Canon law is the beacon that marks out the dynamics of the provisional. He uses it to establish the legitimacy to gather the believers around the faithful bishops, these "angels of the Church who struggles on earth." [3] A legitimacy denied by the Roman hierarchy, incarnation of Babylon. The intent is clear in his correspondence with the "prisoner of Jesus Christ",[4] Jean Soanen, bishop of Senez.

Perhaps too much emphasis was put on the canonical aspect of Bishop Varlet's discourse. Believing it necessary to remain in communion with the Church (it is by making God reign in the souls we escape from Babylon[5], that is to say spiritually), he chose to argue on the need for rules to obtain the conversion of the "stewards of the mysteries of God" (have them pass from injustice to justice) and to reform the Church. But this is not the core of his contribution.

Bishop Charles J. Colbert of Montpellier, is perhaps the one who best captured the traits of Msgr. Varlet. His conviction to see in him "the bishop of a happier century", is expressed by a set of contrasts on his doctrine (strong but measured ideas) and his personality (a courage mixed with patience and gentleness).[6] This is consistent with the perception people had of him in Quebec: a conqueror courageous and ardent[7] on behalf of the gospel,[8] with a great heart[9] that rendered his friendship precious.[10]

Bishop Varlet does not correspond to the image that gave of him the historian Auguste Gosselin: the masked man who merited in Quebec (being elevated to the episcopate) and the real man, the Jansenist rebel who acted in a reprehensible manner in Holland to the point of being excommunicated by three popes.[11] He has nothing either of the "simple man, with no general views and made to be guided," that Maximin Deloche thought of having discovered behind the pencil strokes of Jacob Folkena.[12]

To attain to the true characteristics of the reformer, one must see him arrive in Montreal with his wooden boat, after an unimaginable journey, on lakes and rivers, from Cahokia, Illinois. One must have been witness, as the bishop, the people of the seminary and the members of the cathedral chapter of Quebec, of his zeal for the salvation of souls, that brought the authorities to reinvest in the Indian missions while the trend was rather to abandon them. One must see him set out for Persia with his Arabic grammar and dictionary, eager to communicate the sacred mysteries to Christians he knew in danger of losing faith. Finally, we must remember his great solicitude for the people of the Church of Utrecht who had been sacrificed to the whims of Babylon who is in the Church.

Bishop Colbert, whose letter is from the first years of the establishment in Holland (1727), is a reliable source. What he says about the doctrine of Bishop Varlet summarizes what we must remember: the strength and the measure. The first term supports the Jansenist devotion of the missionary and prophet; the second, the Gallican protest of legal (canonical) tone. One is in line with the courage, the other with that of patience. The specificity of the reform lies in the marriage, difficult to realize, between the two components.

The strong ideas, originated from evangelical piety, tend to shatter the structures by a power of truth which concedes nothing to greed. Those measured, of the doctor of the Sorbonne, moderate desires of heart that the charismatic exaltation could make sink into fanatism. Someone who knows how to balance impulses as divergent as those of the doctor and the prophet had the bark to mark the religious history with his footprint. He took up an unusual challenge: to stay in balance between the radical enthusiasm described in Matt. 13:44-46 (which can lead outside the path of Catholicity) and the temperance of the agape, that St. Clement of Rome strove to teach to the Corinthians, referring to the Acts of the Apostles[13] and the Pastoral Epistles[14] in favor of maintaining the *episkope*, the worthy overseeing of God.[15] From this point of view, the reform initiated by Bishop Varlet is still valid for today's Christians who are torn between evangelical freedom and Catholic fidelity.

Bishop Varlet is a beacon lit on the sea of the imponderable balance of the Church, between Babylon and the Kingdom.

Notes

---

1. D.M. Varlet, op. cit., p. 25.
2. D.M. Varlet, Letter to Pope Benedict XIII, August 4, 1724, op. cit., p. 61.
3. To the Bishop of Senez, September 25, 1735, in Lettres..., BAnQ, p. 149.
4. This is the title Bishop Soanen used at the end of his letters, after his imprisonment.
5. D.M. Varlet, Commentary on the Book of Revelation, op. cit., p. 35-36.
6. Bishop Colbert to Bishop Varlet, November 4, 1727. A.P.R. 3651.
7. Lettres du Canada et de la Louisiane, P.U.Q., p. 64.
8. Idem, p. 61.
9. Idem, p. 63.
10. Idem, p. 64.
11. A. Gosselin, op. cit., p. 333-334.
12. M. Deloche, op. cit., p. 41.
13. Acts 14:23; 20:17 & 28.
14. 1 Timothy 3:1-10, 5:17-22; Titus 1:5-9.
15. Job 10:12; Wisdom 1:6.

APPENDIXES

1
The Five Propositions

From the Bull Cum Occasione, May 31, 1653

1.
Some of God's precepts are impossible to the just, who wish and strive to keep them, according to the present powers which they have; the grace, by which they are made possible, is also wanting. Declared and condemned as rash, impious, blasphemous, condemned by anathema, and heretical.

2.
In the state of fallen nature one never resists interior grace. Declared and condemned as heretical.

3.
In order to merit or demerit in the state of fallen nature, freedom from necessity is not required in man, but freedom from external compulsion is sufficient. Declared and condemned as heretical.

4.
The Semipelagians admitted the necessity of a prevenient interior grace for each act, even for the beginning of faith; and in this they were heretics, because they wished this grace to be such that the human will could either resist or obey. Declared and condemned as false and heretical.

5.
It is Semipelagian to say that Christ died or shed His blood for all men without exception. Declared and condemned as false, rash, scandalous, and understood in this sense, that Christ died for the salvation of the predestined, impious, blasphemous, contumelious, dishonoring to divine piety, and heretical.

2
101 Propositions of Pasquier Quesnel Condemned by the Bull Unigenitus Issued on Sept. 8, 1713

1. What else remains for the soul that has lost God and His grace except sin and the consequences of sin, a proud poverty and a slothful indigence, that is, a general impotence for labor, for prayer, and for every good work?

2. The grace of Jesus Christ, which is the efficacious principle of every kind of good, is necessary for every good work; without it, not only is nothing done, but nothing can be done.

3. In vain, O Lord, do You command, if You do not give what you command.

4. Thus, O Lord, all things are possible to him for whom You make all things possible by effecting those same things in him.

5. When God does not soften a heart by the interior unction of His grace, exterior exhortations and graces are of no service except to harden it the more.

6. The difference between the Judaic dispensation and the Christian is this, that in the former God demanded flight from sin and a fulfillment of the Law by the sinner, leaving him in his own weakness; but in the latter, God gives the sinner what He commands, by purifying him with His grace.

7. What advantage was there for a man in the old covenant, in which God left him to his own weakness, by imposing on him His law? But what happiness is it not to be admitted to a convenant in which God gives us what He asks of us?

8. But we do not belong to the new covenant, except in so far as we are participators in that new grace which works in us that which God commands us.

9. The grace of Christ is a supreme grace, without which we can never confess Christ, and with which we never deny Him.

10. Grace is the working of the omnipotent hand of God, which nothing can hinder or retard.

11. Grace is nothing else than the omnipotent Will of God, ordering and doing what He orders.

12. When God wishes to save a soul, at whatever time and at what ever place, the undoubted effect follows the Will of God.

13. When God wishes to save a soul and touches it with the interior hand of His grace, no human will resists Him.

14. Howsoever remote from salvation an obstinate sinner is, when Jesus presents Himself to be seen by him in the salutary light of His grace, the sinner is forced to surrender himself, to have recourse to Him, and to humble himself, and to adore his Savior.

15. When God accompanies His commandment and His eternal exhortation by the unction of His Spirit and by the interior force of His grace, He works that obedience in the heart that He is seeking.

16. There are no attractions which do not yield to the attractions of grace, because nothing resists the Almighty.

17. Grace is that voice of the Father which teaches men interiorly and makes them come to Jesus Christ; whoever does not come to Him, after he has heard the exterior voice of the Son, is in no wise taught by the Father.

18. The seed of the word, which the hand of God nourishes, always brings forth its fruit.

19. The grace of God is nothing else than His omnipotent Will; this is the idea which God Himself gives us in all His Scriptures.

20. The true idea of grace is that God wishes Himself to be obeyed by us and He is obeyed; He commands, and all things are done; He speaks as the Lord, and all things are obedient to Him.

21. The grace of Jesus Christ is a strong, powerful, supreme, invincible grace, that is, the operation of the omnipotent Will, the consequence and imitation of the operation of God causing the incarnation and the resurrection of His Son.

22. The harmony of the all powerful operation of God in the heart of man with the free consent of mans will is demonstrated, therefore, to us in the Incarnation, as in the fount and archetype of all other operations of mercy and grace, all of which are as gratuitous and as dependent on God as the original operation itself.

23. God Himself has taught us the idea of the omnipotent working of His grace, signifying it by that operation which produces creatures from nothing and which restores life to the dead.

24. The right idea which the centurion had about the omnipotence of God and of Jesus Christ in healing bodies by a single act of His will, [Matt. 8:8] is an image of the idea we should have about the omnipotence of His grace in healing souls from cupidity.

25. God illumines the soul, and heals it, as well as the body, by His will only; He gives orders and He is obeyed.

26. No graces are granted except through faith.

27. Faith is the first grace and the source of all others.

28. The first grace which God grants to the sinner is the remission of sin.

29. Outside of the Church, no grace is granted.

30. All whom God wishes to save through Christ. are infallibly saved.

31. The desires of Christ always have their effect; He brings peace to the depth of hearts when He desires it for them.

32. Jesus Christ surrendered Himself to death to free forever from the hand of the exterminating angel, by His blood, the first born, that is, the elect.

33. Ah, how much one ought to renounce earthly goods and himself for this, that he may have the confidence of appropriating, so to speak, Christ Jesus to himself, His love, death, and mysteries, as St. Paul does, when he says: "He who loved me, and delivered Himself for me" [Gal. 2:20].

34. The grace of Adam produced nothing except human merit.

35. The grace of Adam is a consequence of creation and was due to his whole and sound nature.

36. The essential difference between the grace of Adam and of his state of innocence and Christian grace, is that each one would have received the first in his own person, but the second is not received except in the person of the risen Jesus Christ to whom we are united.

37. The grace of Adam by sanctifying him in himself was proportionate to him; Christian grace, by sanctifying us in Jesus Christ, is omnipotent, and worthy of the Son of God.

38. Without the grace of the Liberator, the sinner is not free except to do evil.

39. The will, which grace does not anticipate, has no light except for straying, no eagerness except to put itself in danger, no strength except to wound itself, and is capable of all evil and incapable of all good.

40. Without grace we can love nothing except to our own condemnation.

41. All knowledge of God, even natural knowledge, even in the pagan philosophers, cannot come except from God; and without grace knowledge produces nothing but presumption, vanity, and opposition to God Himself, instead of the affections of adoration, gratitude, and love.

42. The grace of Christ alone renders a man fit for the sacrifice of faith; without this there is nothing but impurity, nothing but unworthiness.

43. The first effect of baptismal grace is to make us die to sin so that our spirit, heart, and senses have no more life for sin than a dead man has for the things of the world.

44. There are but two loves, from which all our volitions and actions arise: love of God, which does all things because of God and which God rewards; and the love with which we love ourselves and the world, which does not refer to God what ought to be referred to Him, and therefore becomes evil.

45 When love of God no longer reigns in the heart of sinners, it needs must be that carnal desire reign in it and corrupt all of its actions.

46. Cupidity or charity makes the use of the senses good or evil.

47. Obedience to the law ought to flow from the source, and this source is charity. When the love of God is the interior principle of obedience and the glory of God is its end, then that is pure which appears externally; otherwise, it is but hypocrisy and false justice.

48. What else can we be except darkness, except aberration, and except sin, without the light of faith, without Christ, and without charity?

49. As there is no sin without love of ourselves, so there is no good work without love of God.

50. In vain we cry out to God: My Father, if it is not the spirit of charity which cries out.

51. Faith justifies when it operates, but it does not operate except through charity.

52. All other means of salvation are contained in faith as in their own germ and seed; but this faith does not exist apart from love and confidence.

53. Only charity in the Christian way makes (Christian actions) through a relation to God and to Jesus Christ.

54. It is charity alone that speaks to God; it alone that God hears.

55. God crowns nothing except charity; he who runs through any other incentive or any other motive, runs in vain.

56. God rewards nothing but charity; for charity alone honors God.

57. All fails a sinner, when hope fails him; and there is no hope in God, when there is no love of God.

58. Neither God nor religion exists where there is no charity.

59. The prayer of the impious is a new sin; and what God grants to them is a new judgment against them.

60. If fear of punishment alone animates penance, the more intense this is, the more it leads to despair.

61. Fear restrains nothing but the hand, but the heart is addicted to the sin as long as it is not guided by a love of justice.

62. He who does not refrain from evil except through fear of punishment, commits that evil in his heart, and is already guilty before God.

63. A baptized person is still under the law as a Jew, if he does not fulfill the law, or if he fulfills it from fear alone.

64. Good is never done under the condemnation of the law, because one sins either by doing evil or by avoiding it only through fear.

65. Moses, the prophets, priests, and doctors of the Law died without having given any son to God, since they produced only slaves through fear.

66. He who wishes to approach to God, should not come to Him with brutal passions, nor be led to Him by natural instinct, or through fear as animals, but through faith and love, as sons.

67. Servile fear does not represent God to itself except as a stern imperious, unjust, unyielding master.

68. The goodness of God has shortened the road to salvation, by enclosing all in faith and in prayers.

69. Faith, practice of it increase, and reward of faith, all are a gift of the pure liberality of God.

70. Never does God afflict the innocent; and afflictions always serve either to punish the sin or to purify the sinner.

71. For the preservation of himself man can dispense himself from that law which God established for his use.

72. A mark of the Christian Church is that it is catholic, embracing all the angels of heaven, all the elect and the just on earth, and of all times

73. What is the Church except an assembly of the sons of God abiding in His bosom, adopted in Christ, subsisting in His person, redeemed by His blood, living in His spirit, acting through His grace, and awaiting the grace of the future life?

74. The Church or the whole Christ has the Incarnate Word as head but all the saints as members.

75. The Church is one single man composed of many members, of which Christ is the head, the life, the subsistence and the person- it is one single Christ composed of many saints, of whom He is the sanctifier

76. There is nothing more spacious than the Church of God; because all the elect and the just of all ages comprise it.

77. He who does not lead a life worthy of a son of God and a member of Christ, ceases interiorly to have God as a Father and Christ as a head.

78. One is separated from the chosen people, whose figure was the Jewish people, and whose head is Jesus Christ, both by not living according to the Gospel and by not believing in the Gospel.

79. It is useful and necessary at all times, in all places, and for every kind of person, to study and to know the spirit, the piety, and the mysteries of Sacred Scripture.

80. The reading of Sacred Scripture is for all.

81. The sacred obscurity of the Word of God is no reason for the laity to dispense themselves from reading it.

82. The Lord's Day ought to be sanctified by Christians with readings of pious works and above all of the Holy Scriptures. It is harmful for a Christian to wish to withdraw from this reading.

83. It is an illusion to persuade oneself that knowledge of the mysteries of religion should not be communicated to women by the reading of Sacred Scriptures. Not from the simplicity of women, but from the proud knowledge of men has arisen the abuse of the Scriptures and have heresies been born.

84. To snatch away from the hands of Christians the New Testament, or to hold it closed against them by taking away from them the means of understanding it, is to close for them the mouth of Christ.

85. To forbid Christians to read Sacred Scripture, especially the Gospels, is to forbid the use of light to the sons of light, and to cause them to suffer a kind of excommunication.

86. To snatch from the simple people this consolation of joining their voice to the voice of the whole Church is a custom contrary to the apostolic practice and to the intention of God.

87. A method full of wisdom light, and charity is to give souls time for bearing with humility. and for experiencing their state of sin, for seeking the spirit of penance and contrition, and for beginning at least to satisfy the justice of God, before they are reconciled.

88. We are ignorant of what sin is and of what true penance is, when we wish to be restored at once to the possession of the goods of which sin has despoiled us, and when we refuse to endure the confusion of that separation.

89. The fourteenth step in the conversion of a sinner is that, after he has already been reconciled, he has the right of assisting at the Sacrifice of the Church.

90. The Church has the authority to excommunicate, so that it may exercise it through the first pastors with the consent, at least presumed, of the whole body.

91. The fear of an unjust excommunication should never hinder us from fulfilling our duty; never are we separated from the Church, even when by the wickedness of men we seem to be expelled from it, as long as we are attached to God, to Jesus Christ, and to the Church herself by charity.

92. To suffer in peace an excommunication and an unjust anathema rather than betray truth, is to imitate St. Paul; far be it from rebelling against authority or of destroying unity.

93 Jesus sometimes heals the wounds which the precipitous haste of the first pastors inflicted without His command. Jesus restored what they, with inconsidered zeal, cut off.

94. Nothing engenders a worse opinion of the Church among her enemies than to see exercised there an absolute rule over the faith of the faithful, and to see divisions fostered because of matters which do not violate faith or morals.

95. Truths have descended to this, that they are, as it were, a foreign tongue to most Christians, and the manner of preaching them is, as it were, an unknown idiom, so remote is the manner of preaching from the simplicity of the apostles. and so much above the common grasp of the faithful; nor is there sufficient advertence to the fact that this defect is one of the greatest visible signs of the weakening of the Church and of the wrath of God on His sons.

96. God permits that all powers be opposed to the preachers of truth, so that its victory cannot be attributed to anyone except to divine grace.

97. Too often it happens that those members, who are united to the Church more holily and more strictly, are looked down upon, and treated as if they were unworthy of being in the Church, or as if they were separated from Her; but, "the just man liveth by faith" [Rom. 1:17], and not by the opinion of men.

98. The state of persecution and of punishment which anyone endures as a disgraceful and impious heretic, is generally the final trial and is especially meritorious, inasmuch as it makes a man more conformable to Jesus Christ.

99. Stubbornness, investigation, and obstinacy in being unwilling either to examine something or to acknowledge that one has been deceived daily changes into an odor, as it were, of death, for many people, that which God has placed in His Church to be an odor of life within it, for instance, good books, instructions, holy examples, etc.

100. Deplorable is the time in which God is believed to be honored by persecution of the truth and its disciples! This time has come.... To be considered and treated by the ministers of religion as impious and unworthy of all commerce with God, as a putrid member capable of corrupting everything in the society of saints, is to pious men a more terrible death than the death of the body. In vain does anyone flatter himself on the purity of his intentions and on a certain zeal for religion, when he persecutes honest men with fire and sword, if he is blinded by his own passion or carried away by that of another on account of which he does not want to examine anything. We frequently believe that we arc sacrificing an impious man to God, when we are sacrificing a servant of God to the devil.

101. Nothing is more opposed to the spirit of God and to the doctrine of Jesus Christ than to swear common oaths in Church, because this is to multiply occasions of perjury, to lay snares for the weak and inexperienced, and to cause the name and truth of God to serve sometimes the plan of the wicked.

3
Letters Patent issued by Bishop St. Vallier
6 October 1717

We, John, by the grace of God and the Holy Apostolic See, Bishop of Quebec in New France, to all whom these present letters shall come, greeting and blessing in Our Lord.

Although by our Letters Patent of July 14, 1698 we have granted to the Superiors and Directors of the Seminary of Foreign Missions of Quebec a special power to send missionaries among the Tamaroa Indians and to make such residences, settlements, and missions as they would judge suitable, considering that the places where the said Tamaroa Indians live are the key so to speak and the necessary passage to the tribes farther in the interior and so make access easy for them, now <u>M. Varlet, our Vicar-general</u> of missionaries to the Tamaroa Indians, having represented to us that before he can arrive at the said mission a considerable time will have passed without the Seminary of Quebec being able to send any missionaries to fill the place of M. Bergier who died there while laboring for the conversion of the said Indians, he fears that our said Letter Patent of 14 July 1698 may be regarded as expired and that missionaries of some other order may pretend to dispute the possession of the said seminary; he has therefore begged us to give him new letters patent confirmatory of those preceding ones.

We, wishing to favor the zeal of the said Seminary for the conversion of the infidels, and having regard for the representations that have been made to us by M. Varlet, have authorized and do authorize the said Superior and Directors of the said Seminary of Quebec to continue their missions among the Tamaroas, confirming by these patents those which we sent to them the 14th of July 1698 as well as those of the first day of May in the same year 1698 by which we granted to the said Superior and Directors full power to settle themselves and form missions among all the tribes who are on both sides of the river Mississipi and all the length of this river and of its tributaries, confirming moreover the contents of the said letters, revoking by these patents all other letters and powers we may have granted to others, if any such are found contrary to these presents. We reserving the power, when the said missionaries of the Foreign Missions of Quebec abandon the said place, to give the said Mission of the Tamaroas to whom we think fit in order that the souls do not remain abandoned.

Given at Quebec under our hand and that of our secretary, and sealed with the seal of our arms this 6th day of October 1717.

Jean evesque de quebec

FAC-SIMILE OF THE SIGNATURE OF BISHOP SAINT VALLIER.

4
The Holy Trinity in Bishop Varlet's Theology

This text is based on our article *La sainte trinité dans la théologie de Mgr Dominique Varlet à l'origine du vieux-catholicisme* published in I.K.Z., Oct.-Dec. 1983, p. 235-245.

Bishop Varlet sees the Church as a *locus salutis* (place of salvation) between the first and the second comings of Christ. Specific areas such as the role of the Holy Spirit in the acquisition and exercise of the infallibility which gives the Church her authority, reveal a continuity in the Old Catholic discourse from the time the Kerk der O.B.C. was formed till today. There is a similarity of view between Bishop Varlet and the theologians of the Faculty of Berne in that the infallibility does not depend on the living magisterium[1] but on the sanctification of the believers under the influence of the Holy Spirit who makes us translate faith into action in reference to Christ. This appears in the different editions of the Internationale Kirchlische Zeitschfrit (I.K.Z.).

We must however qualify this statement. The Old Catholic theologians of Berne have accentuated the intra-ecclesial dimension of salvation based on a Trinitarian scheme.[2] But Bishop Varlet gives the impression of promoting a more individualistic view. May be understood in that sense the special relationship he establishes between the elect and God, and his relativization of the institutional church in favor of the spiritual reign in the souls of the redeemed.

In this text, we present the Trinitarian perspective of Bishop Varlet's theology and indicate the form it takes in the representation of the Church.

Bishop Varlet on the Three Persons of the Trinity

Let's precise, as a start, that beyond an explicit reference to the Trinity in the *Commentary on the Acts of the Apostles*,[3] we do not find other clear mentions of the term in his work. But this does not render our project vain. There are two reasons to that. First, the experience of Trinitarian life is mentioned in connection with baptism. And this sacrament is central to Bishop Varlet's ecclesiology. It is through baptism that we experience the death-life passage (death to sin and life in Christ)[4] and enter the Body of Christ. Secondly, it is "a form established by Jesus Christ".[5] This reference to Christ is the means through which he states his faith in God the Father, Son and Holy Spirit. Therefore it is necessary to start with the representation of the Son to reach that of the two other persons of the Trinity.

The Son: God Equal to his Father

Bishop Varlet's understanding of the Son is presented in his interpretation of the event of the Ascension: *He was brought into the secret of the Father, from where He came.*[6] This understanding has implications on his idea of Jesus and of his relation to the Father, whom he shares the intimacy. Although He has a *true human nature*,[7]

He is *equal to God the Father*.[8] God does not dwell in him as in the prophets of the Old Testament[9] because He is from all eternity.[10] Following Clement of Alexandria, Cyprian, Eusebius, Tertullian and Origen, he assimilates Him with the Creator-Wisdom[11] who had her delights with the sons of men (Proverbs 8:22-31).

We must take into account a set of appropriations that is not without consequence for what Bishop Varlet says about the Father and the Son. The Messiah[12] accomplishes the redemption in the wake of the act of creation described in Genesis 1: "He makes us retrace in our hearts the *demut*, the likeness of God (Genesis 1:26-27) that sin has erased." [13] Therefore he can say with Dionysius of Alexandria[14] that "Christ is the Son and Lord for those who repent." [15]

Bishop Varlet shares the Christology of the Alexandrian Fathers: an emphasis is placed on the deity. "Our Lord pre-existed his historical insertion as Jesus of Nazareth. He "appeared" to speak of the Kingdom of God." [16] He made miracles by his own force without demanding the Father to give hear to him (He knows that He always does) because it is the same God who acts.[17] The chains that break in the resurrection to let him return to the Father had no power over him.[18] In fact, He is in the world (He ate at Emmaus after the resurrection[19]) without being of it. As the incarnation of the Divine Wisdom, He can have no acquaintance with the wisdom of the humans which is foolish in the eyes of God.[20] The strong emphasis he places on the opposition between the two wisdoms tends to relativize the Jesus of history[21] in favor of Christ as the "Word made flesh who dwelt among us, full of grace and truth; whose glory we have beheld, glory as of the only Son from the Father" (John 1:14). What matters for Bishop Varlet is that in Jesus of Nazareth, the humans discover that they are beneficiaries of an existence for God. The Messiah is the Servant, the *Ebed* announced by Isaiah,[22] who rebuilts the disfigured humans and makes them worthy to appear before God who has created them in His image and likeness.

Although it is not written as such, the representation functions as a surdetermination of the *ruah*[23] of Genesis (1:2) by the *logos* of Proverbs (8:22) and the prologue of St. John's gospel (1:1-18).[24] The divine outpouring which has organized the chaos (Genesis 1:1-2) is personalized in the Creator-Wisdom, then in the Logos, "hail for the hardened and fruits for the goods." [25] In any case, it is from the role of the Divine Word in refiguring the humans (their reintegration into the "Demut" YHWH) that are evoked the traits of the Father and the Spirit.

God the Father as YHWH

The role of the Logos-Wisdom in reinserting into *Demut* is summarized by Bishop Varlet in the terms of *divine adoption*.[26] In Christ we pass from injustice to justice (we are saved) and we acknowledge God as the only Lord (Deuteronomy 6:4).[27] The judgement belongs to Him[28] as well as the final establishment of the Kingdom,[29] whose time He is the only one to know.[30] His judgement will be based on the Alliance of the Horeb and the requirements of the Torah.[31] In order to be the Church expressing the divine will,[32] we must observe the commandments of God, the One Who Is: YHWH." [33] To be in the Reign has for postulate the determining event at Mount Horeb.[34] Bishop Varlet emphasizes the Word of God, the incarnate Logos, who makes us remember the great actions of God for his people; bends the human will to will what the Father wants and reveals his universal concern by the gift of tongues to the apostles (Acts 2:4).[35] The Father enlightens the will.[36] This calls for the action of the Holy Spirit, the consuming fire[37] that was poured abundantly in Jesus Christ,[38] the gift from God's mouth.[39]

The Holy Spirit, "Fire of God" and "Gift from his Mouth"

Bishop Varlet defines the Holy Spirit as "the soul of the Church" [40] and specifies that it is only in the Church that he can be received.[41] But by defining Him later as love[42] and charity,[43] he indicates that he sees Him as the soul of the intra-divine communion.

His lines on the third person of the Trinity are the finest and most telling. The Spirit gives heart to the "trium corpus" and reveals the secret of his intimacy. Fire of God,[44] he is also the gift from his mouth.[45] An equation is established between the Love (or the Father) and the Word which expresses Him (the pre-existing Son). Therefore, while shedding light on the specific function of the Father in relation to the *eschaton* (He will definitely establish the Kingdom[46]), the Holy Spirit informs on the role of the Son. As a Word from God, He calls for the conversion in the time between what is already accomplished and what is yet to come. Prodigy of the Father, whose grace He dispenses, the Holy Spirit is also the breath of the Son. And this, in the post-paschal "pneuma" (for the sanctification of the disciples[47]) as in the plenary infusion of Pentecost (for the missionary preaching[48]). Most of the attributes of the Holy Spirit are related to the "kerygma", by which is continued the work of Christ in his Body, the Church, until He gives everything back to the Father. He is a teacher of the truth;[49] a force of eloquence in the Apostles[50] and of change in the souls that Love penetrates.[51] He is also a teacher of the doctrine: He puts it within the reach of ordinary people.[52]

It is through the Holy Spirit that the Trinity takes a concrete form in serving God's Reign, which is the purpose of the Church.

Church and Trinity

At first glance, Bishop Varlet can give the impression of having an ambiguous view of the Trinity. Goes in that sense the use, seemingly ambivalent, of the term "God" to designate both the Father and the Son. There is also another difficulty. This is the meaning of the expression "Our Lord". Generally associated with the post-paschal confession of faith (St. Peter's speech at the beginning of the Acts of the Apostles), we are naturally inclined to apply it to Christ. However, in Bishop Varlet's theology, it is in principle to the One mentioned in Deuteronomy 6:4 that the lordship is attributed.[53] Further complication. The pre-existing Son is also called "Our Lord" independently of the event of Easter (without being separated from it since the Resurrection is defined as the *great and terrible day* in the Commentary on the Acts of the Apostles[54]). Ambiguity regarding the divine persons (Father and Son, but also indirectly, Holy Ghost) and to some extent, the Christian community. Is it the new Israel, the spiritual people who acknowledging the "coming of the times of grace",[55] definitely seals a covenant that had stayed conditional until then? [56]

Bishop Varlet having not left a constructed discourse on the Trinity, we are limited to fragments which need to be systematized to answer these questions.

Fragments Consistent and Integrable

There is in the work of Bishop Varlet enough indications to articulate his Trinitarian view of the Church. Grouped under the headings "Son-God equal to His Father", "God the Father as YHWH" and "the Holy Spirit, fire of God and gift of his mouth", they are part of an integrative structure. Based on Galatians 4 and Romans 8 (Christ sends the Spirit who makes us call God Daddy[57]), this structure is the Prayer of Jesus (Our Father)[58] reported in Matthew 6:9-13 (par. Luke 11:2-4). Its components are: the fatherhood of God (Matt 6:9), the sanctification of His name (Matt 6:9), the coming of his kingdom (Matt 6:10), the fulfilling of His will (Matt 6 10), the forgiveness of sins (Matt 6:12), the deliverance from evil (Matt 6:13) and God as the eternal principle of the reign, power and glory (Matt 6:13).

a) An Eternal Principle of Power and Glory (Matt 6:13)

Everything originates in the Creator,[59] who pours into the chaos of the origins his organizing energy (the ruah) on which depends the direction of the world as a hymn to his glory. This principled energy has two dimensions: it is the Holy Spirit as glorious living expression and the Logos-Wisdom to whom, by faith, is attributed the meaning of humanity and its history. Bishop Varlet who was trained in Hebrew language and culture,[60] is sensitive to the message of the book of Genesis: God's Word creates what He calls with force, as reflected by the redundancy of the formula /God said ... and it was so/. It is understandable that in this context the event of the Horeb take a decisive importance.

b) Whose Name must be hallowed (Matt 6:9)

The book of Exodus is in line with that of Genesis. God who creates by giving meaning to what He calls can only be the foundation of His creatures.[61] The revelation of the divine name to Moses (I am YHWY) is accompanied by a promise of deliverance (the Hebrews are released from Egyptian oppression). The phrase "I am your God" has for corollary the "you shall be my people" of the first Easter. God revels Himself as the Maker of His Reign (put in concrete form through liberating his people and marked out in the Torah. Therefore to be in YHWH is equivalent to observing the commandments.[62] And this, before and after the arrival of the time when He speaks as Father through his Son.

c) God the Father (Matt 6:9)

This third term is the backbone of Bishop Varlet's theology. It illuminates his vision of salvation and the meaning he gives to the advent of Jesus Christ, to the action of the Holy Spirit, to the role of the Church and to the eschaton, the last things.

The mission of Jesus marks the arrival of the "time of grace ", a time when the Spirit is poured out in abundance. With Christ, the Torah is not repealed but radicalized. The novelty of the Alliance in his Blood[63] is that in Jesus, God of Genesis and Exodus is closer than ever to his people. The Word which created the nation under the old law, but that sin had prevented to bear its fruits, is now before us (1 John 1), destroying the distance that separated us from the redeeming Love. For Bishop Varlet, this is the great wonder. By the election of grace,[64] we enter in the fullness of Christ's intimate relationship with God of Whom he announced the coming of the Kingdom.[65]

d) The Coming of the Kingdom (Matt 6:10)

If Love is in a Son the incarnate Word, it is also a purifying fire[66] and a transforming force.[67] God, through grace, gives Himself as the Word that makes us welcome him as Lord, but also as the Spirit which bends our will to want what He wants. Christ and the Holy Spirit are interrelated in the service of one and the same divine Loving Principle. Where the first calls to repentance,[68] the second engages the process by which is operated the change of life.[69] The Church where occurs the advent of the Kingdom is *locus trinitatis* in that the Spirit makes us put into practice what Christ proclaims of the will of the Father.

e) The Accomplishment of His Will (Matt 6:10)

Christ comes into the world to proclaim the Kingdom of God.[70] It is in relation to God "tremens" become "fascinosum", by the way he has drawn near, that one can understand the mission of Jesus. He appeared to do the Father's will and to show his benevolence for the world. So, the recognition of the Son as Christ and Lord is at the same time, the recognition that in Jesus Servant, God is at work to draw all to Him. Lifted up from the earth, Christ draws us by his cross (John 12:32) that leads to eternity. The Blood shed is the premise of the Ascension which is for Bishop Varlet the standpoint of the vocation of the Christians: to be raised to meet the Lord when he comes.[71]

f) The Deliverance from Evil (Matt 6:13) and the Forgiving of Trespasses (Matt 6:12)

The Church, spiritual reality, is grounded in God and continues on her way provisory in the expectation of the final accomplishment of the Kingdom. It is the reign of God in the converted souls, who recognize Christ under the influence of the Holy Spirit.[72]

Jesus showed that He was the expected Messiah by appearing as the Word of liberation. Deliverance from evil (disease and injustice) and of the root of evil (sin). After his resurrection, He breathes on the disciples to remit their sins[73] and at Pentecost, He sends the Holy Spirit upon the Apostles for the expansion of the Kingdom (the mission). This, as an aspect of the ongoing liberation, the spiritual exodus, made through the "Ebed YHWH", by practicing virtue and struggling against the enemies of salvation.[74]

To Sum Up

There is, in the theology of Bishop Varlet, a consistent Trinitarian perspective. We penetrate it by identifying the purpose of the event Jesus: to proclaim the Kingdom of God. The cause of Jesus is the cause of God in the world, the triumph of His will. His personality is fading in favor of the Word which He embodies. He is the eternal Word of the living God, the foundation of everything, who creates and makes alliance for the good of his creatures.

In Jesus Christ, the Revelation is radicalized in proximity in the Spirit who operates in the manner of "fire". He inflames the gift of the Father's mouth, making it fascinating to humans. So, it is in the outpouring love of God through Christ in the Spirit, that salvation is experienced. The church life is understood in reference to this *locus theologicus* that Bishop Varlet defines in terms of divine adoption. The church life is basically the life in God. The arrival of the times of grace marks the disappearance of the gap that separates the human from the source of his being: YHWH. The opposition to the Bull Unigenitus finds there its justification. Living under grace has for corollary the transformation of society into the Body of Christ. And this transformation can only be based on that, radical, of the individual ablazed by love. To this purpose, prior to Pentecost, from which the missionary vocation originates, there is the post-paschal breath on the disciples for the remission of sins. For Bishop Varlet, this is central. In no way can "the election of grace" that makes sinners become saints be tarnished. Hence the struggle that he has waged against attrition and probabilism. The true conversion is expressed by the sorrow of life, proving that the love for God has at least begun.[75]

We touch here an important aspect of Bishop Varlet's understanding of the Church. She is basically the reign of God in the redeemed souls. A view that Hans Küng expresses in his book <u>On Being a Christian</u> (1974). The foundation of the Church, he wrote, "is not primarily a cult or liturgy, a peculiar constitution, a specific organization with defined functions, but only the faithful assertion that Jesus is the Christ." However, this can only be achieved through conversion for the task of the Church is to "serve" the cause of Jesus (which is that of God) and realize it for herself in the Holy Spirit. She is not the Kingdom but shows that it can be actualized by walking "in the footsteps of Jesus as a provisory Church, conscious of her faults and resolved."

5
Bishop Varlet's Plan of a Method to Study Theology and Church History

Treaty 1   THE RELIGION

- Natural, surnatural, faith.
- Truth of the Christian religion.
- Truth of the Catholic religion.
- The Church: her infallibility, the councils, the authority of the Pope, the decisions of the Bishops, canonicity (how to understand it), the Tradition, the use of reasoning in theology.

Treaty 2   THE ATTRIBUTES OF GOD

- The vision of God.
- The person of God: his will, his liberty, his providence, predestination.

Treaty 3   THE HOLY TRINITY

Treaty 4   THE ANGELS

Treaty 5   THE WORK OF THE DAYS

Treaty 6   THE HUMAN ACTIONS

- Their relation to God.
- The invincible ignorance.
- Probability.

Treaty 7   THE SINS

- Mortal and venial.
- Original.
- Children who have died without baptism.

Treaty 8   THE LAWS

- Customary law.
- Old or ancient law.
- New law.

Treaty 9   GRACE

- History of the constitutions.
- Innocence, original nature, fallen nature, necessity of grace.
- Essence of grace.
- Sufficent grace.
- Possibility of the commandments.
- Grace given to all.
- Deserved grace.
- Agreement of liberty with grace.

Treaty 10   JUSTIFICATION AND MERIT

Treaty 11   THE VERTUES OF FAITH, HOPE AND CHARITY

Treaty 12   THE COMMANDMENTS OF GOD AND OF THE CHURCH

Treaty 13   THE INCARNATION

- The prophets.
- Satisfaction of Jesus Christ.
- The person of Jesus Christ.
- The addition to the trisagion.[76]
- Nature, will and science of Jesus Christ.
- The liberty of Jesus Christ, his descent into hell.
- The worship of Christ and of the saints, the use of pictures.

Treaty 14   THE LAST JUDGEMENT

- Purgatory, hell, heaven, resurrection.

Treaty 15   THE SACRAMENTS

- Their effectiveness, their number, their nature

Treaty 16   BAPTISM

- Circumcision, sacrament of the ancient law.

Treaty 17   CONFIRMATION

Treaty 18   HOLY EUCHARIST

- Paschal Mystery of Christ.
- Manner and Form.
- Real Presence.
- Transubstantiation.
- Sacrifice of the Mass.

Treaty 19 PENANCE
- Matter, contrition, confession, absolution, indulgence, censure.

Treaty 20 ANNOINTING OF THE SICK

Treaty 21 HOLY ORDERS
- Re-ordinations.
- Bishops and Chorbishops.[77]
- Priests and Deacons.
- Celibacy.

Treaty 22 MARRIAGE
- Ministers of the sacrament.
- Matter and Form.
- Indissolubility.
- Empediments.
- Polygamy of the Patriarchs.
- Wedding.

Treaty 23 THE HOLY SCRIPTURE
- The different versions: Greek (Septuagint[78]), Latin (Vulgate[79]), Canonical[80] & Deuterocanonical[81] Books.

6
The Declaration of Utrecht

On September 24, 1889, the Old Catholic churches of Germany and Switzerland have joined forces with the Kerk der O.B.C. of Holland and formed the Utrecht Union. They issued a joint statement summarizing their ecclesiastical principles, and the bishops joined in an episcopal conference chaired by the Archbishop of Utrecht.[82] Here follows the text of the statement called Declaration of Utrecht.

In nomine ss. Trinitatis

Johannes Heykamp, Archbishop of Utrecht.
Casparus Johannes Rinkel, Bishop of Haarlem,
Cornelius Diependaal, Bishop of Deventer,
Joseph Hubert Reinkens, Bishop of the Old Catholic Church of Germany,
Eduard Herzog, Bishop of the Christian Catholic Church of Switzerland,

assembled in the Archiepiscopal residence at Utrecht on the twenty fourth day of September, 1889, after invocation of the Holy Spirit, address the following Declaration.

To the Catholic Church.

Being assembled for a conference in response to an invitation from the undersigned Archbishop of Utrecht, we have resolved henceforth to meet from time to time for consultations on subjects of common interest, in conjunction with our assistants, councillors, and theologians.

We deem it appropriate at this our first meeting to summarize in a common declaration the ecclesiastical principles on which we have hitherto exercised and will continue to exercise our episcopal ministry, and which we have repeatedly had occasion to state in individual declarations.

(1) We adhere to the principle of the ancient Church laid down by St Vincent of Lérins in these terms: 'Id teneamus, quod ubique, quod semper, quod ab omnibus creditum est; hoc est etenim vere proprieque catholicum'. Therefore we abide by the faith of the ancient Church as it is formulated in the ecumenical symbols and in the universally accepted dogmatic decisions of the ecumenical synods held in the undivided Church of the first millennium.

(2) We therefore reject as contradicting the faith of the ancient Church and destroying her constitution, the Vatican decrees, promulgated July 18, 1870, concerning the infallibility and the universal episcopate or ecclesiastical plenitude of power of the Roman Pope. This, however, does not prevent us from acknowledging the historic primacy which several ecumenical councils and the Fathers of the ancient Church with the assent of the whole Church have attributed to the Bishop of Rome by recognizing him as the primus inter pares.

(3) We also reject the dogma of the Immaculate Conception promulgated by Pope Pius IX in 1854 as being without foundation in Holy Scriptures and the tradition of the first centuries.

(4) As for the other dogmatic decrees issued by the Bishops of Rome in the last centuries, the bulls Unigenitus and Auctorem fidei, the Syllabus of 1864 etc., we reject them on all such points as are in contradiction with the doctrine of the ancient Church, and do not recognize them as binding. Moreover we renew all those protests which the ancient Catholic Church of Holland has made against Rome in the past.

(5) We refuse to accept the decisions of the Council of Trent in matters of discipline, and we accept its dogmatic decisions only insofar as they agree with the teaching of the ancient Church.

(6) Considering that the Holy Eucharist has always been the true focal point of worship in the Catholic Church, we consider it our duty to declare that we maintain in all faithfulness and without deviation the ancient Catholic doctrine concerning the Holy Sacrament of the Altar, by believing that we receive the Body and the Blood of our Saviour Jesus Christ Himself under the species of bread and wine.

The Eucharistic celebration in the Church is neither a continual repetition nor a renewal of the expiatory sacrifice which Christ offered once and for all on the Cross; the sacrifical character of the Eucharist, however, consists in its being the perpetual commemoration of that sacrifice and a real representation, being enacted on earth, of the one offering which Christ according to Heb. 9:11-12 continuously makes in heaven for the salvation of redeemed humanity, by appearing now for us in the presence of God (Heb. 9:24).

This being the character of the Eucharist in relation to Christ's sacrifice, it is at the same time a sacrificial meal, by means of which the faithful, in receiving the Body and Blood of the Lord, have communion with one another (1 Cor. 10:17).

(7) We hope that the theologians, while maintaining the faith of the undivided Church, will succeed in their efforts to establish an agreement on the differences that have arisen since the divisions of the Church. We urge the priests under our jurisdiction in the first place to stress, both by preaching and by religious instruction, the essential Christian truths professed in common by all the divided confessions, carefully to avoid, in discussing still existing differences, any violation of truth or charity, and, in word and deed, to set an example to the members of our parishes of how to act towards people of a different belief in a way that is in accordance with the spirit of Jesus Christ, who is the Saviour of us all.

(8) We believe that it is in faithfully maintaining the teaching of Jesus Christ, while rejecting all the errors that have been added to it through human sin, as well as rejecting all the abuses in ecclesiastical matters and hierarchical tendencies, that we shall best counteract unbelief and that religious indifference which is the worst evil of our day.[83]

7
Old Catholic Episcopal Succession
to and from Utrecht Union Bishops
1739-1910

Bishop Varlet on 17 October 1739 consecrated

- Peter Meindaerts, Archbishop of Utrecht, who in 1745 consecrated
- J. van Stiphout, Bishop of Haarlem, who in 1768 consecrated
- Walter van Nieuwenhuisen, Utrecht, who in 1778 consecrated
- Adrian Broekman, Haarlem, who in 1797 consecrated
- Johannes J. van Rhijn, Utrecht, who in 1805 consecrated
- Gisbert C. de Jong, Bishop of Deventer, who in 1814 consecrated
- Willibrord van Os, Utrecht, who in 1819 consecrated
- Johannes Bon, Haarlem, who in 1825 consecrated
- Johannes van Santen, Utrecht, who in 1854 consecrated

Herman Heykamp, Bishop of Deventer
who consecrated in 1873

Gaspard J. Rinkel for Haarlem			Josef H. Reinkens for Germany	
Gerard Gul [84] Utrecht, 1892			Eduard Herzog Switzerland, 1876	
F Hodur PNCC USA 1907	AH Mathew U.K. 1908	JM Kowalski Polish Mariavites 1909 Roman J. Prochniewski 1910	*Priests* R Vilatte & JB Gauthier USA & Canada, 1885, 1889	A Kozlowski Polish USA 1897

Notes

[1] As established by the constitution *Pastor Aeternus* of Vatican I.

[2] H. Aldenhoven, "Die Unterscheideung zwischen einer erkennbar-zugänglichen und einer unerkennbar-unzugänglichen Seite in Gott und die Trinitätslehre...", p. 214-232. Also P.Amiet, "Ortskirche – Universalkirche....", p. 33-45.

[3] D.M. Varlet, paraphrase on Acts 2:38 in <u>Recueil alphabetique</u>, p. 19.

[4] Romans 6:1-23.

[5] Recueil alphabétique, p. 19.

[6] Idem, p. 8.

[7] Loc. cit.

[8] Idem, p. 7, 11, 18, 133.

[9] Idem, p. 138. He refers to the definitions of the Arabic Synod of Bostre (3rd century).

[10] Idem, p. 211.

[11] Idem, p. 26 & 133.

[12] Idem, p. 21 & 220.

[13] Idem, p. 165.

[14] Bishop of Alexandria, Egypt. Born in 265, Dionysius had a vision and converted to Christianity. He entered a catechetical school and studied under Origen, whom he succeeded as master of the school.

[15] Recueil alphabétique, p. 18.

[16] Idem, p. 7.

[17] Idem, p. 21.

[18] Idem, p. 18. Paraphrase on Acts 2:28.

[19] Idem, p. 8.

[20] Idem, p. 39.

21	The man tried in the desert, who rebeled against the vendors of the temple and in whom the Zealot party taught of having found an ally, and who, finally, died on the cross after a life of solicitude for the sinners.
22	D.M. Varlet, Collection sur Isaie…, A.P.R. 3768.
23	The spirit or the breath of God.
24	Recueil alphabétique, p. 159.
25	Idem, p. 4.
26	D.M. Varlet, <u>Première Apologie</u>, p. 17.
27	Recueil alphabétique, p. 6.
28	Idem, p. 9.
29	Loc. cit.
30	Idem, p. 11.
31	Idem, p. 135-136.
32	Idem, p. 16.
33	Idem, p. 204.
34	Desert or mountain of the dried up ground, a general name for the whole mountain range of which Sinai was one of the summits (Exodus 3:1; 17:6).
35	Recueil alphabétique, p. 16.
36	Idem, p. 19.
37	Idem, p. 12-14.
38	Idem, p. 18.
39	Idem, p. 13.
40	Idem, p. 14.
41	Idem, p. 16.
42	Idem, p. 12.
43	Loc. cit.

44. Idem, p. 13-14.
45. Idem, p. 13.
46. Idem, p. 9.
47. Idem, p. 8 & 13.
48. Idem, p. 9, 14 & 16.
49. Idem, p. 9.
50. Idem, p. 16.
51. Idem, p. 5.
52. Idem, p. 6.
53. Loc. cit.
54. Idem, p. 17.
55. Idem, p. 17 & 19.
56. Idem, p. 24.
57. Première Apologie, p. 17.
58. Loc. cit.
59. Bishop Varlet sees the Son work in the Creation with the Father. Commenting on the Epistle of Paul to the Colossians, he attributes the creation of angels to Him. Recueil Alphabétique, p. 133.
60. Bishop Varlet studied Hebrew with Professor Fetis de la Croix at the Collège Royal.
61. Recueil alphabétique, p. 6 & 204.
62. Idem, p. 135-136.
63. Première Apologie, p. 16.
64. This phrase appears at several places in the work of Bishop Varlet with the term *elect* which is corollary to it.
65. Recueil alphabétique, p. 7.
66. Idem, p. 12.

67	Idem, p. 5.
68	Première Apologie, p. 16-17.
69	Loc. cit.
70	Recueil alphabétique, p. 7.
71	Idem, p. 11.
72	Jesus Christ speaks through Him. Recueil alphabétique, p. 166.
73	Recueil, p.8
74	Loc. cit.
75	Idem, p. 165-166.
76	The trisagion is (1) the hymn "Holy God, Holy Mighty, Holy Immortal, have mercy on us," which is sung at Divine Liturgy before the reading of the Apostle and Gospel. On certain feasts it is replaced by the verse "As many as have been baptized into Christ..." or "Before Thy Cross we bow down, O Master...."; (2) the cycle of prayers that begins with the above words and includes the prayer "O Most Holy Trinity, have mercy on us..." and other brief sentences before the Lord's Prayer. http://www.orthodoxpsalm.org/resources/glossary/p-t.html
	The addition is that of the "filioque": 'the Holy Spirit proceeds eternally from the Father and the Son', whereas the Nicene Creed in its unaltered form states that 'the Holy Spirit proceeds eternally from the Father.' The position of Bishop Varlet was that "the Holy Spirit proceeds from the Son because it is nowhere said that the Holy Spirit pours out the Son". *Commentary on the Acts of the Apostles* (2:32), op. cit., p. 18.
77	A chorbishop is a rank of Christian clergy below bishop. The name chorepiscope or chorepiscopus (pl chorepiscopi) is taken from the Greek Χωρεπίσκοπος and means rural bishop. http://en.wikipedia.org/wiki/Chorbishop
78	The Septuagint was a Greek translation of the Old Testament. It contained 46 books: Genesis, Exodus, Leviticus, Numbers, Deuteronomy, Joshua, Judges, Ruth, 1 and 2 Samuel, 1 and 2 Kings, 1 and 2 Chronicles, Ezra and Nehemiah, Tobit, Judith, Esther, 1 and 2 Maccabees, Job, Psalms, Proverbs, Ecclesiastes, the Song of Songs, the Wisdom of Solomon, Sirach (Ecclesiasticus), Isaiah, Jeremiah, Lamentations, Baruch, Ezekiel, Daniel, Hosea, Joel, Amos, Obadiah, Jonah, Micah, Nahum, Habakkuk, Zephaniah, Haggai, Zachariah and Malachi.

[79] The present Vulgate contains elements which belong to every period of its development, including (1) an unrevised Old Latin text of the Book of Wisdom, Ecclesiasticus, 1 and 2 Maccabees, and Baruch; (2) an Old Latin form of the Psalter, which Jerome corrected from the Septuagint; (3) Jerome's free translation of the Books of Job and Judith;(4) Jerome's translation from the Hebrew Old Testament excluding the Psalter;(5) an Old Latin revision of the Gospels from Greek manuscripts; (6) an Old Latin New Testament, revised. Some of the books mentioned belong to a division known as Deuterocanonical or Apocrypha, normally considered books of Jewish origin which lie outside the canon of the Old Testament. http://www.gotquestions.org/Latin-Vulgate.html

[80] A list or set of Biblical books considered to be authoritative as scripture.

[81] Deuterocanonical books is a term used since the sixteenth century in the Catholic Church and Eastern Christianity to describe certain books and passages of the Christian Old Testament that are not part of the Hebrew Bible. The term is used in contrast to the protocanonical books, which are contained in the Hebrew Bible. This distinction had previously contributed to debate in the early Church about whether they should be read in the churches and thus be classified as canonical texts. The Deuterocanonical books are considered canonical by Catholics, Eastern Orthodox and Oriental Orthodox, but are considered non-canonical by Protestants.
http://en.wikipedia.org/wiki/Deuterocanonical_books

[82] Kurt Stalder, *Der ekklesiologische und kirchenrechtliche Gehalt des Utrechter Union der Altkatholischen Kirchen*, in Oesterreichiches Archiv für Kirchenrecht, Vol. 31, No. 4, 1980, p. 368 ff.

[83] This is a translation made from the original text in German (cf. I.K.Z. 84, 1994, p. 40-42) published on the website of the Utrecht Union.
http://www.utrechter-union.org/english/ibc_foundations5.htm.

[84] Archbishop Gul also consecraterd Bishop H.J.T. van Vlijmen for Haarlem (1916) who consecrated the next Archbishop of Utrecht: Franciscus Kenninck (1920). He consecrated bishops for Austria (A. Schindelaar, 1925), Czekoslovakia (A. Paschek, 1924) and Yugoslavia (M. Kalogjera, 1924),

CHRONOLOGY

1678: Born in Paris, France, on March 15.

1698: Student at Saint Magloire Seminary in Paris.

1699: Admitted as a member of the Congrégation des Prêtres du Calvaire (October 6).

1706: Doctor of Theology from Sorbonne University. Ordained a priest and assigned to parishes in Paris suburbs.

1708: Parish priest at Conflans 14 miles from Paris.

1711: Asked to be admitted into the Société des Prêtres des Missions Étrangères (S.M.É.) in order to devote himself to the evangelization of Indians of New France.

1712: Resigned as parish priest and came to put himself at the disposal of the S.M.É. Designated to go to restore the mission to the Tamaroa Indians at Cahokia in New France (now East St. Louis, Illinois).

1713: Sailed from Brest on March 28 and on June 6 arrived at Fort Louis, Louisiana (now Mobile Bay, Alabama) where he did pastoral work.

Bull *Unigenitus Dei Filius* proclaimed by pope Clement XI on September 8. Condemned as heretical (Jansenist) 101 propositions drawn from the book *Réflexions morales sur le Nouveau Testament* (1699) written by Oratorian priest Pasquier Quesnel.

1715: Took advantage of an expedition organized at the beginning of the year by Antoine de la Mothe Cadillac, Governor of Louisiana, to go to Cahokia to establish himself as Superior of the Sainte Famille Mission and Vicar General of the Diocese of Quebec for the Mississippi and Illinois region.

1717: Four French bishops deposited in the Sorbonne a notarized act which was an appeal from the Bull Unigenitus to a general council of the Church (March 5).

On 24 March left for Quebec City to recruit missionaries and to consolidate his position in the face of claims put forward by the Jesuits, who deplored the presence of priests of the Seminary of Quebec in a region that they considered reserved for them. Reached Quebec City 11 September and on October 6 received from the Bishop, Msgr. Jean de Saint-Vallier, confirmation of the privileges granted in 1698 for the Tamaroa Indian mission.

1718: Successful in persuading the Seminary to give him reinforcements: priests Goulven Calvarin, Rene Thaumur de La Source, and Jean Paul Mercier left for Cahokia on May 10. But Varlet himself was never to see the Illinois region again.

Appointed as Co-adjutor to the Bishop of Babylon in Persia (Bagdad, Irak), Louis-Marie Pidou de Saint-Olon. Left Quebec City on September 29. Was at La Rochelle on November 23 and a fortnight later in Paris.

1719: Consecrated in S.M.É. Chapel, Paris, on Sunday, February 19. One of the consecrating prelates was Louis François Duplessis de Mornay, Co-adjutor Bishop of Quebec. On the same day, informed of Bishop Saint-Olon's death and urged to leave for his diocese of Babylon.

Left Paris on March 18. On his way to Persia stopped in Amsterdam. At the request of the Cathedral Chapter of Utrecht, between 17 and 23 April, confirmed 604 persons who had not been able to receive the sacrament due to conflict with Rome.

1720: Upon his arrival in Persia on March 26, he found himself interdicted by a decree of the Congregation for the Propagation of the Faith (Propaganda Fidei) from all episcopal functions. Church authorities in Rome were offended because, they claimed, he had administered the sacrament of confirmation in Holland without permission. Also because when he left Paris, he had neglected to call upon Papal Nuncio Martino Bentivoglio, between whose hands he was supposed, as prescribed, to declare his allegiance to the Bull Unigenitus condemning Jansenism.

1721: Went back to France, arriving on July 21. Made contacts in order to have the interdiction cancelled. Spent the rest of the year with Appelant bishop of Auxerre, Msgr. Charles de Caylus.

1722:	Returned to Holland. Was in Amsterdam in the month of February. Counted on being able to work for his justification. It did not take long for circumstances to lead him to identify his cause with that of the Dutch Jansenists. On March 19, sent a Memorandum to the Roman Curia.
1723:	Became an *Appellant* against the bull *Unigenitus* on February 15. Was to remain so despite the efforts made by the S.M.É. to regularize his situation.
1724:	On October 15, he consecrated Cornelis Steenoven, who had been elected Archbishop of Utrecht by the Cathedral Chapter on April 27, 1723. On that year was published his *Appel à la Cour pontificale* of February 15, 1723. Also published: *Suite à l'Appel*, *Plainte à l'Église catholique*, *Lettre à Benoît XIII* and *Première Apologie*.
1725 :	On January 15, *Deuxième lettre au pape Benoît XIII* (published in 1727). Papal brief *Qua Sollicitudine* (February 22) declared illicit the consecration of Msgr. Steenoven and pronounced the excommunication of Bishop Varlet and all those involved in the election and the consecration of the archbishop. *Protestation et Appel* (March 15) followed by *Lettre au Concile de Rome* and *Troisième Lettre au pape Benoît XIII* (March 23).

Lettre à un missionnaire du Tonquin (August 24). On September 30, consecrated Cornelis Barchman-Wuytiers, chosen as successor to Msgr. Steenoven deceased 3 April.

1726: *Deuxième plainte à l'Église catholique* (August 1).

1727 : Participated in a synod held in Utrecht (June 16) to elect a bishop for the see of Haarlem. Acted as Suffragan to Archbishop Barchman-Wuytiers. Left Amsterdam for Schonauwen. Published his *Deuxième Apologie*.

1733: Death of Archbishop Barchman-Wuytiers at Rijnwijk (May 13). There were rumors that he could succeed him but on July 22, Theodore van der Croon was elected as successor. First of a series of strokes (July 20). Removed to Rijnwijk.

1734: Dispute with the Cathedral Chapter over usury. Retired to Zwolle (March to July). Consecration of Archbishop Elect van der Croon delayed untill October 28.

1735: Brief of pope Clement XI against him (February 17). *Réponse à la lettre de M. de Senez* (September 9, published in 1737).

1736 : *Lettre à M. de Montpellier* (June 7). *Lettre... sur les erreurs avancées dans quelques nouveaux écrits* (October 25, published in 1742).

1739: Death of Archbishop van der Croon (June 8). Consecrated Peter J. Meindearts (October 18) elected as successor (August 3).

1742: Passed to his eternal rest on May 14 at Rijnwijk. Buried in the Cloister Yard of St. Mary's Church, Utrecht. His spiritual testament was published on July 8.

INDEX

A

Abandoned, deprived church : 125, 193, 273

Abandoned souls : 49, 91, 108, 113, 115, 117

Abandoned works : 40, 44, 88, 103, 117

Abraham : 128, 163, 180, 263

Académie Française : 30

Acadia : 90

Accuser : 123, 124

Ackerman, R. : 257

Acta et decreta secundae Synodi Ultrajectensis : 229-236

Actant and Actor : 198, 199

Acton, John : 257

Ad Sacram, bull : 80

Adrian I : 194

Adrian II : 194

Agapetus, pope : 277

Aguesseau, J.B. Paulin d' : 82

Akkoy, Gerard : 143

Aldenhoven, Herwig : 10, 246, 248, 250, 258, 264, 266, 317

Alet, bishopric of : 33, 79

Alexander VII : 80, 145, 147, 199

Alexander the Great (of Macedonia) : 177

Alexandre, Noël : 82, 153, 200

Alexandria (Egypt): 317

Alford, Henry : 204

Algonquian(s) : 47, 90

Allmang, E. : 86, 96, 257

Alterocentrism : 138

Altkatholisch(e) : see Old Catholic

Altkatholizismus : see German Old Catholics

Amerindians : 46, 51, 53, 119, 185

Amersfoort : 95

Amiet, Peter : 10, 246, 248, 250, 265, 266

Amsterdam : 35, 36, 58, 59, 62, 94-96, 98, 111, 113, 114, 122, 148, 231, 155, 327-329

Anabaptism, Anabaptists : 99

Ancient Church : see Early Church

Ancients and Moderns (Quarrel of the) : 30, 31, 81

Anderwert, Fridolin : 222

Angels (Invocation of) : 89, 307

Anglican Church (Communion), Anglican(s) : 13, 43, 68, 98, 196, 226, 253, 259, 261, 267, 268
- Bonn Agreement with the: 13, 219, 227-229, 261, 268, 269
- Orders: 227

Anna (Ivanovna), Empress of Russia : 67

Angoulême : 62

Antichrist : 89, 171, 174, 181

Anti-Infallibilism, Anti-Infallibilist(s) : 216

Anti-Millenarians : see Millennium

Anthropology, Anthropological : 248-251

Apostolic succession: 9, 10, 13, 73, 216, 219, 221, 223, 229, 230, 245, 251, 256, 257, 261, 315

Appeal to a General Gouncil, Appelant(s) : 3, 9, 13, 21, 34, 37, 54, 60, 64, 68, 72, 73, 80, 82, 95, 105, 117-121, 143, 144, 326-328

Aquinas, Thomas : see St. Thomas Aquinas

Arabic : 40, 143, 276

Arenberg, Marie Anne, Princess of : 100

Arianism : 203

Aristobulus : 174

Aristophanes : 31

Aristotle, Aristotelian : 31, 201

Arles, Rostagne of : 150

Armorial general de France : 16

Arnauld, Antoine : 19, 23, 26, 28, 30, 31, 32, 34, 35, 79, 80, 83, 93, 145, 146, 201, 215, 235

Ascalon : 94

Ascension : 175, 178, 251, 296, 304

Asfeld, Jacques V. d' : 82

Asnière : 42, 66, 201
- Cérémonial : 41, 44, 88

Assembly of the French clergy : 33, 41, 77, 80, 87, 88

Astranquan : 95

Athenians : 167

Attrition, Attritionism : 37, 38, 151, 231, 235, 274, 306

Audet, F. Émile : 92

Augustinian, Augustinism : 34, 35, 54, 77, 83, 108, 118, 175, 176, 182, 232, 251

Augustinus, book : 13, 19, 33, 80, 83, 199, 232

Austria : 226, 260, 321

Authority
- Among the Protestants: 196
- Confusion of the levels, types of: 131
- Spiritual, characterized by humility and charity, and different from the temporal authority that uses coercive force: see Bishops & Pope
- Wordly domination of Rome and its consequences (dogma, discipline and morals): 131, 240, 241

Auvergne, Princess of : 75

Auxerre, bishopric of : 62, 327

Aymon, Jean : 98

B

Babylon : 55, 57, 58, 59, 67, 71, 74, 84, 94-98, 122, 170, 174, 203, 215, 216, 243, 275, 277, 326, 327

Bachoud, Louis : 95

Bacinski, Augustin : 260

Baghdad (Irak) : 57

Baius, Michel : 33, 83

Baltzer : 220

Barberini, Antonio : 256

Barcos, Martin de : 93

Barnabas: see Fedele

Barrin : 129, 195

Bash : 95

Basnage, Jacques : 43, 89, 165, 176

Bastille : 82, 88

Bavaria : 220

Bay, Michel de : see Baius.

Bayeux : 62

Beast : 89, 180, 183

Beauvais, bishopric of : 82

Bec Helloin, Abbey of : 90

Bégon, Michel : 108, 109

Béjart, Armande : 25

Bekken, Dean : 257

Belgian(s), Belgium : 63, 258

Belief : see Faith

Bellarmine (Bellarmino), Robert : 158, 202

Bellefond, Bernardin Gigault, marquis de : 25, 79

Bellegarde, Gabriel du Pac de : 86, 192, 193

Benedict VIII : 194

Benedict XIII : 95, 105, 192, 196, 197, 200, 274

Benedictine(s) : 35, 44, 55, 57, 58, 205

Bengel, Johann Albrecht : 179, 206

Bentivoglio, Martino : 327

Bergier, Marc : 44, 50, 90, 92, 110, 293

Berne : 222-225
- Old Catholic Faculty (Department): 10, 246-248, 258, 295
- University of: 5, 10

Berruyer, Isaac Joseph : 231, 233

Bertrand, Louis : 93

Bérulle, Pierre de, Berullian : 37, 38, 39, 77, 86

Bible : 20, 42, 97, 135, 136, 179, 180

Bible interpretation : 35, 39, 89, 104, 144, 166, 176
- Allegorical (conventional) : 168, 172, 174, 175, 203. 205
- Biblicist, Biblist : 179-182
- Bishop Varlet's method of : 165
- Conventional, traditional : 168
- Critical exegesis : 206
- Figurism, Figurist(s), Figurative : 165, 172, 176, 177, 179, 182, 204, 207, 213-215
- Hermeneutic : 165
- Its link to ecclesiology : 165, 172, 173
- Litteral : 174
- Millenarist : 168, 175, 178
- Non-Allegorical : 176

Bindschedler-Robert, Denise : 11

Bishop(s): 41, 195, 252, 307
- Actorize the requirements of grace: 141
- Are the angels of the Church: 201, 275
- Are called to personal sanctification: 141
- Are the operators of the church infallibility: 141, 239
- Derive their authority from Jesus Christ: 131, 196, 239
- Interpreters of the councils: 130
- Judges of the faith: 131
- Must assume the lordship of Jesus: 72, 141, 186
- Must conform to the canons: 131, 196, 200, 239
- Must give a good example: 201
- Must preach repentance: 201
- National: 60
- Rights of the: 196
- Spiritual authority characterized by humility and charity: 131, 136, 159, 198, 240
- Suffragan: 66, 156, 201, 329
- Their role as stewards (of mysteries of God): 149, 153, 240, 275
- Their judgements: 196
- Their jurisdiction: 80, 148, 149
- Their obligation to preach the Gospel: 128
- Their role in the economy of the Church: 130, 141

Bishop of Rome : see Pope

Bismark, Otto von : 221

Blondel, David : 41

Bock, Hieronimus de : 100

Boidot, Philippe : 171

Boileau, Nicolas : 30, 79, 81

Bon, Johannes : 315

Bonn
- Agreement : see Anglican Church
- City : 220, 225

Book of Revelation : see New Testament

Borde, Vivien de la : 43, 200, 215

Borromeo, Charles : 19, 37, 38, 236, 241

Bossuet, Jacques Bénigne : 146, 158, 243, 249, 264

Bostre, Synod of : 317

Bosveld, Jacob : 30

Bourgeois, Bourgeoisie : 25, 79

Bourges : 82

Breslau : 220

Brest : 45, 325

Breton Strait : 107

Brisacier : 84

Broekman, Adrian : 315

Brothers, William Francis : 268

Broue, Pierre de la : 37

Brown, Graham: 261

Brown, John Henry Hobart : 258

Bruggeman, J. : 64, 65, 84, 93, 97

Brussels, Internuncio of : 58, 61, 94, 116, 118, 148, 149

Budapest : 259

Busembaum, Hermann : 231, 236

Byeveld, Bertholomew J. : 100

C

Cadillac, Antoine Laumet de la Mothe : 45, 90, 91, 326

Cahokia (Illinois): 44, 47, 48, 49, 50, 85, 92, 93, 103, 276, 325, 326

Caille, Claude : 84

Calmet, Augustin : 157, 202

Calvaire (Calvary)
- Prêtres du / Priests of : 19, 26, 27, 29, 31, 32, 81, 171, 325
- Mont : 26

Calvarin, Goulvern : 326

Calvin (Jean), Calvinism, Calvinist : 33, 41, 43, 97, 98, 153, 178

Camus, Étienne le : see Le Camus.

Canada : 52, 57, 58, 81, 82, 90-92, 94, 103, 108

Canon(s) / church law : 39, 61, 86, 117, 120, 187, 188, 223, 232, 259, 308
- Authority of the : 86, 115, 116
- Pope bound to observe : 86
- Their observance prevents conflicts and divisions : 124, 188, 200

Canonical, legal : 118, 119, 124, 159, 188, 275, 277

Canonist(s) : 59, 87

Canterbury
- Archbishop of : 13, 67, 98, 261

Cap-Français (Cap-Haitien): 45

Capuchins : 95

Carfora, Carmel H. : 268

Carmelite Fathers : 122

Carreyre, J. : 255-257, 264

Cartesianism, Cartesian : 201

Carthage : 150

Carthusians : 64, 66

Case of conscience : 36, 85, 145, 199

Catechism : 53, 89, 110
- Of England: 99, 196

Catholicity : 277
- Criterium of : 154

Catullus : 205

Caulet, François de: 79, 83

Caylus, Charles de : 59, 95, 327

Celestine I : 194

Celibacy : 89, 258

Censure : 146-148, 193

Chaise-Dieu, Abbey of: 96

Chambéry : 98

Charity : 233, 235
- Destroyed by conflicts and divisions: 141
- Exercized under the influence of the Holy Spirit: 128
- Propensity to seek after common good: 186, 196
- Necessary for Christian actions: 135

Charpentier, Hubert : 19, 26, 27

Chartres : 41, 88

Chassaigne, Antoine de la : 172, 179

Chenu, Marie-Dominique : 132, 197

Chicago : 224

China : 40, 87, 88

Chinese Rite controversy : 39, 40, 87

Chiniquy, Charles : 258

Chorbishop : 320

Christ
- Accomplishes the promises: 166
- Divinity of : 252
- Elevates humans by degrees: 104, 138, 168, 187, 237
- His lordship: 103, 123, 127, 250
- His merits: 128, 137, 159, 234

- His reign (of 1000 years) on earth: 168, 170, 173, 181, 204
- His return in glory (at the Last Day): 171, 180, 181
- His Spirit: 157
- Imitation of: 72, 104, 125, 140, 187, 193, 237
- Is God Equal to the Father: 127, 296, 301
- Is the way to salvation: 252
- Made reparation for our sins: 128, 135, 137, 159, 180, 186, 233, 240, 263, 265
- Makes us enter justice: see Justification
- Only Mediator: 234
- Redeeming love of God: 138, 237, 303
- Suffering Servant: 138-140, 298
- The saints will reign with Him during the millennium: 170, 181
- Will end the injustice which is in the Church: 274
- Will free the elect: 170, 181, 183, 274
- Will introduce the redeemed in the heavenly kingdom: 204

Christian Catholic Church
- Of Canada (Quebec) : 224, 253, 258, 259
- Of Switzerland : 11, 223, 258

Christianity
- Primitive : see Early Church

Christocentrism : 39

Christology, Christological : 86, 118, 188, 297

Church
- Accuser: 123, 125
- Ages, periods of the: 175, 248
- Alternative: 10, 213, 214
- Alterocentered: 132
- And State: 173
- Apostolicity of the: 129
- Authority in/of the: 86, 88, 129, 131, 239, 248, 251
- Babylon/the Beast is in the: 165, 170, 240, 274, 276
- Body of Christ: 124, 130, 136, 137, 140, 248, 250, 266, 300
- Body of the Three Persons: 247
- Can be degraded by alterations of doctrine: 104
- Common Mother: 104
- Communio Sanctorum: 214, 247, 251

- Democratic view of the: 77
- Domineering : 10
- Entire body of the faithful: 255
- Faith community: 132
- Has her infallibility from the Word infallible: 266
- Her mission diactated by Scripture and Tradition: 75
- Holiness of the: 129, 136, 137, 187, 246, 247, 252
- Indefectibility of: 117
- Infallibility of the: 117, 129, 130, 137, 159, 195, 231-233, 240, 346, 251, 263, 266, 295, 307
  - Not of the Pope: 202
- Liberties of the: 124
- Life of: 183, 247, 266
- Locus salutis, theologicus, trinitatis: 132, 134, 249, 295, 304, 305
- Many things oppose the will of God in the: 175
- Mystery of: 159
- Must produce the fruits of the Holy Spirit: 104
- National: 61
- New community-based model of: 213
- Non-dominating: 132
- Order of: 124, 149, 150, 188, 189, 215
- Polity: 214
- Reign of God in the souls: see Reign of God
- Rest of Israel: 183
- Sacerdotal model of exclusive mediator replaced by participatory democraty of believers: 214
- Sacrament of salvation: 10, 104
- Servant: 10, 123-125, 132, 195
- Spiritual renewal of the: 203
- State of division in the: 110, 213
- Subordinate to Scripture and Tradition: 87, 235
- Transfer /Church-Israel/: 182
- Trinitarian: see Holy Trinity
- Undivided: 257
- Unity of the: 130, 141
- Universal: 141, 187, 188
- Wellbeing of the: 141

Church Fathers : see Patristics

Cicero : 31, 205

Cistercians : 64, 96

Clement IX : 145-147, 199

Clement XI : 13, 20, 85, 87, 94, 113, 147, 325, 329

Clerical establishment
- Contested: 213
- Cupidity of: 214, 241, 244
- Forces of evil incarnated in the: 213
- Loss of confidence in the: 213
- May impede salvation: 214
- Wordly object of: 238

Clericalism : 95

Coat of Arms : 16

Cockerman, A.W. : 257

Codde, Peter : 36, 80, 86

Coello, Claudio : 59

Cogné, Daniel : 78, 79

Cognet, Louis : 77, 80, 85, 86, 202, 257

Colbert, Charles J. : 37, 262, 275, 278

Cole, Alan M. : 269

Collège Royal : 40, 82, 319

Collection Réforme catholique (BAnQ) : 80, 86

Collette, Regent of De Valk College : 193

Cologne
- Assembly of: 221
- Old Catholic Congress of: 229, 242, 264

Colombière, Joseph C. de la : 93, 108, 109

Commandments of God : 89, 104, 234, 299, 302, 308

Commentaries : 143, 199

Commodanius : 173, 205

Communion (Ecclesial)
- Conditioned by unity of faith: 130, 131, 239, 241-243, 249
- Relates to faith and morals: 130, 239

Compagnie des Indes : 90

Competence, Competencies (Christian/Ecclesial): 128, 136, 137, 214, 237, 240, 273, 274

Conciliar, Conciliarism : 34, 39, 87, 256

Condom, bishopric of: 57

Conflans : 43, 44, 325

Congar, Yves : 265

Conscience
- Autonomy of: 214
- Erroneous: 235

Constance
- Diocese of: 258
- Old Catholic Congress of: 226

Constantine, emperor: 173, 174

Constitution civile du clergé : 23

Contrition : 37, 86, 235, 274

Controversy : 20, 144, 161

Conversion : 127, 137-139, 159, 203, 275, 300, 306
- Church establishment can be obstacle to: 213
- Makes us will what God wants: 139, 237
- Role of the Holy Spirit in: 137, 237

Convulsions, Convulsionists : 72, 73, 100, 139, 162, 179, 203, 211, 214
- Biblical understanding of: 73
- Pathos of: 215, 216
- Supernatural manifestation: 73, 161, 162

Conzemius, Victor : 243, 264, 266

Corinthians : 277

Corneille, Pierre : 24, 26, 78, 79

Cornelius, Adolf von : 220

Côté, O'Neill : 259

Council(s)
- General: 68, 77, 233
- Of Basel: 222
- Of Constance: 84
- Of Embrun: 96
- Of Limoges: 194
- Of Nicea: 261
- Of Ries: 89
- Of Rome: 174, 175, 192, 195, 196
- Of Trent: 19, 37, 77, 89, 134, 135, 145, 148, 150, 157, 200, 241, 244
- Of the Vatican (I): 117, 221, 222, 243, 244, 257-260, 317
- Of the Vatican (II): 132
- Superior over the pope: 117

Counter-Reformation : 19, 37, 77, 84, 202

Cour, de la : see Jubé, Jacques

Credita Nobis, brief : 93

Creed : 247

Croatia, Croatian, Croats : 225, 260

Croix, Fétis de la : 40, 82, 319

Crozat, Antoine : 45, 91

Crispus : 173

Cuba : 261

Cum Occasione, bull : 281

Cupidity : See Greed

Czech, Amandus : 260

Czech Republic : 260

Czechoslovakia : 225, 226, 321

Czernohorski-Fehervary, Tomasz : 259

D

Dalenoort : see van Dalenoort

Damasus, pope : 174

Daniel, prophet : 205, 206

David : 180, 182

Dederen, Raoul : 256, 260, 261

Degert, A. : 83

Deloche, Maximin : 81, 191, 276, 278

Democraty, Democratic : 117, 214

Denmark : 226

Descartes, René : 31, 33, 79, 82

Despagne, Pierre : 178, 206, 207

Désessarts, Alex : 204

Désessarts, J.B. : 97

Detroit, River, Fort of : 52, 91

Deventer : 73, 100, 221, 225

Devotee(s), Devotion, Devout : 85, 104, 113, 116, 145, 277

Diependaal, Cornelius : 310

Dilhe : 96

Dionysius (of Alexandria) : 297, 317

Discipline
- Of the Church : 252, 267
- Of the clergy : 89

Doctrine : 10, 143, 185, 257, 267
- Alteration of : 141, 230, 243
- Body of : 217, 229, 230, 245
- Cohesion of : 252
- For Rome, its holiness comes from the founders of the Church: 129
- Of Grace : 83, 84, 132, 134, 184, 186, 231, 232
- Of incarnation : 132, 231
- Of Pelagius : 134
- Of redemption : 132
- Of St. Augustine : 146
- Of the Holy Fathers : see Patristics
- On original sin : 134
- Order of the : 141

Dogma(s)
- Of the Church : 187
- Of the Immaculate Conception of Mary: 244

Dolgoruki, Princess Irena Petrovna and family : 67, 69, 98

Döllinger, Ignaz von: 220, 243, 248, 256, 265

Dominicans : 87, 222

Donatus, Donatism, Donatist(s) : 172, 194

Donker, Theodore : 66

Drappier, Guy : 43

Drolet, Michel : 258

Druffel, August von : 221

Dubois, A.J. de Brigode : 58, 62, 66, 96, 99

Duguet, Jacques-Joseph : 34, 83, 158, 172, 204, 215

Dupin, Louis Ellies : 82, 98

Dürer, Albrecht : 152

Dutch (Merchants) Party : 72, 97, 151, 200, 201

Dutch Old Catholics : 74

E

Early Church : 43, 174, 242, 244, 268, 269

Eastern Christians : 67, 69

Ecclesiology : 10, 39, 87, 124, 129, 144, 175, 176, 178, 182, 185, 215, 248-251, 265-267, 274, 296
- Alternative : 211, 213-217, 241
- Christocentered : 87

- Ecclesiocentrism : 132
- Gallicano-Jansenist paradigm : 211-214, 229, 244, 245
- Persistence of Varletian theses on : 229

Ecumenism, Ecumenical, Unity talks : 43, 68, 98, 233, 267

Eekhof, A. : 268

Egocentrism : 138

Egypt, Egyptian : 84, 302

Elijah, prophet: 171, 203, 204, 255

Embrun : 96

England : 68, 224, 259

Epicurianism, Epicurian : 27, 80

Episcopal Church : 261

Episcopal succession: see Apostolic succession.

Episcopate : 43, 58, 89, 121

Episcopè : 277

Episcopi vagantes (wandering bishops) : 13

Epistle to the Romans : see St. Paul.

Erie, lake : 52

Eschatology, Eschatological, Eschaton : 131, 196, 204, 240, 248-251, 299
- Brings out of Babylon which is in the Church: 170
- Millenarian predictions and: 171
- To have God as the ultimate end: 196, 198, 201, 235

Esope : 31

Étemare, J.B. Le Sesne de Ménilles : 215

Ethiopian : 143

Euripid : 31

Evangelization : 46, 51, 53, 69, 325

Evolution of society : see Social changes

Evora : 84

Excommunication : 62, 72, 121, 125, 185, 220, 232, 276

Exegesis : see Bible interpretation

F

Faculty of theology of Paris : 28, 39, 54, 67, 82, 145-147

Faith
- Content of the revelation: 230
- Core/ Essentials of the: 228, 252
- Deposit of the: 68, 124, 188
- Dogmas of the: 200
- Errors relating to: 231
- Falling away from Catholic: 252, 253, 259, 267-269
- Fidelity to the: 153
- First grace and source of all others: 128
- Given once for all: 124, 154, 188, 242, 243, 249
- Justification by: 128, 233, 234
- Must be translated into action: 273
- Necessary for salvation: 128, 135
- Of the undivided Church: 13, 257
- Purity of the: 195, 204
- Rule of: 202, 235
- Sacred mysteries: 230
- Unity of the: 68, 140, 242, 243
- Word of: see Kerygma

Faithful (the): 135, 195, 196

- Are actors of God's reign: 140, 213, 214
- Are encouraged to read the Holy Scripture: 213, 214
- Guard faith and morals: 135, 153, 154
- Must be instructed in the mystery of religion: 135

Fallersleben, H. von : 244

Fathers of the Church: see Patristics

Fedele, Barnabas : 94, 95

Féhel, abbé : 85

Felicianow : 259

Ferland, J.B. Antoine : 92

Feydeau, Mathieu : 82

Figurism : see Bible interpretation

Filioque : 265, 266, 320

Fleury, Claude : 157, 202

Flores (Fiore), Joachim of : 175, 176, 205, 206, 265, 274

Folkena, Jacob : 276

Fond du Lac : 258

Fontenelle, Bernard le Bovier de : 30, 81

Foreign Missions : see Missions Étrangères.

Formulary of Alexander VII : 37, 77, 80, 145-147, 153

Fort de Buade : 91

Fort-Louis (Louisiana): 45, 325

Fox (Indians) : 52

Franciscan(s) : 52, 259

Franco-Americans : 223, 258

Frankfurt : 220

Freewill : 84, 85, 159

French
- Ambassador : 71
- Bishops : 62
- Clergy : 77, 117
- Dissidents : 36
- In North America : 108, 223
- Old Catholics : 226
- School of spirituality : 77, 145
- Society : 78
- Theological circles : 36
- Their influence in Utrecht : 97, 200

French Canadians : 258

Fribourg : 222

Friedrich, Johannes : 220

G

Gallican Articles (Liberties): 21, 33, 54, 77, 78, 83, 87

Gallican, Gallicanism : 13, 20, 23, 34, 35, 41, 54, 58, 72, 77, 84, 87, 94, 95, 97, 117, 193, 202, 243, 244, 262, 277

Gallicano-Jansenist : see Ecclesiology

Galois, Philippe : 28

Garneau, François-Xavier : 55, 90, 93

Garraghan, Gilbert : 92

Gassendi, Pierre : 27, 80

Gaudium & Spes, constitution : 132

Gaugler, Ernst : 246

Gauthier, Jean-Baptiste : 223, 315

Gauthier, Léon : 11, 249, 266

Gazier, Augustin : 83

Gelasius I : 194

German Old Catholics : 73, 100, 117, 216, 219, 221, 222, 226, 242, 256, 267

Gers : 57

Ghent : 82

Gibert, Jean-Pierre : 59

Gibbon, Edward : 173

Girardin, Pierre de : 98

Glandelet, Charles : 53, 55, 93, 108

Gnostics : 173, 205

God : 160-163, 168, 180, 185, 198, 235, 251, 263, 295-306
- Actant of His reign : 140
- Attributes of : 159, 160, 162, 187, 307
- City of, built by : 205, 208
- Essential Soul : 205
- YHWH : 138, 298, 301, 302

Godeau, Antoine : 157, 202

Gondy, Claude Marguerite de : 25

Gospel(s) : 42, 85, 103, 115, 117, 128, 133, 135, 166, 167, 204, 250, 276

Gosselin, Auguste : 31, 58, 82, 90, 94, 276, 278

Gouda : 99

Grace : 168, 196, 231-234, 264, 281, 283-291, 308
- And freewill : 85, 134
- Controversy on : 23, 134
- Efficacious: 84, 85, 144-147, 159, 214, 232
- Election of: 183
- Gives divine adoption : 135, 137, 242, 298
- Gives the spirit of Jesus Christ: 137
- Gives to humankind its true dignity: 85, 237
- Induces sentiments of humility: 117, 134
- Is received in the Church: 134, 187
- Makes us desire eschatological goods: 137, 139, 237
- Makes us do good works: 233
- Makes us know and love the truth: 110, 237, 238, 242
- Necessary: 147, 159, 233, 252
- Predestinates to salvation: 214
- Produces in us both the will and the doing of God: 139, 234, 237
- Requires personal purification : 137
- Sanctifying: 247, 306
- Sufficient: 159
- Vivifies the Church: 247

Grancolas: 88

Greed : 160, 263, 274
- Associated with the empire of the Beast: 180
- Impediment to sanctification: 241
- Is source of all ills, of evil in the Church: 132

Greeks : 232

Gregory VII: 175, 194

Greimas, A.J.: 122, 194, 198

Grenoble, Morale de : 153, 201

Gres-Gayer, Jacques : 98

Greswell, Edward : 204

Groman, E. Owen : 257

Groulx, Lionel : 94

Guérin de Tencin : see Tencin

Guilbert, Pierre : 82

Gul, Gerard : 224, 225, 259, 321, 315

Guy, Basil : 80, 81, 99, 100

H

Haarlem : 66, 73, 94, 09, 100, 143, 221, 225, 321, 329

Habert, Louis: 34, 83

Hamadan: 95

Hardon, John A.: 256

Hardouin, Jean : 231, 233

Harlay, Achille de: 25

Harlay, François de: 33

Harpe, Bénard de la: 91

Hautmesnil, Catherine Chrétienne de: 109

Hautefontaine, abbey of : 82

Haute-Loire : 96

Hebrew : 40, 143, 202, 302, 319

Hefele, Charles : 220

Helder : 216

Helluin, Marie : 25

Herzog, Eduard : 223, 224, 259, 311, 315

Hesiod, poet: 31

Hesselius: 153

Heykamp, Hermann : 100, 221, 311

Heykamp, Johannes : 221, 259, 311

Hierarchy : see Clerical establishment

Hilarus, pope : 151, 194, 200

Hilgers : 220

Hirscher, J.B.: 222

Hodur, Franciszek : 224, 252, 315

Holland : 49, 58, 59, 61, 67, 77, 85, 86, 88, 94, 98, 104, 113, 116, 118, 119, 130, 148, 151, 154, 178, 202, 219, 235, 276, 328

Holy Cross, church/sanctuary of: see Sainte-Croix, sanctuaire de la.

Holy Family Mission : 45, 48, 103, 326

Holy Fathers: see Patristics

Holy Mysteries : 47

Holy Scripture : 97, 99, 119, 157, 179, 185, 204, 230, 232, 233, 267, 269, 290, 310
- Accessible to the believers: 202
- Authority of: 252
- Deuterocanonical books: 310, 321
- Different versions of the: 310, 320-321
- Eschatological aspects of: 172
- Is a rampart against the abuses of papal authority: 87
- Its interpretation by the Church: 86, 235
- Its link with Tradition: 133, 235, 242
- Rules of understanding: 204
- Supremacy of: 274

Holy Spirit : 132, 166, 167, 182, 186, 187, 248, 250, 251, 266
- Actualize salvation: 239
- Animates the devotion and zeal of the elect: 104, 180
- Builds the Body of Christ: 266
- Communicates grace: 137, 140, 168, 187, 247, 251
- Conflicts and divisions sin against the: 141
- Force which makes us change: 138, 166, 237, 304
- Fulfillment of prophecies: 182
- Gives infallibility and indefectibility to the Church: 117, 247, 248
- His rapport to eschatology: 138
- His role in the exercise of infallibility: 130, 239, 247, 252
- Is the consummation of the kingdom of God on earth: 175
- Is the fulfillment of the prophecies: 182
- Leads us to imitate Christ: 186, 237
- Makes God reign in the souls: 251, 299, 304
- Makes us act according to the law of charity: 138, 140, 186, 239, 240, 299
- Makes us estimate our ordeals: 139
- Makes us live under grace: 248
- Makes us see salvation: 103, 138, 237, 248, 273, 304
- Only in the Church do we have the: 103
- Operator of charity: 140, 240
- Operates the reference to Christ: 136, 237, 248, 304
- Proceeds from the Father: 250, 266
- Proceeds from the Son: 250, 266
- Recreates us spiritually: 104
- Sanctifies the Church: 129, 130, 136, 247, 248, 252
- Transforms greed into charity: 237

Holy Trinity, Trinitarian : 175, 195, 231, 247-250, 266, 295-306

Holy Wisdom: 104, 138

Homosexuality: see Sexuality

Honasse, Benoît : 66

Hospitallers of St. Joseph, sisters : 108

Huron, lake : 52

Huissen : 64

Hulse, Hiram Richard : 261

Hungary : 259

Hurtubise, Pierre : 51, 53, 55, 58, 79, 82, 87, 89, 90-94, 201, 256

Hypocrisy : see Pharisaism

I

Illinois : 39, 50, 51, 53, 90-92, 103, 111, 326

Independent churches, groups, ministries : 256-260

India : 69

Indians : 47, 50, 90, 276, 325

Indochina, mission of : 63, 69, 71

Indulgences : 232

Infallibility : see Church
- Fruit of a life sanctified by the Holy Spirit: 136
- Dogma of the: 100, 117
- Its rapport with authority: 131, 145
- Papal claim of: 13, 202

Innocent I: 120

Innocent III: 194

Innocent X: 147, 199

Innocent XIII : 59, 61, 83, 95, 121

International Council of Community Churches : 224, 253

Iran : 58, 95

Isaac : 263

Isaiah : 97, 105, 133, 206, 238

Isfahan (Ispahan), bishop, diocese of : 58, 94, 120, 122

Isle-Dieu : 107

Israel : 84, 174, 180, 181, 263

Italy : 226

J

Jablonski, Michal Ludwik : 259

Jacob: 180, 263

Jacobs, J.Y.H.A. : 96

Jacques, Émile : 23, 79, 80, 81, 82, 83, 85, 86

Jal, Auguste : 78, 256

Jansen, Cornelis (Jansenius) : 13, 19, 33, 36, 37, 57, 77, 80, 83, 85, 144, 158, 231, 232, 241
- Right and fact of: 85, 146, 199, 232

Jansenism, Jansenist(s) : 13, 19, 20, 23, 26, 27, 28, 29, 31, 32, 34, 35, 36, 37, 38, 39, 54, 55, 63, 72, 73, 77, 79, 80, 83, 84, 85, 86, 88, 98, 100, 117, 134, 140, 145, 146, 172, 176, 179, 183, 197, 199, 200-202, 215, 216, 232, 236, 238, 240-243, 256, 276, 277, 325, 327, 328
- Second Jansenism: see Gallicano-Jansenist

Jarry, E. : 81

Jerusalem : 205

Jesuitism, Jesuit(s) : 19, 35, 40, 49, 50, 52, 53, 54, 58, 80, 84, 95, 122, 129, 131, 134, 198, 201, 202, 231, 233, 235, 242, 326

Jesus : see Christ

Jews : 167, 168, 171

Joan I (of Navarre), Queen : 87

John VIII: 150, 194

John XXIII: 132

Jong, Gisbert C. de : 315

Jubé, Jacques (dit de la Cour) : 40, 41, 42, 43, 44, 66, 67, 73, 82, 88, 89, 155, 201

Judah, kingdom of: 180

Judgement(s) : 170, 171, 181, 183, 309

Juénin, Gaspard : 34, 83, 84

Jurgens, Madeleine : 78

Jurisdiction
- Of the bishops: 148, 149
- Of the cathedral chapter: 148, 150, 151
- Ordinary: 148-151

Justice
- Brought by Jesus Christ: 273
- Role of the apostolate (ministry) in the accomplishment of: 273

Justification : 89, 125, 128, 159, 233, 234, 240, 242, 252, 264, 273, 298, 308

K

Kalogera, Marko: 225, 321

Kaskaskia: 91

Keller, Augustin: 222

Kemp, Willibrord: 155, 201

Kempis, Thomas A.: 193

Kenninck, Franciscus: 225, 226, 227, 262, 321

Kenosis: 125, 188, 195

Kersey, John: 257

Kerygma (Kerygmatic)
- Its rapport to salvation: 238, 300
- Link to koinonia: 130, 140, 300
- Word of God, of faith: 129, 133

Keussen, Rudolf: 246, 251, 265

Kingdom : 137, 277, 303
- Against Babylon in the Church: 170, 183
- And the institutional church: 172-174, 175, 178, 238, 262, 273, 274, 295
- Compromized by the absence of preaching: 128
- During the millennium: 165, 204
- Eartly, litteral, visible: 168, 173, 178-183, 204
- Of Christ: 165, 168, 178-183, 204
- Spiritual reality: 178

Kireev, Alexander: 259

Knoodt: 220

Koinonia: 130, 140, 249, 266

Kowalski, Tymotheusz: 260

Kowalski, Jan Michał: 225, 259, 315

Kozlowska, Feliksa: 259

Kozlowski, Anton: 224, 315

Krahl, Werner: 246

Krämer, Liliane & Max: 12, 264

Kreiser, Robert: 203, 204, 207, 211, 255

Küng, Hans : 306

Küppers, Werner: 246, 247

Küry, Adolph: 226

Küry, Urs: 245-247, 256, 264, 265

L

La Bruyère, Jean de : 31

Lachine, Rapids of : 52

La Croix, Claude : 231, 236

La Croix, Fétis de : see Croix, Fétis de la.

Lactancius : 173

Lactaneius : 173, 205

Lafiteau, Pierre François : 68, 98

Laflèche, College of : 54

La Fontaine, Jean de : 31, 81

Lagerwey, E. : 263

La Grange, Charles Varlet dit : see Varlet, Charles.

La Grange, Marie : 24

Lambeth Conference : 227

Laicism, laity : 41, 42, 97, 198, 214, 215, 222
- Ceremonies translated from Latin to vernacular: 198
- Its heteredox influence in the altkatholizismus: 258

Lamorte, André : 203, 204

Lan, François Hyacinthe de : 154, 201

Langelier, Moise : 258

Langen, Josef : 220

Langle, Pierre de : 37

Last Day : 171, 173

La Rochelle : 45, 107, 326

Laval, François de Montmorency : 54, 82

Lavallée, Jean-Guy : 84

Lavisse, Ernest : 81

Laxism, Laxist : 151
- And probabilism : 135

Lebanon : 84

Le Bec, André : 259

Le Camus, Étienne : 54, 57, 93, 201

Le Clerc, Pierre : 231-233, 261

Leduc, Anne Françoise : 108

Leenders-Stouthandel, Agatha : 255

Lefebvre, A.M. : 79

Le Gros, Nicolas : 97, 215

Lemaire, F. : 99

Le Noir, Jean : 82

Lent : 89

Leo IV : 194

Letters Patent : 50, 51, 92, 293-294

Levant : 84, 120

Le Vessor, Michel : 31

Liberal Catholic Church : 259

Lionne, Artus de : 40

Liturgy : 41, 42, 43, 89

Livesey, James : 203

Loan : 33

Lohof, Jaque : 74

London : 225

Longueville, Duchess of : 32

Lossen, Max : 220

Louis XIV : 20, 33, 78, 79, 94, 199

Louisiana : 39, 45, 46, 48, 81, 90, 103, 325-326

Louvain : 59, 60, 64, 82, 83, 95, 96

Loyson, Hyacinthe : 261

Lucius III : 205

Lucretia : 31

Lust : 233-235

Luther (Martin), Lutheran(s) : 178, 206, 267

Luxemburg : 13

Lyons : 233

M

Maan, P.J. : 96, 98, 255

Macon : 62

Magisterium : 130, 214

Maignelay, Marquis de : 25

Malabar, islands of : 69

Malebranche, Nicolas : 31, 82

Malet, A. : 264

Malines : 43, 82

Manichean(s) : 99

Marbillon : 43

Marest, Gabriel : 49, 92

Mariavites : 224, 225, 259, 260

Martene, Edmond : 43

Martimort, Aimé Georges : 82, 83, 87

Martin I : 194

Martin, Joseph : 258

Mass :
- Anaphora : 42
- Confiteor : 42
- Offertory : 42, 89
- Secret : 42, 89

Massillon, Jean-Baptiste : 57

Mathew, Arnold Harris : 13, 224, 253, 259, 261, 315

Matignon, Jacques Goyon de : 57

Maxfield-Miller, Elizabeth : 78

Mazotta, Nicolai : 231, 236, 262

Meindaerts, Peter : 73-75, 97, 200, 230, 315, 330

Menochius (Menochio), Giovanni: 158, 202

Merchants Party : see Dutch Party.

Mercier, Jean-Paul : 53, 92, 93, 103, 109, 326

Mercier, Louis : 258

Merlac, André de : 55

Metz : 62

Michaud, Eugène : 122, 194, 201, 246, 251, 266

Michigamea : 91

Michigan, lake : 52

Michilimakinak : 52

Middle Ages : 248

Middlehoff, Kees : 257

Milan, city : 37, 159

Millennarism
- Bishop Varlet and: 168-170, 181, 182
- Differences from Non-Millenarism, Anti-Millenarians: 204
- Doctrine of: 170-174, 203
- Ecclesiogical applications : 169
- Prophetic teaching: 171, 173
- Spiritualist ideology: 172

Millenarian(s), Millenarist : 10, 144, 159, 168-171, 176, 179, 203, 262, 265

Millennium : 168-170, 173, 178, 181-183, 203
- Described in Scripture: 165
- Expresses the triumph of the saints: 165
- Manifested in the conversion of the Jews: 165, 171, 181, 183, 204
- Perfect justice established: 165
- St. Augustine and the: 175
- The hope of the elect is founded in it: 165
- Triumph of the Church/Babylon destriyed: 171, 203

Ministry : 10, 39, 193
- Continuity of: 113-116

- Discontinuity: 113, 116, 117

Miracles : 73, 100, 127, 139, 161, 168, 211, 213, 214, 255

Mission(s), Missionary(ies): 103, 277, 304, 326
- Critique of the Church: 103
- Defence of the truth: 103, 123
- Keeping the sacred deposit: 103
- Of the East: 143, 144
- Prophetic: see Prophecy
- Redemptive: 207, 213, 214
- Traditional acception: 39, 40, 45, 49, 50, 51, 53, 69, 79, 80, 81, 87, 88, 103, 113, 114, 117
- Work to reform the Church: 104

Missions Étrangères (Foreign Missions)
- Prêtres des, Priests of : 10, 58
- Séminaire des : 44, 57, 88, 293-294, 327
- Société des (S.M.É.) : 10, 44, 57, 88, 293-294, 325-328

Mississipi : 44, 45, 90, 294, 326

Mobile, Alabama : 45-48, 50, 90, 91, 107, 191, 325

Möhler, Johann : 220

Moingwena : 91

Mokry, Jean-Claude : 267

Molière, J.B. Poquelin dit : 24-27, 78, 79, 81

Molina, Luis de : 35, 84, 85, 134, 197

Molinism, Molinist(s) : 84, 85, 135, 197, 201

Moltman, Jürgen : 133, 197

Montgeron, Louis Basile Carré de : 162, 203

Montigny, François de : 58, 59, 94

Montpellier : 62, 143, 147, 155, 157, 259, 262, 275

Montreal : 52, 55, 108, 109, 223, 276

Mont-Valérien : 19, 26-29, 31, 32, 81

Morals, Christian conduct : 10, 89, 166, 263
- Purity of: 195
- Rules of: 199

Moreau, priest of Thouars : 198

Moreri : 256

Mornay, Louis F. Duplessis de : 57, 93, 327

Moscow : 67, 69, 119

Moses: 171, 234, 288, 302

Moss, Claude B.: 86, 95-97, 216, 229, 245, 256, 258-261

Muller, Charles : 257, 258, 263, 264

Münich: 220
- Old Catholic Congress of: 222, 229, 242
- School of history: 220

Munzinger, Walter : 222

Museum Catharijneconvent, Utrecht : 11

N

Nantes
- Edict of : 26, 33
- Library of : 68

Nanteuil, Castle of : 24

National churches, groups : 112, 216, 219

Native people : 46, 47, 49, 50

Navarre, Collège de : 39, 40, 82, 87

Neale, John M.: 86, 95-99, 192, 255, 256, 261-263

Neercassel : see van Neercassel.

Néez, L.: 99

Neil, Stephen: 261

Nemkovich, Robert M. : 252

Neoplatonicism : 173

Nepos, Cornelius : 173, 205

Neo-testamentarization of the Old Testament : see St. Augustine

Neri, Philip : 77

Neumayer, François : 231, 236

Netherlands, The : 58, 63, 64, 73, 86, 88, 103, 120, 186, 215, 225

New France (Nouvelle-France) : 3, 23, 45, 53, 54, 57, 58, 79, 85, 90, 91, 93, 103, 107, 113, 201, 293, 325

New Testament : 38, 206, 304
- Acts of the Apostles : 41, 105, 157, 165, 168, 170, 178, 181, 197
- St. Paul's epistles : 157
- Other epistles : 157, 188
- Synoptics : 157, 158, 166, 181, 204
- St. John's gospel : 157
- Book of Revelation : 157, 158, 165, 168-170, 174, 203, 274

Niagara Falls : 52

Nicholas I : 194

Nicole, Pierre : 35, 157, 201, 215

Nijmegen, Treaty of : 36

Noailles, Louis Antoine de : 43, 44, 57, 58, 67, 144

Nobility : 24, 78

North America : 253, 259

Notre Dame, Congregation of: 109

Nuncio (internuncio)
- In Brussels: 58, 61, 94, 116, 118, 148, 149
- In Cologne: 94
- In Paris: 118, 193, 327

O

Old Catholic(s)
- Appellation: 221
- Church: 9, 10, 13, 127, 215, 217, 227, 229, 243, 245, 248, 252, 261
- Doctrine: 257
- Episcopate : 27, 259
- Groups : 13, 117
- Line of succession: 100, 315
- Movement: 216, 226, 242, 253, 259
- Position: 159, 202, 229, 241, 249, 251
  - Continuity with Bishop Varlet's theology: 202, 243, 264, 295
- Protest: 219-222, 243, 257, 264
- Reflection: 250, 267, 295

Old Catholicism : 11, 23, 139, 189, 211, 269
- Seen as removed from principles claimed in 1889: 245, 253

Old Regime : see Ancien Régime.

Old Roman Catholic Church(es): 13, 253, 259

Old Testament : 156, 168, 182, 208, 234, 273, 297, 320, 321
- Psalms: 156, 158, 180, 182, 320
- Pentateuch: 97, 129, 156, 158, 168, 180, 320
- Prophets: 133, 156, 170, 174, 180, 182, 320

Olivier, Antoine: 100

Ontario
- Lake : 52
- Province: 258

Orange, Frederick Henry, Prince of : 78

Oratoire, Congregation of the, Oratorians : 20, 33, 36-39, 69, 77, 82, 86, 325

O'Reiley, Helena : 93

Origen : 158, 172, 174, 175, 297

Original sin : see Sin

Orthodox Churches : 13

Orval
- Abbey in Luxemburg: 64, 82
- Monks of: 65

Overseeing
- May become instrument of oppression: 114, 118
- Must conjoin the believers to eschatological goods: 131

Orzell, Lawrence J. : 13, 260, 267, 268

Oud-Bisschoppelijke Clerezij (O.B.C.) / Clergé vieil-épiscopal: 10, 14, 23, 63, 64, 80, 109, 111, 117, 118, 127, 188, 200, 201, 216, 219, 221, 229, 241-245, 251, 264, 273, 295

Ovid : 31

P

Palestine : 84

Palmer, Douglas B. : 255

Pamiers, bishopric of : 33, 62, 79

Papacy, Papal : see Pope

Papias : 173

Palladium : 194

Parables
- Bad fish in the net with the good: 183
- Good Samaritan / Priest and levite: 85
- Prodigal son: 85
- The wheat and the tares: 183

Parenesis : 129, 140

Paris
- Archbishop of : 37
- City of : 24, 26, 30, 33, 36, 40, 43, 50, 52, 58, 59, 64, 69, 78, 79, 325-327
- Parliament : 203
- Seminary : see Saint Magloire
- University of : see Sorbonne

Parenesis : 129, 140

Pâris, François de : 72, 161, 162, 203, 214

Parmentier, M.F.G.: 261

Parochism : 97, 198

Parousia : 251

Pascal, Blaise : 19, 79, 80, 81, 201

Pascheck, Aloïs: 225, 321

Pastor Aeternus, Constitution: 242, 243, 257, 317

Pastoral exhortation: 109

Patristics : 20, 39, 89, 104, 124, 143, 146, 157-159, 187, 188, 202, 220, 232, 297

Paul III : 77

Pavillon, Nicolas : 54, 79, 83, 93

Pelagius, Pelagianism : 84, 197, 281

Pelletier, Abraham : 258

Pentecost, J.D. : 173, 204

Peoria : 91

Perreault, Charles : 30, 81, 185

Persecution : 166, 183, 216, 274

Persia : 58, 60, 110, 111, 118, 119, 122, 170, 185, 276, 326, 327

Peter II, Tsar of Russia : 67, 98

Petitpied, Nicolas : 41, 82, 85, 88, 200, 215

Pharisaism (ecclesial), Pharisaic : 266
- Antithesis of justice: 273, 274
- Scandal: 116

Pichon, Jean : 231, 235

Pieper, Josef : 249

Pierling, Paul : 98

Pimiteoui : 109

Pindar : 31

Pius IV : 232

Plante, Guy : 86, 93, 94, 201

Plato : 174

Pliny the Young : 31

Plock (Poland) : 225, 259

Pneumatology, Pneumatological : see Holy Spirit

Polish churches, groups : 13, 224, 225, 252, 253, 259, 260, 267-269
- See Mariavites

Poncet : 97

Pontchâteau, M. de : 35

Poorvo Communion : 267

Pope : 9, 39, 57, 61, 62, 71, 77, 78, 80, 86, 93, 187, 220, 232, 276
- Authority of the: 14, 131, 159, 77, 240
- Bound by the rescripts of the councils: 84, 87, 131, 239
- Can compromise the advent of the Kingdom: 273
- Dogmas of infallibility and universal jurisdiction of the: 144, 202, 219-222, 241, 243, 257, 260, 264
- Epiphenomenon of the episcopal college: 131, 239
- Gardian of unity: 120, 239
- Grievances against the: 238
- His jurisdiction must not restrict that of bishops: 131, 148-150, 239
- Is not infallible: 195
- Must preserve the good order of the Church: 131, 150
- Responsible for the "communicatio in sacris" and the respect of church rules (canons): 119, 130, 141, 148, 195
- Responsible for safety of doctrine and purity of discipline: 200

Port-Louis : 45, 90, 107

Port-Royal :
- Abbey of: 19, 29, 30, 32, 65, 82, 84
- Archives/Collection of: 11, 64, 65, 84
- École de/School of: 26, 79
- Religious (Solitaires) of / Port-Royalists: 26, 27, 34-36, 80, 83, 263
- Société des Amis de: 11

Portugal, Portuguese : 71, 84

Poulet, Georges F. : 55, 57, 58, 94

Pragmatics : 128, 239

Prague : 222

Preaching
- Its rapport to faith: 133
- Its rapport to salvation: 128

Préclin, Edmond : 23, 41, 68, 80-86, 88, 89, 95-99, 200

Predestination : 77, 134, 159, 232, 234

Pre-Nicean : 173, 274

Presbyterian, Presbyterianism : 41, 97

Presbytero-episcopal influence, trends : 68, 95, 117

Pride : 123

Priests, Priesthood : 41, 43, 89

Primacy (of honour) : 13

Primitive Christianity, Church : see Early Church

Priory of Notre Dame, Conflans : 90

Probabilism, Probabilist : 135, 140, 159, 231, 236, 274, 306

Procedure (ecclesiastical) : 154

Prochniewski, Roman Jakub : 225, 259, 315

Promises (Old Testament) : 137, 140, 165, 175, 179-182
- And the institutional, visible church: 175
- And the millennium: 165, 180
- Their fulfillment began with the resurrection of Christ: 137, 178
- Their rapport to national Israël: 179

Propaganda, Congregation of the : 59, 94, 95, 192, 327

Prophecies: 172, 174, 179, 180, 205, 206, 273

Prophet(s), Prophetic : 104, 117, 118, 127, 133, 180, 241, 248, 249, 277, 297

Propositions condemned : 13, 54, 80, 146, 147, 183, 199, 231, 232, 241, 281, 283-292, 325

Protestantism, Protestant(s) : 26, 35, 41, 43, 60, 77, 88, 89, 98, 153, 157, 196
- Communicatio in sacris with: 252, 267

Prussia : 221

Prüter, Karl : 257

Q

Qua Sollicitudine, Brief : 62, 116

Quebec: 108
- Bishop of: 44, 50, 54, 185, 201, 276, 293
- Chapter of: 54, 93, 276
- Church of: 9, 54, 55, 113, 115, 275, 276
- City of: 45, 49, 50-52, 90-92, 275, 276, 326
- Coadjutor Bishop: 57, 93
- Diocese of: 45, 49, 53, 55, 326
- Province of: 258
- Ritual of: 54
- Seminary of: 90-93, 48-53, 108-111, 226, 293-294, 326

Quesnel, Pasquier : 13, 20, 27, 32-35, 41, 62, 63, 83, 86, 93, 95-97, 111, 117, 215, 325

Quinault, Philippe : 78

R

Rache, Francis Rudolf de Landas Berghes de : 260, 261, 268

Racine, Jean : 26, 27, 79, 81, 201

Ragueneau, Marie : 25

Rambaud, Alfred: 93

Rationalism (liberal): 245, 258

Rattisbone: 243

Redemption: 128, 179, 213, 233, 251, 273, 297

Réflexions morales..., book : 13, 20

Reform: 216, 221, 222, 226-228, 277
- Doctrinal: 132, 134
- Liturgical: 41, 198, 258
- Moral: 131-135
- Movement of: 19
- Of the Church: 131, 132, 240, 255, 275
- On Ancient Church model: 227, 245
- Pastoral: 132, 135
- Program of: 127, 214, 229, 230, 237, 238, 265
- Spiritual: 211
- Work of: 207

Reformation : 166, 178, 179, 220, 228
- English : 198, 261

Reformer : 103, 108, 188, 258, 276

Refuge, Refugees : 63-66, 71, 96, 186

Régale, droit de / right of : 26, 33, 79, 83

Regalism, Regalist : 54

Regiminis Apostolici, Constitution : 199

Reign of God : 124, 125, 188, 300, 304, 306
- Actant and actors of: 139, 140
- Advent, accomplishment of: 121, 139, 140, 165
- In the souls: 165, 178, 182, 242, 263, 264, 273, 275, 306

Reims : 60

Rein, Harald : 267

Reinkens, Josef H.: 100, 220-223, 229, 241, 242, 263, 264, 311, 315

Religion : 89, 132, 135, 158, 230, 307

Respectuous silence : 145, 146

Restout, Jean : 162

Reusch, Heinrich : 220

Revelation, book of: see New Testament

Revival : 168, 203, 211

Rhéaume, Anselme : 90

Rheinfelden : 223

Rhodes : 62

Richer, Edmond, Richerism, Richerist(s) : 20, 34, 35, 39, 41, 68, 77, 83, 89, 95, 97, 99, 201

Rijnwijk : 3, 63-66, 71, 74, 96, 156, 186, 201, 329, 330

Rijksaarchief Utrecht : 11, 34

Rinkel, Gaspard J. : 311, 315

Ritter, Mortiz : 220

Robillard, Anselme : 258

Romanet, Catherine de : 27

Rome, church, court, curia, see of : 9, 23, 33, 34, 58, 60, 61, 68, 69, 71, 72, 83, 86, 87, 93-95, 116, 119, 122-125, 129-132, 139, 140, 148, 159, 186, 196-200, 222, 231, 235, 240, 241, 244, 273, 274, 327

Rosalie, Bishop of : 69, 88

Rotterdam : 98

Rouen : 24

Rouse, Ruth : 261

Rovenius : 86

Royal Archives of Utrecht : see Rijksaarchief

Royal Navy : 90

Rueil : 26-28

Rules
- For the trial of bishops: 119
- Inherited from the Tradition and the Holy Fathers: 120, 141
- Inviolable: 120, 141
- Of faith: 135, 230, 233, 235, 243, 244
- Of the Church: 120, 150, 156
- Of discipline: 124, 230
- Of morals: 124, 135, 230-234, 243
- Useful against the ambition of the hierarchy: 130, 148, 275

Russian Orthodox Church : 63, 67-69, 259

S

Sacraments: 198, 227, 230, 235, 268, 309-310
- Annointing of the sick: 310
- Baptism: 89, 137, 246, 296
- Confirmation: 58, 59, 85, 89, 94, 113-115, 148, 273, 309, 327
- Holy Eucharist (Communion): 35, 88, 159, 176, 202, 206, 235, 244, 255, 264
  - Transsubstantiation: 206
- Holy Orders: 261
- Marriage: 310
- Penance: 37, 38, 85-87, 99, 199, 231, 235, 241, 310
- Standards for reception of the: 236

Saint André des Arts, church : 28, 29, 32

St. Ambrose of Milan: 159

St. Anne (Kankakee), Illinois: 258

St. Athanasius: 159

St. Augustine: 97, 105, 137, 158, 159, 172, 194, 202
- His condemnation of Pelagius: 84, 197, 208, 262
- His neotestamentarization of the Old Testament: 182
- On happiness: 137
- On grace: 77, 83, 137, 146
- On the chaining of, victory over Satan: 182, 204
- On the Church and the ministry: 175
- On the original sin: 197

St. Bernard of Clairvaux: 193

St. Clement of Alexandria: 173, 297

St. Clement of Rome: 277

Saint Côme, Michel de : 90

St. Cyprian: 150, 194, 297

Saint Cyran, Jean du Vergier de Hauranne, Abbot of : 19

St. Cyril of Jerusalem : 159

St. Eusebius of Caesarea : 159, 174

St. Francis of Sales : 84

St. Germain L'Auxerrois : 24

St. Gregory the Great: 99, 149, 150, 194, 196, 200

St. Gobain : 33

St. Ignace, Michigan : 91

St. Ignatius of Loyola : 84

St. Irenaeus of Lyons: 173

St. Jerome : 158

St. John Chrysostom : 158, 159, 166, 194

St. John the Evangelist : 169, 203

St. Justin Martyr: 97, 105, 159, 173

St. Lawrence, river : 52

St. Leo the Great: 130, 194

St. Louis East, Illinois : 44, 325

St. Luke : 167

Saint-Magloire, Séminaire : 31, 38, 43, 82-84, 88, 96, 98, 145, 172, 200, 204, 325

St. Mary's Church Cloister, Utrecht : 65, 74, 330

St. Matthew : 97

St. Medard Cemetery : 73, 179

St. Nicolas des Champs, church : 25

Saint-Olon, Louis Marie Pidou de : 57, 94, 326, 327

St. Paul : 41, 166
- Fidelity to the truth: 104
- His Epistle to the Colossians: 319
- His Epistle to the Corinthians: 167
- His Epistle to the Philippians: 195
- His Epistle to the Romans: 38, 97, 105, 114, 128, 130, 133, 137, 170, 192
- His Epistle to Timothy: 167
- In the Acts of the Apostles : 167

Saint-Paul-aux-Bois : 33

St. Peter: 149, 166, 300

St. Peterburg : 95

St. Sulpice, priests of : 52

St. Thomas Aquinas: 153, 157, 175, 202, 232

St. Vallier, Jean de la Croix de : 50, 51, 54, 55, 57, 86, 92-94, 108, 111, 201, 293, 294, 326

St. Vincent of Lerins : 188, 202, 249, 264

St. Vanne, abbey of : 202

St. Virgil of Arles : 150

Sainte-Beuve, Charles Augustin de : 80, 153

Sainte Croix, Sanctuaire de la : 26, 27, 29

Sainte Famille Mission : see Holy Family Mission

Sainte-Marthe, Abel Louis de : 33, 36, 82

Salle, René Robert Cavalier, sieur de la: 39

Salvation : 9, 83, 134, 140, 185, 205, 239, 242, 251
- Certainty of: 89
- Given by God in Jesus Christ: 140
- Hierarchy and faithfull must collaborate in the work of: 140
- Occurs, is experienced in the Church: 103, 265, 266
- Of souls: 46, 53, 205, 276
- Uncertainty of: 202
- The Holy Spirit makes us see it in the Church: 248, 250

Satan, Satanic : 139
- Attached to the Cross: 175
- Chained during the millennium: 169, 170, 181, 182
- Defeat of: 204
- Opposed to the reign of God: 170
- Power of: 169, 170
- Pretentions of: 122, 123
- Temporarily released at end of millennium: 170, 181

Sauer, Eric : 179, 204-206

Savoy, Irène : 267

Schaff, Philipp : 173, 204

Schindelaar, Adalbert : 225, 321

Schism, Schismatical, Schismatics : 38, 86, 122, 214, 232, 256

Schömberg, Frederick Hermann, Marshal of France : 24, 25, 78

Schömberg, Hans Meinard : 78

Schonauwen : 3, 63-67, 97, 186, 201, 329

Schute, Friedrich von : 222, 257, 258

Scranton (Pennsylvania) : 224
- Declaration of: 267, 269

Scripture : see Holy Scripture

Secularism, Secularist : see Laicism

Séez : 82

Séminaire Saint-Magloire : see Saint Magloire Seminary

Senez, bischopric, diocese of : 62, 82, 93, 96, 105, 143, 147, 154, 201, 275

Sens : 82, 88

Sexuality, Sexual
- Orientation : 267
- Same-sex unions : 252, 259, 267, 268

Shallis, Ralph : 170, 203, 205

Shamake : 95

Shea, John G. : 91

Sicily : 205

Siam : 69, 88

Sin : 308
- Agains the lordship of Christ: 123, 186
- Ignorance does not excuse from: 236
- Of Adam, original: 84, 89, 134, 197, 233, 263
- Remission of / Deliverance from: 135, 234, 297, 304

Sinai : 318

Sisters of the Visitation : 82

Slicher : 60

Slovakia : 226, 252, 260, 268

Soanen, Jean : 37, 64, 82, 93, 96, 275, 278

Social changes : 267

Society of the Precious Blood : 223

Soissons : 233

Solomon, biblical king : 180

Solothurn (Switzerland) : 222

Sophocles : 31

Sophism(s) : 230, 263

Sorbonne : 26, 32, 39, 49, 60, 67, 82, 85, 98, 145, 146, 154, 233, 277, 325, 326

Soteriology, Soteriological : 128, 136, 138, 195, 239, 248, 251

Souls : 46, 117, 137, 139, 238, 251

Source, René Thaumur de la : 53, 93, 103, 110, 326

Spanish mystics : 77

Sri Lanka : 259

Stalder, Kurt : 11, 246, 248, 265, 266, 321

Steenoven, Cornelis : 34, 35, 61-63, 86, 95, 96, 111, 116, 127, 199, 241, 328

Stieve, Felix : 220

Structural analysis : 118

Supremacy
- Papal claim of: 13

Suspense : 58, 59, 86, 95, 113, 116, 118-121, 125, 148, 185

Sutton, Anne : 78

Sutton, Edward : 78

Sweden : 226, 267

Switzerland, Swiss : 98, 219, 222, 225, 226, 245, 258, 267

Syllabus of Errors (of Pope Pius IX) : 244

Synod, Synodal, Synodalism : 41, 98, 150, 192, 199, 200, 217, 252, 258, 274

Syria, Syriac : 40, 84
- Patriarchate of Antioch: 259

Szulgowicz, Maria Beatrijcze : 259

T

Talon, Jean: 94

Tamaroa(s) : 44, 45, 48-51, 88, 90, 91, 293, 325, 326

Tans, J.: 97

Targny, Louis : 179, 207

Tartars : 99

Tatford, Frederick A.: 173, 204-308

Taveneaux, René : 96, 97, 179, 197-200, 203-208, 256

Teaching : 143, 156
- Of the Bible: 136
- Theological
  - Content of: 135

Tencin, Pierre-Paul Guérin de : 96

Terence : 31

Terrasson, Gaspard : 69, 99

Tertullian : 97, 105, 158, 159, 173, 247, 297

Têtu, Henri : 93

The Hague : 98, 201

Theodoret : 159

Thessalonica, archbishop of : 130

Theology
- Bishop Varlet's theological sum, principles, synthesis, system: 127, 128, 136, 185, 236-240, 245, 248, 256, 265, 266, 273, 277
- Linked to a critique of the Church: 133
- Linked to the Word of God: 132, 133
- Moral: 135
- Mystical: 185, 203
- Of creation: 267, 319
- Of hope: 133
- Of the signs of the times: 132, 197
- Plan of study of : 157, 158, 202, 307-310
- Prophetic role of: 133
- School of : 65
- Teaching of: 156

Theophore : 123, 194

Thiboult, Thomas : 53, 55, 93, 111

Thomism, Thomist : 84

Tichonius : 172

Tillemont, Louis Sébastien Le Nain de : 29

Tonkin : 35, 86, 88, 99, 105, 143

Tradition : 146, 233, 249, 267, 269, 307

Trela, Jonathan : 257

Trinity : see Holy Trinity

Tremblay, H.J. : 88

Tremblay, M. : 90

Tronson, Louis : 93

Troyes : 62, 255

Truth
- Can be held captive (of injustice...): 104, 133
- Defence of the: 122, 125, 134, 139, 140, 215, 216, 238, 240, 273, 274, 277
- Defended by humble people: 123, 139
- Defended by the prophet(s): 104
- Fidelity to the: 104, 123, 243
- Given once for all: 104, 243, 249
- Is Jesus Christ: 250
- Revealed: 39, 132
- The Gallican claim is isotope to it: 274

Turkey : 84

Ultramontanism, Ultramontane : 9, 13, 14, 20, 77

Unigenitus, bull : 9, 13, 20, 34, 35, 37, 38, 54, 55, 58-60, 64, 68, 69, 72, 80, 84, 111, 117-121, 129, 135, 143, 144, 147, 193, 200, 211, 242, 244, 283-292, 305, 325-328
- Casts shadow on the doctrine of grace: 129, 147
- Challenges traditional dogma: 134
- Darkens the theology of the Church: 147
- Destroys the theology of St. Paul's epistle to the Romans: 134
- Gallicano-Jansenist opposition to: 211
- Is a sign of the universal apostasy at the end of times: 170
- Leads to laxism: 135, 151
- Presents church doctrine in a form not suitable: 132
- Repressive: 111
- Resistance to: 23, 213, 274

- State law in France: 111, 170, 171, 256
- Undermines the doctrine of efficacious grace: 144, 147

United Kingdom : 225

United States : 223, 224

Urban VIII : 256

Usury : 66, 72, 97, 151-155, 185, 201, 329

Utrecht
- Agreement of: 257
- Archbishops of: 11, 13, 71, 72, 86, 88, 96, 152-154, 185, 200, 221, 227, 260
- Bishops Conference of: 11, 226, 257-260, 267
- Chapter of: 9, 23, 59-62, 71, 72, 86, 94, 96, 114, 115, 127, 150-155, 161, 185, 200, 201, 211, 215, 216, 242, 273, 327-329
- Church of: 60-64, 66, 68, 72, 82, 86, 91, 114-116, 143, 144, 151, 187, 192, 200, 216, 219, 227, 231, 241-244, 257, 262, 263, 276
- City of: 65, 74, 98, 100, 224
- Clergy of: 9, 36, 60, 82, 145
- Contentious jurisdiction: 115, 116
- Convention & Declaration of: 159, 202, 243-245, 257, 311-313
- Metropolitan see of: 58, 60, 63, 66, 77, 86, 130, 151, 200, 215, 219
- Pope Patriarch of: 98
- Reform of: 113
- Synod of: 74, 229-243, 256, 262, 263, 329
- Union of: 11, 13, 219, 225, 226, 229, 245, 246, 251, 252, 257, 259-261, 266-268, 315
  - European body: 253
  - Modernist direction of: 260

V

Vaillant, Pierre : 255

Vaissière, abbé de : 88

Vallée, Marie, mother of Bishop Varlet : 24, 28, 40, 45, 52, 80, 81, 85, 88, 90-92, 191

Van Bijlevelt, Jean : 61

Van Cock, Theodore : 86

Van Dalenoort, Willem : 62, 96, 154, 201

Van der Croon, Theodore : 71-73, 97, 99, 151, 154, 155, 161, 329, 330

Van de Ven, A.J. : 64, 65, 84, 93, 96, 97

Van Erkel, Johannes : 62, 96

Van Espen, Z. Bernard : 59, 60, 95

Van Kleef, Bastian A. : 80, 82, 85, 86, 88, 90, 94-100, 204, 256

Van Kley, Dale K. : 203

Van Neercassel, J.B. : 36, 38, 86, 235, 236

Van Nieuwenhuan, Walter : 315

Van Os, Willibrord : 315

Van Rhijn, Johannes : 315

Van Santen, Johannes : 315

Van Schooten, Kees : 11

Van Stiphout, J. : 315

Van Vlijmen, H.T.J. : 321

Van Woestenberg, J.A. : 192

Varlet, Achille : 24, 25, 27, 28

Varlet, Anne-Marie : 40, 94, 99

Varlet, Charles : 24, 25, 78

Varlet, Hector : 24

Varlet, Jean-Achille : 40, 46, 90-92, 191

Varlet, Marie-Justine : 24, 25

Vatican : see Rome

Vaugrigneuse : 40

Venne, Jean : 2

Verheul : 216

Viaixnes, Thierry de : 35, 62, 66, 85, 94, 95, 98

Vicar apostolic : 54, 69, 86, 93, 94, 116, 149, 150, 200

Vicar general : 47, 90, 96. 185, 201, 326

Vilatte, René : 223, 258, 259, 315

Villermola, Michel de : 55

Villiers, L. Paris Vaquier de : 66, 74, 155, 201

Vineam Sabaoth Domini, bull : 85

Virgil : 31

Visser, J. : 86

Vitasse, C. : 82

Vivant, dean of Paris : 88

Vlierbeek, abbé de : 85

Voltaire, François M. Arouet dit : 68, 98

W

Wake, William : 67, 98

Wassemberg, Ignaz H. von : 222, 258

Weber, Theodor : 224, 259

Wedgwood, James I. : 260

Williams, Bernard M. : 257

Witte, Aegidius de : 43

Wisconsin : 258

Women in ministry : 252, 260, 266-268

Word of God : 274, 299, 303, 305
- Embodied in the faith community: 132
- Prepares the advent of the kingdom: 133

World Council of Churches : 13, 224, 253

World Council of National Catholic Churches : 268

Wuytiers, J.C. Barchman : 36, 63, 66-69, 71, 74, 82, 88, 96, 97, 151, 152, 161, 201, 216, 241, 255, 329

X, Y, Z

Xenophon : 31

Yugoslavia : 321

Zoborowski, Robert : 259

Zosimus : 194

Zwolle : 73, 329

BIBLIOGRAPHY

1
Works of Bishop Varlet

Published:

Lettre de Monseigneur l'évêque de Babylone à Monseigneur l'évêque de Montpellier pour servir de réponse à l'ordonnance de Monsieur l'archevêque de Paris rendue le 8 novembre 1733 au sujet des miracles opérés par l'intercession de Monsieur de Pâris, à Utrecht, aux dépens de la Compagnie, 1736.

Lettre de Monsieur l'évêque de Babylone aux missionnaires du Tonquin, à Utrecht, chez la veuve Chrysostome Lafuite, 1734.

Lettre de Monseigneur l'archevêque d'Utrecht et de Monseigneur l'évêque de Babylone à Monseigneur l'évêque de Senez au sujet du jugement rendu à Embrun contre ce prélat, à Utrecht, aux dépens de la Compagnie, 1738.

Première Apologie de Monseigneur l'évêque de Babylone, Nicolas Potgieter, Amsterdam, 1724.

Deuxième Apologie de Monseigneur l'évêque de Babylone, Nicolas Potgieter, Amsterdam, 1727.

Réponse de Monseigneur l'évêque de Babylone à Monseigneur l'évêque de Senez, Utrecht, 1736.

Testament Spirituel de M. Dominique-Marie Varlet, évêque de Babylone, Nouvelles Ecclésiastiques, Paris, July 8, 1742.

Manuscripts:

A - <u>Commentaries</u>:

Constituted of a statement and/or a query

- Mémoire sur la manière d'écrire aux évêques.
- Mémoire sur l'établissement d'un évêque de Haarlem.

Constituted of a reflection and/or a criticism

- Observations sur l'écrit "Discussio brevis, an Ecclesiae Haarlemensi praeficiendus sit episcopus »
- Observations sur l'instruction de Bissi.
- Remarques sur le traité contre l'usure.
- Remarques sur l'histoire de C. Lenfant : Schisme des protestants.
- Remarques sur un écrit concernant les prétentions du chapitre d'Utrecht.

Demonstrating the falsity of what another has written

- Réfutation de la lettre de R.D.N. à un étudiant de Cologne sur sa réputation.
- Réfutation des dialogues de M. de Cambrai.

Written in response to a question or request

- Réponse à un écrit qui a pour objet de prouver... dans l'affaire de Haarlem.

Made of annotations on texts

- Annotations sur l'Écriture Sainte.
- Annotations et extraits sur les affaires de l'Église.
- Annotations sur divers sujets d'ordre historique, théologique et moral.
- Annotations sur le mandement du cardinal de Noailles du 2 août 1720 sur la bulle Unigenitus.
- Annotations sur les mémoires du refus des bulles.

In draft form

- Plan d'une méthode pour étudier la théologie et l'histoire de l'Église.

Narrating facts of his life

- Journal du voyage vers Babylone.
- Journaux du Tonquin.

Collected and classified in a documentary intent

- Collections sur l'épître aux Romains, sur Isaie, Justin, Tertullien et saint Augustin.

B - <u>Letters</u>:

- His general correspondence including letters relating to the missions of the Seminary of Quebec and the East as well as those related to the resistance against the Bull Unigenitus, the Appeal to the General Council and the affairs of the Church of Utrecht.

C - <u>Other Writings</u>:

- Acte de protestation contre l'élection de Gérard Akkoy.
- Divers écrits sur les langues arabe, éthiopienne et hébraique.
- Expostulatio de calumniosa libello sparso 8 aprilis 1724 et appendix appellationis interpositae.
- Pièces sur les affaires de l'Église de Hollande.

D - <u>Bibliography</u>:

- Jacob Bosveld, <u>Bibliotheca Varletiana</u>, Kribber & Weyde, Utrecht, 1748.

2
Books, Articles, Testimonials About Bishop Varlet or Having Relation to Him and His Work

Aman, E., *Varlet, Dominique-Marie*, <u>Dictionnaire de théologie catholique</u>, Vol. 15, p. 2535-2536.

Cogné, Daniel, *Les armoiries de Mgr Dominique-Marie Varlet, 1678-1742*, <u>L'Héraldique au Canada</u>, XVI,2, June 1982.

Deloche, Maximin, *Un missionnaire français en Amérique au 18e siècle. Contribution à l'histoire de l'établissement des Français en Louisiane*,

Bulletin de la section de géographie du Comité des travaux historiques, Paris, XLV, 1930, p. 39-60.

De Villiers, L. Paris Vaquier, In Obitum Illustrissimi ac Reverendissimi in Christo Patris D.D. Dominici Mariae Varlet, Babylonensis Episcopi, Schonauwen, The Netherlands, June 21 1742.

Guy, Basil, Domestic Correspondance of Dominique M. Varlet, Bishop of Babylone, E.J. Brill Editor, Leyden, The Netherlands, 1986.

Hurtubise, Pierre, *Dominique-Marie Varlet, missionnaire en Nouvelle-France, 1713-1718*, Revue de la Société canadienne d'histoire de l'Église catholique, 35, 1968, p. 39-60.

Hurtubise, Pierre, *Relations inédites des missions de l'Illinois, 1720-1724*, Église et Théologie, 8, 1977, p. 265-291.

Hurtubise, Pierre, *Varlet, Dominique-Marie*, Dictionnaire biographique du Canada, Vol. II, 1969, p. 691-693.

Jal, Auguste, *Varlet, Dominique-Marie*, Dictionnaire critique de biographie et d'histoire, Paris, 1867, p. 726-729.

Lopez, Davide, *L'opera di Dominique Marie Varlet*, Cattolici senza Roma, Facolta di Littere e Filosofia, Universita di Milano, July 2007, p. 23-24.

Michaud, Eugène, *Les deux apologies de Dominique-Marie Varlet, évêque de Babylone*, Revue internationale de théologie (R.I.T.), Berne, 1902, p. 478-503.

Michaud, J.F. & L.G., *Varlet, Dominique-Marie*, Biographies universelles anciennes et modernes, 2nd ed., Tome 42, Louis Vives, Paris, p. 649.

Moreri, E., *Varlet, Dominique-Marie*, Le Grand Dictionnaire, 1759, Tome X, p. 481.

Rhéaume, Anselme, *Mgr Dominique-Marie Varlet*, Bulletin de recherches historiques, III, 1897, p. 18-22.

Thériault, Serge A., *Dominique-Marie Varlet, de l'Église de Québec à la réforme d'Utrecht*, Revue d'histoire de l'Amérique française (R.H.A.F.), Vol. 36, No. 2, September 1982, p. 195-212.

Thériault, Serge A., Dominique-Marie Varlet. Lettres du Canada et de la Louisiane, 1713-1724, Presses de l'Université du Québec, 1985.

Thériault, Serge A., *De Charles Chiniquy à l'évêque Varlet: une évocation à l'occasion du 125e anniversaire de la réforme catholique franco-américaine, 1858-1983*, Aujourd'hui Credo, United Church of Canada, Vol. 30, No. 12, December 1982, p. 20-22.

Thériault, Serge A., Entre Babylone et le Royaume. Vie et œuvre de Dominique-Marie Varlet, grand vicaire de l'évêque de Québec et père de l'épiscopat vieux-catholique d'Utrecht, Th.D. Dissertation, Old Catholic Faculty of Theology, University of Berne, May 1983.

Thériault, Serge A., *L'articulation christologique comme forme de la thématique ecclésiologique dans trois textes de Dominique-Marie Varlet aux origines du vieux-catholicisme*, I.K.Z., Berne, Vol. 80, No. 389, 1990, p. 40-58.

Thériault, Serge A., *La pastorale dans le jansénisme : la figure de Mgr Dominique-Marie Varlet*, I.K.Z., Berne, July-September 1985, p. 180-188.

Thériault, Serge A., *La sainte Trinité dans la théologie de Mgr Dominique-Marie Varlet aux origines du vieux-catholicisme*, I.K.Z., Berne, October-December 1983, p. 234-245.

Van Kleef, Bastian A., *Dominicus Maria Varlet*, R.I.T., Berne, LIII, 1963, p. 78-104, 149-177, 193-222.

3
Books which speak of Bishop Varlet

A - *In connection with the Church of Quebec (Roman Catholic)*

Audet, F. Émile, Les Premiers établissements français du pays des Illinois, Fernand Galot, Paris, 1938, p. 42.

Baillargeon, Noël, Le Séminaire de Québec, de 1685 à 1760, Presses de l'Université Laval, Québec, 1977, p. 398-407.

Delangez, Jean, The French Jesuits in Lower Louisiana (1700-1763), Washington, Studies in American Church History, the Catholic University of America, 1935, p. 71-74.

Gagnon, Serge, Le Québec et ses historiens de 1840 à 1920, Presses de l'Université Laval, Coll. Cahiers de l'histoire, 1978, p. 262-302.

Garneau, François-Xavier, Histoire du Canada, Librairie Félix Alcan, Paris, 1913, Tome 1, p. 235.

Giraud, Marcel, Histoire de la Louisiane française, Presses universitaires de France (P.U.F.), Paris, 1966, Tome III, p. 375.

Gosselin, Auguste, L'Église du Canada depuis Mgr de Laval jusqu'à la Conquête, Laflamme & Proulx, Québec, Tome 1, p. 331-335.

Plante, Guy, Le Rigorisme au 18e siècle. Mgr de Saint-Vallier et le sacrement de pénitence, J. Duculot, Gembloux, 1970, p. 154.

Shea, John G., The Catholic Church in Colonial Days, 1521-1763, J.G. Shea Ed., New York, 1886, p. 556.

B – *In Connection with the Church of Utrecht*:

Bellegarde, Gabriel Dupac de, Histoire abrégée de l'Église métropolitaine d'Utrecht, J.A. van Woestenberg, 1852, p. 269 ff.

Leclerc, Gustave, Zeger-Bernard van Espen et l'autorité ecclésiastique, Pas Verlag, Zurich, 1964, p. 98-101, 103, 106, 358.

Moss, Claude B., The Old Catholic Movement, Apocryphile Press, Berkeley, 2005, p. 119-131.

Neale, J.M., A History of the So-Called Jansenist Church of Holland, Aporcyphile Press, Berkeley, 2005, p. 241, 243-247, 256, 264, 266, 277.

Verhey, B.W., L'Église d'Utrecht, Hoogland Printer, Delft, 1981, p. 58-59, 61-62, 68-73, 75, 85, 149.

C – *In Connection with Jansenism*:

Cognet, Louis, Le Jansénisme, P.U.F., Paris, 1975, p. 105.

Jacques, Émile, Les Années d'exil d'Antoine Arnauld, 1679-1694, Publications universitaires de Louvain, 1976, p. 720.

Kreiser, B. Robert, Miracles, Convulsions and Ecclesiastical Politics in Early 18th Century Paris, Princeton University Press, 1978, p. 79, 372-373.

Palmer, Douglas B., The Republic of Grace: International Jansenism in the Age of Enlightenment and Revolutions, Ph.D. dissertation (History), Ohio State University, 2004, p. 5 & 37.

Préclin, Edmond, Les jansénistes du 18e siècle et la constitution civile du clergé, Paris, 1929, p. 201-207.

Taveneaux, René, Jansénisme et prêt à intérêt, Librairie philosophique J. Vrin, Paris, 1977, p. 60, 62, 65, 67-70, 140, 142-143, 150-153, 217, 220-221.

Taveneaux, René, Le Jansénisme en Lorraine, 1640-1789, Librairie philosphique J. Vrin, Paris, 1960, p. 26-27, 540, 594.

4
Books and Articles on Gallicanism, Jansenism and Old Catholicism

Ackermann, R., *Un partenaire peu connu du dialogue oecuménique: l'Église vieille-catholique*, La Croix, July 16, 1979.

Aldenhoven, Herwig, *Das Konzil von Basel in alkatholischer Sicht*, Theologische Zeitschrift, Vol. 38, 1982.

Aldenhoven, Herwig, Der ekklesiologische Selbstverständnis der Altkatholischen Kirchen, op. cit., p. 402-403.

Aldenhoven, Herwig, Die Unterscheideung zwischen einer erkennbar-zu-gänglichen und einer unerkennbar-unzugänglichen Seite in Gott und die Trinitätslehre..., p. 214-232.

Aldenhoven, Herwig, *Geist Gottes − Geist Christi, Verlag Otto Lembeck*, Frankfurt, 1981, Beiblatt zur ökumenischen Rundschau, No. 39.

Aldenhoven, Herwig, *The Filioque in the Old Catholic Churches (...) and the Ecclesiastical opinions,* Beiblatt zur Oekumenischen Rundschau, June 1981.

Allemang, E., *L'Église janséniste d'Utrecht,* Annuaire pontifical catholique, 1912.

Amiet, Peter, *Ortskirche − Universalkirche, Amt un Bezeugung der Wahrheit,* I.K.Z., January-March 1982, p. 33-34.

Amiet, Peter, *Zum altkatholischen Kirchenverständnis,* Beiblatt zur Oekumenische Rundschau, op. cit.

Bruggeman, J. & van de Ven, A.J., Inventaire des pièces d'archives françaises se rapportant à l'Abbaye de Port-Royal-des-Champs et son cercle et à la résistance contre la bulle Unigenitus, Martinus Nijhoff, The Hague, 1972.

Carreyre, J., *Église d'Utrecht* in Dictionnaire de théologie catholique, XV, columns 2390-2446.

Cole, Alan M., The Old Catholic Phenomenon, Avon Books, London, 1997.

Conzemius, Victor, *Aspects ecclésiologiques de Döllinger et du vieux-catholicisme,* Revue des sciences religieuses, Nos. 2-3-4, 1960.

Colonia, P., Bibliothèque Janséniste, Vol. II, p. 139-140.

Cossette, Joseph, *Jean Talon, champion au Canada du gallicanisme royal,* R.H.A.F., *IX,3, 1957.*

Gauthier, Léon, *Actualité de saint Vincent de Lérins*, Kracht in Zwakheid van een kleine Wereldkerk, Amersfoort, The Netherlands, 1982, p. 104-105.

Gauthier, Léon, *Pour le 25e anniversaire de l'intercommunion anglicane et vieille-catholique*, IKZ, 46, 1956, p. 133-149.

Gauthier, Léon, *Qui sont les vieux-catholiques?* in Chemins vers la vérité, Labor & Fides, 1980, p. 7-27.

Gazier, Augustin, Histoire générale du mouvement janséniste, Paris, 1922, Tome 1.

Gedenkbook 1723-1923, *Eenn feest der verkiezing van Cornelis Steenoven tot Aartsbisschop van Utrecht*, 1923.

Gres-Gayer, Jacques, Paris-Cantorbéry (1717-1720). Dossier d'un premier oecuménisme, Paris, Beauchesne, 1989.

Groman, E.O., *An Old Catholic History*, in God's Field, August 1978.

Groulx, Lionel, *Le gallicanisme au Canada sous Louis XIV*, RHAF 1,1, June 1947

Guilbert, P., Mémoires historiques et chronologiques sur l'Abbaye de Port-Royal-des-Champs, Utrecht, 1755-1756.

Kenninck, Franciscus, *Le Clerc und Pinel im Urteil der Utrechter Kirche*, IKZ, April-June 1949, p. 69-93.

Keussen, Rudolf, *Der Katholizismus und seine Ideale*, I.K.Z., 1924.

Küry, Urs, Chemins vers la vérité, Labor & Fides, Geneva, 1980.

Küry, Urs, *Christus und die Kirche in der theologischen Lehre*, I.K.Z., Vol. 46, 1957, p. 35-66.

Le Gros, Nicolas, Du renversement des libertés de l'Église gallicane, 1717.

Maan, P.J., C.J. Barchman Wuytiers Erzbischof von Utrecht, van Gorcum & Co., Uitgevers Assen, 1949.

Martimort, Aimé-Georges, Le Gallicanisme, P.U.F., Paris, 1973

Middlehoff, Kees, *Les vieux-catholiques souhaitent jouer les intermédiaires entre les Églises*, Informations catholiques internationales, No. 424, 1973.

Montgeron, Louis Basile Carré de, La Vérité des miracles opérés par l'intercession de M.de Pâris, démontrée contre M. l'archevêque de Sens, Libraires de la Compagnie, Utrecht, 1737.

Muller, Charles, Esquisse historique du mouvement vieux-catholique dans les pays de langue allemande, Schautz Publisher, Geneva, 1897.

Orzell, Laurence J., *Disunion of Utrecht. Old Catholics Fall Out over New Doctrines*, Touchstone, Chicago, May 2004.

Parmentier, M.F.G., *Evangelical Anglicans and Old Catholics in 1931*, Kracht in Zwakheid van een klein Wereldkerk, Oud-Katholieke Seminarie, Amersfoort, 1982.

Edmond Richer, De ecclesiastica et politica potestate, Ioannem Petis-pas Ed., Paris, 1612.

Rein, Harald, *Report of the (Swiss Church) Commission "Church & Homosexuality"*, Supplement No. 4, Présence catholique-chrétienne, Switzerland, Vol. 98, No. 6, July-August 2006.

Reinkens, Josef H., *Pastoral Letter of August 11, 1872* in Revue Internationale de théologie, Jan.- March 1901, p. 1-6.

Sainte-Beuve, C.A. de, Port-Royal, Bibliothèque de la Pleiade, Paris, tome III, p. 575-76.

Schulte, J.F. von. Der Altkatholizismus, Giessen, 1887.

Stalder, Kurt, *Der ekklesiologische und kirchenrechtliche Gehalt des Utrechter Union der Altkatholischen Kirchen*, in Oesterreichiches Archiv für Kirchenrecht, Vol. 31, No. 4, 1980.

Stalder, Kurt, *Ekklesiologie und Rechtsstruktur der Utrechter Union der altkatholischen Bishöfe*, Kracht in Zwakheid van een kleine ereldkerk: De Oud-Katholieke Unie van Utrecht, Amersfoort, 1982.

Tans, J., *Kerkpolitiek tussen gallicanism en Verlichting*, Kracht in Zwakeid van een kleine Wereldkerk, Oud-katholiek Seminarie, Amersfoort, 1982.

Targny, L., Mémoire sur l'état present des réfugiés en Hollande... and Mémoire sur le projet janséniste.

Taveneaux, René, Jansénisme et politique, Armand Collin, Paris, 1965.

Taveneaux, René, Jansénisme et prêt à intérêt, J. Vrin, Paris, 1977.

Tavenaux, René, Le Jansénisme en Lorraine, 1640-1789, Paris, 1960.

Tighe, William J., *Old Catholics, New Doctrines. The Demise of the Union of Utrecht*, Touchstone, January-February 1999.

Van de Ven, A.J., *La communauté cistercienne de la Maison de Rijnwijk près d'Utrecht*, I.K.Z., Berne, April-June 1949.

5
Archives

Archives Nationales de France
- Document LL1591: Registre... de MM. les Prêtres du Calvaire

Archives of the Archdiocese of Quebec
- Mandements des évêques de Québec (Têtu & Gagnon), I, 495.

Archives of the Seminary of Quebec
- Missions, 105 b.

Archives of the Vatican
- Holding of the Secretariat of State: Nonciature de France, 234, 389.

Bibliothèque et Archives Nationales du Québec
- Collection Réforme catholique (P103)
  - Series Dominique-Marie Varlet (S1)
  - Series Fonds Vilatte (S4)

- Édits et ordonnances royaux, déclarations du Conseil d'état du Roy pour le Canada, Tome 1

Bibliothèque Municipale de Nantes, France
- Manuscript No. 2113, Folio B

Library and Archives Canada

- Collection de l'Abbaye de Port-Royal-des-Champs (microfilm), 1692-1744, MG17-A23.
- Letter dealing with the bishopric of Babylon, Archives of the Congregation « de Propaganda Fide », Rome, vol. 615 (1718). 1719, microfilm MG17-A25.
- Memorandum on the affair of D.M. Varlet, December, 17, 1719, MG17-A1.
- Mémoires sur les missions du Canada, Archives des colonies, B, Vol. II, May 19, 1865, p. 283.

Records Office, London
- Edgmont, MSS 67

Royal Archives of Utrecht (Rijksarchief Utrecht)
- Fonds Port-Royal d'Amersfoort.

State Archives, Holland
- Political Correspondance, Tome 350, Folio 55.

6
Methods of Analysis Used

Theriault, Serge A. & Juery, Rene, <u>Analyse structurale des textes</u>, Asticou Publisher, Coll. Université du Québec, Gatineau, 1980.

ABBREVIATIONS & ILLUSTRATIONS

List of Abbreviations

A.P.R.   Archives of Port Royal

BAnQ   Bibliothèque et Archives Nationales du Québec

C.R.C.   Collection Réforme Catholique, BAnQ

I.K.Z.   Internationale Kirchliche Zeitschrift

L.A.C.   Library and Archives Canada

O.B.C.   Oud-Bisschoppelijke Clerezij

O.C.   Old Catholic

P.N.C.C. Polish National Catholic Church

P.U.F.   Presses Universitaires de France

P.U.Q.   Presses de l'Université du Québec

R.H.A.F. Revue d'histoire de l'Amérique française

R.I.T.   Revue Internationale de Théologie

S.M.É.   Société des Missions Étrangères

414

List of Illustrations

The illustrations used in this book are all in the public domain (copyright expired or released) or belong to the author, except those indicated otherwise.

Page

15: Bishop Dominique Marie Varlet, 1678-1742.
Museum Catharijneconvent, Utrecht

16: Bishop Varlet's Coat of Arms.

19: Cornelis Jansen (Jansenius), Bishop of Ypres, Belgium, 1585-1638. Front conver of his book *Augustinus*. Jean Duvergier de Hauranne, Abbot of Saint-Cyran, 1581-1683.

20: Pasquier Quesnel, Oratorian priest, 1634-1719. Front cover of his book *Réflexions morales sur le Nouveau-Testament*, Tome 3, published in 1693.

24: Charles Varlet, Sieur de La Grange, 1635-1692

25: Friedrich Hermann Schomberg, Marshal of France, 1616-1690

26: The Calvary at Mont Valerien
http://www.montfort.org.uk/ifm/ifmsouth3.htm#MontVal

28: Antoine Arnauld, Port-Royalist, 1612-1694.

32 : Nuns being removed from the Abbey of Port-Royal

36: Johannes B. van Neercassel, Achbishop of Utrecht under the title Bishop of Castoria, 1623-1686.

42: Inside View of the Parish Church of Asnières, France.
http://fr.wikipedia.org/wiki/Fichier:C389glise_Sainte-Genevive_-_nef.jpg

44: Louis Antoine, Cardinal de Noailles, Archbishop of Paris, 1651-1729. View of Conflans (France) and its parish church.

46: Map of New France at its apogee.
http://en.wikipedia.org/wiki/File:Nouvelle-France_map-en.svg
Signature Varlet Vicar General
From J.G. Shea book The Catholic Church in Colonial Days,1886

47: Replica of the old French Fort at Mobile, Alabama.
http://www.associatedcontent.com/image/103603/

48: Log Church of the Holy Family at Cahokia, Illinois.

49: Algonquin Indians.
http://www.usgennet.org/usa/mo/county/stlouis/native/indian.htm

51: Old Seminary of Quebec.
Daniel Abel, http://www.danielabel.net

54: Jean de la Croix de St. Vallier, 2nd Bishop of Quebec 1653-1727.

57: Louis François Duplessis de Mornay, Coadjutor Bishop of Quebec. Succeeded St. Vallier as Ordinary 1663-1741.

59 : Charles de Caylus, Bishop of Auxerre, 1669-1754.

62 : Cornelis Steenoven, Old Catholic (O.C.) Archbishop of Utrecht, 1662-1725.
Museum Catharijneconvent, Utrecht

63:     Cornelis Barchman Wuytiers, O.C. Archbishop of Utrecht, 1693-1733. *Museum Catherijneconvent*

64:     House at Rijnwijk, Holland.
http://home.zonnet.nl/kastelenutr/fotos/Rijnwijk2_Mourot.jpg

65:     House at Schonauwen, Holland.
http://bruno.tunderman.com/gravure20kasteel.jpg

71:     Theodore van der Croon, O.C. Archbishop of Utrecht 1668-1739. *Museum Catharijneconvent*

72:     François de Pâris, deacon, 1690-1727.

73:     Peter J. Meindaerts, O.C. Archbishop of Utrecht 1684-1767. *Museum Catharijneconvent*

74:     Vault of St. Mary Church Cloister in Utrecht, where Bishop Varlet was buried.

109:    Michel Bégon, Intendant of New France, 1669-1747. Joseph Ceré de la Colombière, Grand Vicar of Quebec 1651-1723.

113 :   Clement XI, pope from 1700 to 1721.

115 :   Confirmation by Pietro Antonio Novelli, 1779.

121:    Map of Iran with localisation of Isfahan.
http://biglizards.net/Graphics/ForegroundPix/IranMapSized.gif

125:    Painting of the Holy Trinity that was hanging in St. Louis O.C. Church in Green Bay, Wisconsin.

128:    Painting of a Jansenist crucifix (where the arms are stretched vertically in line with the total collapse of the body).

138:    Tetragrammaton *YHWH* from the window above the main altar in Karlskirche on the south side of Karlsplatz, Vienna.

149:    Cathedral Chapter of Orleans and King Robert le Pieux, 11th century.
http://www.corpusetampois.com/cls-11-helgaldus-vitarotberti-fouquet-robert2orleans.jpg

152:    Usury by Albrecht Dürer, 1471-1522.

157:    Claude Fleury, priest, 1643-1723.

158:    Jacques Bénigne Bossuet, Bishop of Meaux 1627-1704.

159:    The triumph of St. Augustine by Claudio Coello, 1642-1694.

162:    Conversion of Louis Basile Carré de Montgeron at the tomb of Deacon François de Pâris by Jean Restout.

166:    St. Peter preaching.

169:    Picture depicting the Millennial Age (Rev. 20).
http://www.resortrader.com/Alys/0_Images/TIChild1.jpg

172:    Jacques Joseph Duguet, professor, 1649-1733.

175:    St. Joachim of Flores (Fiore), biblical exegete and mystic, 1132-1202.

179:    Johann Albrecht Bengel, biblical exegete, 1687-1752.

220:    Ignaz von Döllinger, church historian, 1799-1890.

221:    Josef Hubert Reinkens, 1st O.C. Bishop of Germany, 1821-1896. Johannes Heykamp, O.C. Archbishop of Utrecht, 1875-1892.

223:    Eduard Herzog, 1st O.C. Bishop of Switzerland (1841-1924). René Vilatte, missionary in North America (1854-1929). Jean-Baptiste Gauthier, French Canadian Priest (1853-1922).

224:    Gerard Gul, Archbishop of Utrecht (1847-1920), E. Herzog, Theodor Weber of Germany (1836-1906) and Anton Kozlowski (Polish Americans), 1857-1907.

225:    Arnold Harris Mathew, O.C. Bishop of Great Britain (1853-1919), Jan Michal Kowalski, 1st Mariavite O.C. Bishop of Poland (1871-1942) & Roman Jakub Prochniewski, 2nd Mariavite Bishop (1872-1954).

275 :   Charles J. Colbert, Bishop of Montpellier, 1667-1738.

294:    Signature of Bishop Jean de St. Vallier
        Book by J.G. Shea, The Catholic Church in Colonial Days

www.ingramcontent.com/pod-product-compliance
Lightning Source LLC
Chambersburg PA
CBHW030132170426
43199CB00008B/46